APPENDIX

N

CASTALIA HOUSE

FANTASY
The Green Knight's Squire by John C. Wright
Iron Chamber of Memory by John C. Wright
Summa Elvetica by Vox Day
A Throne of Bones by Vox Day
A Sea of Skulls by Vox Day

SCIENCE FICTION
City Beyond Time by John C. Wright
Somewhither by John C. Wright
The End of the World as We Knew It by Nick Cole
CTRL-ALT REVOLT! by Nick Cole
Back From the Dead by Rolf Nelson
Victoria: A Novel of Fourth Generation War by Thomas Hobbes

MILITARY SCIENCE FICTION
Starship Liberator by David VanDyke and B. V. Larson
Battleship Indomitable by David VanDyke and B. V. Larson
The Eden Plague by David VanDyke
Reaper's Run by David VanDyke
Skull's Shadows by David VanDyke
There Will Be War Volumes I and II ed. Jerry Pournelle
Riding the Red Horse Volume 1 ed. Tom Kratman and Vox Day

FICTION
Brings the Lightning by Peter Grant
Rocky Mountain Retribution by Peter Grant
The Missionaries by Owen Stanley
An Equation of Almost Infinite Complexity by J. Mulrooney

NON-FICTION
SJWs Always Lie by Vox Day
Cuckservative by John Red Eagle and Vox Day
Equality: The Impossible Quest by Martin van Creveld
A History of Strategy by Martin van Creveld
Compost Everything by David the Good
Grow or Die by David the Good

AUDIOBOOKS
A History of Strategy narrated by Jon Mollison
Cuckservative narrated by Thomas Landon
Four Generations of Modern War narrated by William S. Lind
Grow or Die narrated by David the Good
Extreme Composting narrated by David the Good
A Magic Broken narrated by Nick Afka Thomas

APPENDIX

JEFFRO JOHNSON

CASTALIA HOUSE

Appendix N

Jeffro Johnson

Published by Castalia House
Kouvola, Finland
www.castaliahouse.com

Cover: Scott Vigil

ISBN: 978-952-7065-18-1

Contents

Introduction   i

1   *The Dying Earth* by Jack Vance   1

2   *Three Hearts and Three Lions* by Poul Anderson   5

3   *The High Crusade* by Poul Anderson   11

4   *The Eyes of the Overworld* by Jack Vance   17

5   *A Princess of Mars* by Edgar Rice Burroughs   29

6   *Jack of Shadows* by Roger Zelazny   35

7   *At the Earth's Core* by Edgar Rice Burroughs   41

8   *The Pirates of Venus* by Edgar Rice Burroughs   47

9   *Nine Princes in Amber* by Roger Zelazny   53

10   *Conan of Cimmeria* by Robert E. Howard   59

11   *Creep, Shadow!* by A. Merritt   67

12   *The Moon Pool* by A. Merritt   75

13   *Kothar—Barbarian Swordsman* by Gardner Fox   81

14   *Changeling Earth* by Fred Saberhagen   87

15   *The Face in the Frost* by John Bellairs   95

16   *Dwellers in the Mirage* by Abraham Merritt   103

17   *Lest Darkness Fall* by L. Sprague de Camp   113

18 *The Blue Star* by Fletcher Pratt   127

19 *Kyrik: Warlock Warrior* by Gardner F. Fox   135

20 *The King of Elfland's Daughter* by Lord Dunsany   145

21 *Hiero's Journey* by Sterling Lanier   151

22 *Star Man's Son* by Andre Norton   159

23 *Ill Met in Lankhmar* by Fritz Leiber   163

24 *The Complete Cthulhu Mythos Tales* by H. P. Lovecraft   169

25 *The Broken Sword* by Poul Anderson   177

26 *The Maker of Universes* by Philip José Farmer   185

27 *The Sword of Rhiannon* by Leigh Brackett   191

28 *A Martian Odyssey and The Complete Planetary Series* by
    Stanley G. Weinbaum   197

29 *The Jewel in the Skull* by Michael Moorcock   203

30 *The Trail of Cthulhu* by August Derleth   209

31 *Swords Against Darkness III* edited by Andrew J. Offutt   215

32 *The Carnelian Cube* L. Sprague de Camp and Fletcher Pratt   223

33 *The Warrior of World's End* by Lin Carter   227

34 *The Shadow People* by Margaret St. Clair   233

35 *The Fallible Fiend* by L. Sprague de Camp   243

36 *The Stealer of Souls* by Michael Moorcock   247

37 *The Legion of Space* by Jack Williamson   253

38 *Sign of the Labrys* by Margaret St. Clair   259

39 *The Best of Fredric Brown* edited by Robert Bloch   265

40 *Stormbringer* by Michael Moorcock   271

41 *Battle in the Dawn* by Manly Wade Wellman   277

42 *The Complete Compleat Enchanter* by L. Sprague de Camp and Fletcher Pratt   283

43 *The Hobbit* and *The Lord of the Rings* by J. R. R. Tolkien   291

Afterword: Appendix N Matters   299

Appendix A: *Adventurer Conqueror King System*   305

Appendix B: *Dwimmermount*   313

Appendix C: *The Annotated Sorcerer*   319

Appendix D: A Conversation with Ken St. Andre   331

About the Author   339

Introduction

by John C. Wright

Imagine if you had lived in a house for decades, as had your father before you, and grandfather, and you thought you knew all its halls and chambers. Idly, some rainy day, or when the snow has covered all the roads, you take up a lantern and go to see what is stored in those old boxes in the cellar, or where that one small door you never opened before leads.

You pry the door open, and it groans on rusted hinges, and beyond are caves of wonder, heaped with treasure. Here, like a column of fire, stands a strange genii and other spirits bound to serve your family. They are willing to carry you whirling through the air like an autumn leaf, in less time than it takes to gasp in awe, to far and fabled lands beyond the cerulean ocean, to elfish gardens of dangerous glamor, to jeweled mountains, alabaster cities, or perfumed jungles dreaming in the moonlight where ancient fanes to forgotten gods arise. The genii explains that all these things are yours, your inheritance. You have merely to claim them.

Or, to make the image more true to life, let us say that you are exploring the attic, and you find a handcrank connected to an orrery, worked by a silver key you have always worn but never heretofore found to fit any lock. Turning the crank, you move the model of planets on their epicycles back to an earlier position: trumpets blare and lamps blaze, and now parts and opens the dome of what you had, until now, thought was the sky above your house.

You find yourself in the middle of larger heavens than you knew, with gem-bright suns of many colors, constellations rearing, moons and worlds like colored ornaments, and bearded stars in the high depths of space like runners with torches. And there are worlds beyond those worlds.

Here you find your grandfather, in armor of gold with a sword of white fire, still young and strong, and discover him to be a sorcerer prince, or a dark elf, or a warrior angel, whose ichor runs in your veins as well. All this explains that strangeness that has haunted you all your life.

So it is with all readers and fans of science fiction and fantasy, weird tales and amazing stories who have never looked at the older books from which the younger books spring up. These are tales from beyond the shelves you know, realms unexplored yet oddly familiar.

Jeffro Johnson was the man with that silver key to unlock the older heavens or call up the genii you inherited from the past. It started simply enough: he wrote a series of columns taking as his theme the books listed in Appendix N of the older rules for *Advanced Dungeons & Dragons* written by Gary Gygax.

And the list is nothing exceptional: nearly anyone alive in those days (as I was) and was familiar with fantasy or science fiction reading of the time (as I was) asked to compile a list of the essential books and authors would, no doubt, have issued nearly the same list. The world was smaller in those days, and we who read science fiction were a breed apart, in our own quarter, and a bookish fan could have read or been familiar with all the talented writers in the field, and many of the untalented.

But like the man who explores his own basement and find a treasure trove, or opens his ceiling and finds the heavens rolled back like a scroll, Jeffro Johnson made an astonishing discovery: the things he had been told about the old books, the old pulps, the old days were misleading, or even false.

Because there was good stuff here!

Like a single spark in the dry leaves, other columnists and other readers began to reread the Appendix N books, and find that sense of wonder some writers seem willfully to wish to extinguish. Some modern books, sadly, are like a Xerox of a Xerox, and the freshness of the original is lost. Some are written in rebellion against ideas and themes in older works, but the nature of the rebellion is hidden from any reader to whom the old worlds are closed.

The genres were not demarked so clearly then, and the guards at the borders separating one kingdom from another were wont to nod and sleep, or wave through the wonder-hungry traveler without checking his papers. Works written in established worlds, Star Trek and Star Wars or Warhammer back-grounds, were utterly unknown.

Now imagine that there are some (they are rare, but they are real) whose mission is to bar you from those books, and see to it that you never enjoy the luxuries of your inheritance, or drink from the winebottles your grandfather laid down in his cellar long ago. All fashion of sneering accusation spills from these Grand Inquisitors, most of it senseless, telling you either that the artistic tastes or the personal flaws of those writers or those times render their work unfit.

Ignore the Thought Police. Read. Decide. Learn to enjoy what you enjoy. Because the heritage belongs to us all. And who knows? You may find the books that your favorite author read as his favorite books when he was young. All these worlds are yours. You have merely to claim them.

The Dying Earth

by Jack Vance

The writing of Jack Vance is striking, inventive, and vividly descriptive. His stories are superb, but his books haven't always been easy to track down. Consequently, he's often remembered just for inadvertently providing the template for the magic system in *Dungeons & Dragons*. In that game, a magic-user could spend time studying to learn a set number of spells. When he cast them, he would forget them and then have to study them again. This was termed either "Vancian magic" or "spell memorization" depending on who you gamed with. In D&D circles, it was often accepted as just being the way things worked with hardly anyone demanding an in-depth explanation of it. Outside the *D&D* scene, it was often deemed to be strange, childish, or even "unrealistic."

But it turns out that only a fraction of Jack Vance's ideas was lifted from *The Dying Earth* to be grafted onto the first fantasy role-playing game. And few people would be surprised by this oft-quoted passage:

> *The tomes which held Turjan's sorcery lay on the long table of black steel or were thrust helter-skelter into shelves. These were volumes compiled by many wizards of the past, untidy folios collected by the Sage, leather-bound librams setting forth the syllables of a hundred powerful spells, so cogent that Turjan's brain could know but four at a time.... What dangers he might meet he could not know, so he selected three spells of general application: the Excellent Prismatic Spray, Phandaal's Mantal of Stealth, and the Spell of the Slow Hour.*

This one, however, is an entirely different matter:

> *At one time a thousand or more runes, spells, incantations, curses, and sorceries had been known. The reach of grand Motholam—Ascolais, the*

Idle of Kauchique, Almery to the South, the Land of the Falling Wall to the East—swarmed with sorcerers of every description, of whom the chief was the Arch-Necromancer Phandaal. A hundred spells Phandaal personally had formulated—though rumor said that demons whispered at his ear when he wrought magic. Pontecilla the Pious, then ruler of Grand Motholam, put Phandaal to torment, and after a terrible night, he killed Phandaal and outlawed sorcery throughout the land. The wizards of Grand Motholam fled like beetles under a strong light; the lore was dispersed and forgotten, until now, at this dim time, with the sun dark, wilderness obscuring Ascolais, and the white city Kaiin half in ruins, only a few more than a hundred spells remained to the knowledge of man. Of these, Mazirian had access to seventy-three, and gradually, by stratagem and negotiation, was securing the others.

Considered in the light of the stories in this collection, it's absolutely staggering.

While the real-world development of *Dungeons & Dragons* mirrors this source material in that a few odd spells are named after the wizard that developed them, there really is a lot more going on here. Not only has Jack Vance constructed a detailed far future science-fantasy setting, but he has also crafted an apocalyptic origin story to account for its magic system. His true genius lies in how he established an extremely hard upper limit to the number of available spells in his world. The spell-casters in his tales all hunger after more and greater knowledge precisely because they have so little at their disposal. They pursue it with every ounce of cunning they can muster. But about the only way most of them can get it is by taking it from their rivals!

Such a premise has not been explored overmuch in either fantasy or gaming. Indeed, games are naturally focused more on *how* exactly the rules mechanics work; the settings are often whatever they need to be in order to make the game playable and accessible. There is often no real economy of magic or magical knowledge, and players are often granted new powers automatically whenever the requisite number of experience points are obtained. This gradual evolution in a player-character's abilities is a key factor driving people to engage in ongoing campaigns of weekly game sessions that last for years at a time. Few people want to clutter up the fun by adding more restrictions and impediments to the rush that goes with leveling up.

But imagine if there were only a set number of spells in one of those massively multiplayer online role-playing games. If the only way to gain new spells were to raid other magic-users for their spell books, the result would be a bloodbath. This one alteration would not only completely change the nature of the game, but it would also destroy whatever semblance of civilization was in existence at the start of play—all because every magic-user in the game would have this tremendous incentive to obtain the equivalent of Maziran's seventy-fourth spell! Anyone with a spell they don't already have would be on their hit lists....

Of similar significance is the commonly overlooked fact that mathematics is the key to discerning the "real" nature of Vancian magic. In many games, the designers come up with some sort generic "magicky" type skill or else have it powered by an arbitrary "mana" force. Other people, hankering for a sense of authenticity, work out systems based on pacts with demons and so forth. In contrast to this, Jack Vance is explicit about his magic's being susceptible to discoverable laws:

Within this instrument resides the Universe. Passive in itself and not of sorcery, it elucidates every problem, each phase of existence, all the secrets of time and space. Your spells and runes are built upon its power and codified according to a great underlying mosaic of magic. The design of this mosaic we cannot surmise; our knowledge is didactic, empirical, arbitrary. Phandaal glimpsed the pattern and so was able to formulate many of the spells that bear his name.

But in the *Dying Earth* setting, a general knowledge of how mathematics applies to magic is almost completely lost. The consequences of a scenario that culminates into a science fantasy analog to *Lord of the Flies* go far deeper than what a casual reading would indicate:

In all my youth this ache has driven me, and I have journeyed from the old manse at Sfere to learn from the Curator... I am dissatisfied with the mindless accomplishments of the magicians, who have all their lore by rote.

The wizards, then, are nearly all charlatans. They're like jazz musicians that can only learn a set number of songs, can't improvise on a set of chord changes, and forget what little they do know at the end of a set. They're like engineers that can only solve a few well-known problems and who can only actually tackle a fraction of what was previously solvable. They are like the most typical math student of today who has knowledge of only a handful of tricks, is barely able to recognize when to apply them, and is essentially innumerate when separated from his calculator. Despite their trappings of learning and lore, these wizards amount to little more than barbarian looters of a fallen empire.

This, too, is staggering. It also explains one of the classic divides in role-playing game design. Early editions of *D&D* placed no restrictions on the intelligence of magic-user characters. Your character can be a complete idiot and still cast "Sleep" just as well as other more brilliant mages. When guys like Ken St. Andre and Steve Jackson created their own variations of the fantasy role-playing game concept, they found it natural to limit a character's available spells based on his intelligence level. *The Fantasy Trip* went so far as to require you to roll against IQ in order successfully to cast a spell. While this was appealing to a lot of gamers, it is clearly a completely different take on magic from what we see here. Mages like Maziran were not limited by their intelligence, but by the contents of their spell books and by how many spells they could fit in their brains at once. The spells themselves were differentiated by the duration of the "space-twisting syllables" it took to invoke them. And instead of being limited to a specific number of slots for each of a dozen or so spell levels, Maziran could learn "four of the most formidable, or six of the lesser spells" at one time.

The elements of Jack Vance's work glimpsed in early role-playing games can at first seem strange and nonsensical, but they really do make sense when viewed in their original context. The science fantasy setting, the characters, and the action in *The Dying Earth* all flow directly from the premises of the magic system. Of course, had *Dungeons & Dragons* been more faithful to those premises, it could not have presented the vaguely medieval world that was key to its wide-ranging appeal. The selective pillaging of Vancian concepts makes sense in retrospect, but it's ironic that the life of Jack Vance recapitulates that of his own creation. He's not unlike the wizard Phandaal with only a handful of his hundred spells surviving into general usage. He deserves so much more than that.

Three Hearts and Three Lions
by Poul Anderson

One reason I enjoy reading the older science-fiction and fantasy stories is that they are so much more often free from overt politicization. For a good bad example, look no further than the *Next Generation Star Trek* episode that has Tasha Yar attempting to explain to Wesley Crusher why it is that people get hooked on drugs. Though she stops short of cracking an egg on an overheated console, it's still cringe inducing. It was a small mercy to science-fiction fans that her character was killed off in the following episode lest we had to endure sermonettes about her disturbing childhood on Turkana IV....

The original series actually topped that in "The Omega Glory," when Kirk harangued the bible-clinging, flag-venerating Yangs over their parochial views of the Constitution: *These words and the words that follow were not written only for the Yangs, but for the Kohms as well!* Yes, after dealing with a disastrous violation of the prime directive on a war-torn world, Kirk pretty much can't leave the planet without making that point that, in effect, "inside every gook there is an American trying to get out."[1] It's almost surreal.

This sort of sanctimonious "after-school special" type of approach to storytelling is bad not simply because it is so transparent. It's bad because it displaces deeper and truer things: things that induce wonder and that have the capacity to thrill the soul. In the attempt to be "relevant" or topical, it's all too easy to sacrifice timelessness. It's not just the odd scene that's off the mark either—the entirety of the plot is often structured in such a way as to deliver these ludicrous punchlines. It's a waste, reducing what should be epic adventure down to the level of shaggy dog story.

It's surprising just how different golden age literature can be from this. Humanity, for instance, has not always been portrayed as being destined to succumb to a self-induced apocalypse. Going further back in time, you're so much more likely to find the sort of muscular, can-do attitude that put men on the moon. While this occasionally borders on hubris, I personally wouldn't mind seeing our manifest destiny to the stars make a comeback. Similarly, in fantasy in the days before the influence of countless Tolkien imitators, you were so much more likely to find a sense of alien wildness to the faerie elements. Across all genres, you could find traditional notions of vice and virtue that could lend works a mythical or even parabolic tone.

Poul Anderson's 1961 novel *Three Hearts and Three Lions* is perhaps unique in that it successfully knits *all* of these things together into a particularly satisfying package. This is possible because it's a fairy tale wrapped within a frame of science fiction. The protagonist is whisked from the midst of a World War II skirmish and thrust into a fantasy world. He turns out to be a figure of some importance there but lacks the necessary memories to function intelligently in the new milieu. Though he retains fragmentary knowledge of the nature of his otherworldly abilities, it turns out that his mastery of reason and basic science facts are the key to getting him and his newfound friends out of the trouble that he blunders into time and again. While it occasionally comes off a bit pat, it is nevertheless good fun; the payoff at the end is certainly worth hanging around for.

Of course, a number of people are going to be reading and recommending this book because it is the literary antecedent of the paladin class from the first edition *AD&D Player Handbook*. Certainly, the laying on of hands, the warhorse, and the Holy Sword are all here. The biggest discrepancy is that Gygax made the "protection from evil" ability always on and primarily benefiting the paladin himself. Poul Anderson actually has it being much more powerful and protecting the party's entire camp if certain preparations are followed, though it can be spoiled if the paladin so much as curses or entertains impure thoughts. The latter could be hard to avoid given the alluring nature of the various elf women, nymphs, and evil sorceresses that are on the prowl!

Less often remarked upon is the fact that this book is the source for the alignment system of *Basic Dungeons & Dragons*. For those that have no experience with tabletop role-playing games, I may be unable to convey just how strange and divisive this element really was. You see, in what tended to be a vaguely naturalistic setting, players in the game would set forth into the wilds to kill monsters, to win treasure, and to evade diabolical traps. But for some reason,

Gary Gygax felt it necessary to demarcate what was essentially the spiritual allegiance of every character, monster, and plane of existence in the game. When other designers tried their hand at the medium, this was often the first thing they eliminated, but it remains an integral part of gaming culture to this day. And while the earlier wargame crowd that pushed lead figures on the sand tables in their basements tended to behave more like supreme court justices whenever they had to resolve a rules dispute, role-playing gamers often ended up becoming small time theologians or moral philosophers because of the innumerable issues alignment inevitably brought into play.

At any rate, you will find in *Three Hearts and Three Lions* the basis for the original three-point alignment system of Gary Gygax's famous and influential game. What we see here is so different from what role-players take for granted that it can be positively staggering to people who grew up with the game.

At one extreme, we have Chaos... which here is not always synonymous with evil. As its name would lead you to believe, it really does actually have elements of randomness and unpredictability to it:

You canna tell wha' the Faerie folk will do next. They canna tell theirselves, nor care. They live in wildness, which is why they be o' the dark Chaos side in this war.

The alignment most preferred by the typical adolescent role-player is Neutral, and here it turns out to be a bit more cranky and cynical than what we see in, say, the attitude of Treebeard from *The Two Towers*. Furthermore, it is dialog like this, and not that from *The Lord of the Rings*, that led to dwarfs being depicted as being short Scots:

We'll ha' naught to do wi' the wars in this uneasy land. We'll bide our aine lives and let Heaven, Hell, Earth, and the Middle World fight it oot as they will. And when yon proud lairds ha' laid each other oot, stiff and stark, we'll still be here. A pox on 'em all!

And Lawful is more of a combination of mundanity, civilization, and (surprisingly) Christianity:

Holger got the idea that a perpetual struggle went on between primeval forces of Law and Chaos. No, not forces exactly. Modes of existence? A terrestrial reflection of the spiritual conflict between heaven and hell? In any case, humans were the chief agents on earth of Law, though most of them were so only unconsciously and some, witches and warlocks and evildoers, had sold out to Chaos. A few nonhuman beings also stood for Law. Ranged against them was almost the whole Middle World, which seemed to include realms like Faerie, Trollheim, and the Giants– an actual creation of Chaos. Wars among men, such as the long-drawn struggle between the Saracens and the Holy Empire, aided Chaos; under Law all men would live in peace and order and that liberty which only Law could give meaning. But this was so alien to the Middle Worlders that they were forever working to prevent it and to extend their own shadowy domain.

Contrast this with Tom Moldvay's edit of the original *D&D* rules: Lawful is characterized as being predictable and having a concern for the group over the individual. Chaos is about selfishness and capriciousness. The crucial element that has been dropped from this spectrum is not the Gygaxian good/evil axis of *AD&D*, but rather the influence of Christianity and Faerie at either extreme:

In olden time, richt after the Fall, nigh everything were chaos, see ye. But step by step 'tis been driven back. The longest step was when the Savior lived on earth, for then naught of darkness could stand and Pan himself died. But noo 'tis said Chaos has rallied and mak's ready to strike back.

Here, Christianity is antithetical to Faerie magic. Elves cannot touch iron, cannot bear the sight of a crucifix, and are physically hurt when the name of Jesus is invoked. Neutral creatures of the middle world are often fantastic: they lack magical abilities, but they have "no fear of iron or silver or holy symbols." Incredibly, the influence of the Law/Chaos spectrum spills over into the physical geography of Poul Anderson's fantasy world:

Well, you see, the world of Law—of man—is hemmed in with strangeness, like an island in the sea of the Middle World. Northward live the giants, southward the dragons. Here in Tarnberg we are close to the eastern edge of human settlement and know a trifle about such kingdoms as Faerie and Trollheim. But news travels slowly and gets dissipated in the process. So we have only vague distorted rumors of the western realms—not merely the Middle World domains out in the western ocean, like Avalon, Lyonesse, and Huy Braseal, but even the human countries like France and Spain.

The impotence of Chaos in a direct confrontation with the faithful and the pure of heart means that it must adopt a multifaceted strategy in undermining Law. As a consequence, we see a threat that is quite different from the orc armies of Sauron and his wraithish minions:

> *Chiefly, methinks, the Middle World will depend on the humans who'll fight for Chaos. Witches, warlocks, bandits, murderers, 'fore all the heathen savages o' the north and south. These can desecrate the sacred places and slay such men as battle against them. Then the rest o' the humans will flee, and there'll be naught left to prevent the blue gloaming being drawn over hundreds o' leagues more. With every advance, the realms o' Law will grow weaker: not alone in numbers, but in spirit, for the near presence of Chaos must affect the good folk, turning the skittish, lawless, and inclined to devilments o' their own.... As evil waxes, the very men who stand for good will in their fear use ever worse means o' fighting, and thereby give evil a free beachhead.*

This is utterly fantastic. Yet it also rings true. *For we wrestle not against flesh and blood, but against principalities, against powers, against the rulers of the darkness of this world, against spiritual wickedness in high places.*[2] The contrast between hearing that idea in a homily and getting the exact same thing in an adventure story is stark. And yet non-Christian readers don't seem to feel lectured to when they come to these passages any more than they do when they read how Sam carried Frodo up the slopes of Mount Doom[3] or when the wise turned out to be far less effective than a few rustic hobbits.[4] When telling a story, neither Tolkien nor Poul Anderson needs ever mount a soapbox in order to get their points across. They inspire rather than insult their readers precisely because they leave their readers the freedom to determine the actual applicability of the message.

In like manner, Gary Gygax stripped off the post-apocalyptic elements of Jack Vance's magic and the Christian and Faerie aspects of Poul Anderson's alignment structure so that dungeon masters could far more easily adapt these systems to diverse campaign worlds of their own creation. This Frankenstein's monster approach to game design lends *Dungeons & Dragons* a depth that its competitors often lacked even if it was often hard to understand by players that were unfamiliar with the literary sources. Nevertheless, this is how things are done when creators actually trust their audiences to read and interpret for themselves. It's a pity that such confidence is the exception now rather than the rule.

Notes

1. This astounding assertion was immortalized in Stanley Kubrick's 1987 film *Full Metal Jacket*.

2. Ephesians 6:12.

3. *Bear ye one another's burdens, and so fulfil the law of Christ.* —Galatians 6:2

4. *But God hath chosen the foolish things of the world to confound the wise; and God hath chosen the weak things of the world to confound the things which are mighty.* —1 Corinthians 1:27

The High Crusade
by Poul Anderson

One of the longstanding debates in gaming circles is which of the core *Dungeons & Dragons* classes are the least necessary to the game. Few people challenge the place of either fighting-men[1] or magic-users on the roster. Indeed, Steve Jackson's first role-playing game was built around just those two archetypes, which isn't surprising given that they neatly encapsulate the two poles of the swords and sorcery genre. Consequently, the discussion tends to boil down to whether one has more enmity for the thief or the cleric.

Now... the thief class takes a lot of flak in spite of the enduring appeal of characters like Robin Hood and Bilbo Baggins. Yet not only was it a latecomer that wasn't even in the original three "little brown books" that made up the original "White Box" rule set, but its system of skills and abilities was seen as taking away from actions that everyone tended to try during the earliest game sessions.[2] For instance, fighting-men might take a stab at being stealthy by removing their armor and then scouting ahead for the party. When the thief class came along with an explicit chance to "move silently," a lot of people leaped to the conclusion the other classes couldn't attempt such a thing anymore. This made for some hard feelings, and fixing the design issues implied by this class's existence is such a hassle that maybe it's best to just drop it altogether!

In the same vein, the cleric class comes in for a good deal of grief in spite of the fact that it was one of the original three classes in the game. In more recent editions, people don't mind having one in the party, but they can't always find someone willing to *play* one. (Few people want to be relegated to the role of a glorified medic; they want to get out front and *do* stuff, not just play a support role!) But really, the original class is downright odd. They can't use edged weapons for some reason, and they have a bizarre adaption of the Vancian magic system with the effects drawn largely from biblical accounts. They're just weird, and the archetype doesn't turn up in fantasy literature in anywhere near the same frequency as the other classes. For a lot of people, the cleric is the obvious choice for the odd man out.

Reading Poul Anderson's *The High Crusade*, however, it quickly becomes apparent that, if you're going to be faithful to the game's medieval roots, then the two core classes would have to be the fighting-man and the cleric—a stark difference from Steve Jackson's *The Fantasy Trip*. This just isn't in line with how most people view the game though. This is ironic given that the earliest iterations of what would become *Dungeons & Dragons* were actually a fantasy supplement to the medieval miniatures rule set *Chainmail*. It was an explicit goal of those rules to inspire people to gain a greater familiarity with the actual history of the Middle Ages.[3] This aspect of the hobby gradually faded into obscurity when fantasy gaming took on a life of its own. Of course, the fewer medieval elements you incorporate into your game setting, the less sense the cleric is going to make.

Fans of the oft-maligned class will be gratified to discover that *The High Crusade* is actually narrated by a cleric. Purists, on the other hand, will be disappointed to see that he wields a battleaxe during the first chapter. At first glance, it's hard not to jump to the conclusion that this title made Gary Gygax's "Appendix N" book list because of its likely part in inspiring the game's tendency to fuse science-fiction and fantasy elements together. Indeed, the cover looks like something straight out of "Expedition to Barrier Peaks." But Poul Anderson has done much more than provide an unusual theme for a dungeon adventure. He's turned the standard alien invasion on its head by having the humans thwart the would-be oppressors on first contact. An alien scout vessel is quickly overrun... by medieval Englishmen! When they get their hands on high-tech weaponry and figure out what they can do with it, their first thought is to gather up the entire village, board the spacecraft, and take an extended vacation that would include invading France and taking back the Holy Land!

When the narrator is tasked with teaching the sole surviving alien Latin so that they can force him to explain how to properly "sail" the ship, hilarity ensues:

"You brought this on yourself," I told him. "You should have known better than to make an unprovoked attack on Christians." "What are Christians?" he asked. Dumbfounded, I thought he must be feigning ignorance. As a test, I led him through the Paternoster. He did not go up in smoke, which puzzled me. "I think I understand," he said. "You refer to some primitive tribal pantheon." "It is no such heathen thing!" I said indignantly. I started to explain the Trinity to him, but had scarcely gotten to transubstantiation when he waved an impatient blue hand. It was much like a human hand otherwise, save for the thick, sharp nails. "No matter," he said, "Are all Christians as ferocious as your people?" "You would have had better luck with the French," I admitted. "Your misfortune was landing among Englishmen."

This is some seriously funny stuff, very nearly in the same vein as the best material of Douglas Adams. The fact that it is a straightforward science-fiction story with realistic medieval characters only makes it funnier. While one might expect this sort of tongue-in-cheek delivery to get tiresome after a while, the plot moves along quickly enough that it gradually fades into the background. The Englishmen are soon (and inadvertently) deep in the process of taking over the alien empire that would have otherwise subjugated humanity. And while the reader naturally identifies with the humans as he reads, it gradually becomes clear that there is an additional angle to Poul Anderson's handiwork:

Actually, the Wersgor domain was like nothing at home. Most wealthy, important persons dwelt on their vast estates with a retinue of blueface hirelings. They communicated on the far-speaker and visited in swift aircraft of spaceships. Then there were other classes I have mentioned elsewhere, such as warriors, merchants, and politicians. But no one was born to his place in life. Under the law, all were equal, all free to strive as best they might for money or position. Indeed, they had even abandoned the idea of families. Each Wersgor lacked a surname, being identified by a number instead in a central registry. Male and female seldom lived together more than a few years. Children were sent at an early age to schools, where they dwelt until mature, for their parents oftener thought them an encumbrance than a blessing. Yet this realm, in theory a republic of freemen, was in practice a worse tyranny than mankind has known, even in Nero's infamous day. The Wersgorix had no special affection for their birthplace; they acknowledged no immediate ties of kinship or duty. As a result, each individual had no one to stand between him and the all-powerful central government. In England, when King John grew overweening, he clashed both with ancient law and with vested local interests; so the barons curbed him and thereby wrote another word or two of liberty for all Englishmen. The Wersgor were a lickspittle race, unable to protest any arbitrary decree of a superior. "Promotion according to merit" meant only "promotion according to one's usefulness to the imperial ministers."

Yes, after being the butt of so many jokes and tongue-in-cheek remarks, our "primitive" narrator has a few observations to make about the culture of the alien people he is so cheerfully invading. The shortcomings of the alien society are in fact almost painfully familiar to the typical reader of the twentieth century. Poul Anderson has deftly turned the tables on us: *we* are the punch line. It is thought provoking, to say the least, but it's a mere prelude to the coming knockout blow:

"Well?" demanded Sir Roger. "What ails you now?" "If they have not yet gone to war," I said weakly, "why should the advent of a few backward savages like us make them do so?" "Hearken, Brother Parvus," said Sir Roger. "I'm weary of this whining about our own ignorance and feebleness. We're not ignorant of the true Faith, are we? Somewhat more to the point, maybe, while the engines of war may change through the centuries, rivalry and intrigue look no subtler out here than at home. Just because we use a different sort of weapons, we aren't savages."

Granted, the tale depends on a great many implausibilities, but the fact that there's an element of truth here is the key to what makes it so funny. You see, it's not just that medieval people can be interesting if they are portrayed a little more faithfully to their real-life character and attitudes. It's that they may even have been *better* than us in ways we rarely contemplate. And maybe the things that seem the strangest about them now were actually perfectly reasonable cultural adaptions that addressed the essential problems of their time! Whether you agree or not, it's certainly an audacious premise—exactly the sort of mind-blowing concept I look for in a good science-fiction novel.

Fans of science fiction and fantasy too often embrace just the surface elements of their respective genres. Whether it's aliens in rubber suits or historical characters that have barely disguised twentieth-century world-views, there is a tendency to dumb things down to a level where it becomes glorified dress up. Steampunk, for instance, has a fairly aggressive tendency in that direction.[4] What's more disappointing, however, is when a lazy ignorance of fundamental cultural differences gives way to an outright contempt for the historical antecedents. A recent episode of *Doctor Who* provides a good example of that. Matt Smith practically spits out the words in his 2012 Christmas special: "Oh dear me, how very Victorian of you." His hatred of an entire period of history is taken as self-evident and is not even supported in the context of the episode's events. It not only falls flat, but it is also incoherently sanctimonious.

It doesn't have to be this way. The fact that Poul Anderson could make taking the opposite tack look so effortless is a big part of why he deserves his title as a grandmaster of science fiction. This book is just as fresh and exciting as it was when it came out over fifty years ago. It is rightly regarded as a classic of the field. The fact that it graphically illustrates why interstellar feudalism is such a good fit for *Traveller*'s Third Imperium setting only makes it better.

Notes

1. This slightly more archaic term is used both in *The High Crusade* (see the beginning of chapter six) and also in the original version of *Dungeons & Dragons*. Later editions of the game would use the slightly watered down "fighter" in its stead.

2. See "The Trouble with Thieves" by James Maliszewski in *Knockspell #2* for a good rundown on the arguments surrounding the introduction of the thief class.

3. "Besides providing you with an exciting and enjoyable battle game, we hope that these rules will interest the wargamer sufficiently to start him on the pursuit of the history of the Middle Ages. Such study will at least enrich the life of the new historian, and perhaps it will even contribute to the study of history itself." – *Chainmail* by Gary Gygax and Jeff Perren, page 8.

4. See Steampunk Scholar's "I'll be Holmes for Christmas, or Sherlock Holmes and the case of the missing holiday" for more on that.

The Eyes of the Overworld
by Jack Vance

Just by reading a few influential books from fifty years ago, we've seen magic that could reduce civilizations to chaotic wastelands just on the basis of the incentives it created. We've seen clerics boldly face down alien marauders, secure in the knowledge that demons and devils cannot harm them. We've seen science and myth collide, elves fall back at the sight of a crucifix, and medieval knights subdue an interstellar empire. It's downright astounding. Fantasy back then was actually *fantastic*. It just wasn't the kind of world where Greedo would need to shoot first, where vampires and werewolves would be tamed into overwrought boyfriends, or where anyone would feel that Frodo had to be reduced to mere baggage at the Ford of Rivendell instead being able to turn and face five Nazgul as he lifted his sword, and cried, "By Elbereth and Lúthien the Fair, you shall have neither the Ring nor me!"

There is a raucousness about the literature that inspired the earliest role-playing games that is even more remarkable when compared with today's standard fare. It was compelling, no doubt, but it quickly devolved into something else. There's plenty of speculation with regard to the actual cause of the changes. A lot of people would be inclined to blame the gatekeepers, for instance. I'm sure a guy like Neal Postman could argue these sorts of cultural shifts are purely a function of technology, but my own pet theory would be that the "cult of the new" has had much the same effect on literature that it has had on board games.

While I realize that there are a lot of different angles on this, I'm going to set all of these speculations aside for now and try focusing entirely on trends in fantasy from the perspective of tabletop gaming alone. The first thing you need to know is that the men who laid the groundwork for the role-playing hobby had an incredible appetite for books. You may have been in a comic book shop on a Wednesday when the new shipment came in and the most dedicated fans in your town are right there to get the latest installment of everything they're into. Well, Gary Gygax and James M. Ward were like that with *books:*

> *One fateful Tuesday, I was poring through the racks, picking up the newest Conan and Arthur C. Clarke novels. When I reached the end of the racks, I had seven books in my hand. There was a gentleman doing the very same thing beside me. When he got done, he and I had the exact same books in our hands. We laughed at the coincidence and he started talking about a game he had just invented where a person could play Conan fighting Set. I was instantly hooked on the idea. A few weeks later I was regularly going over to Gary Gygax's house to learn the game of Dungeons & Dragons.[1]*

Note that the main selling point of the game at its inception was that it was not merely an adaption of their favorite stories to game form. No, the "lightning in the bottle" that Gary Gygax had gotten hold of was, in fact, the apex of genre fiction.[2] He was opening up an entirely new method for creating worlds and allowing people to enter them. We take it for granted today, but J. Eric Holmes was not exaggerating when he declared that it was a "truly unique invention, probably as remarkable as the die, or the deck of cards, or the chessboard."[3]

Its influence is pervasive. At the time of the release of *E.T.*, it was nearly ubiquitous. Hardly a multi-million dollar video game is released today that does not incorporate design concepts that were pioneered in Gary Gygax's basement. And while a great many authors got their start playing tabletop role-playing games[4], many more picked up their basic assumptions about what fantasy was all about indirectly from people who practically ate, drank, and breathed *Dungeons & Dragons* and its descendants. Given all that, it's ironic that a great many of those who pontificated about the shortcomings of "Vancian magic" back in the day would have been unfamiliar with Jack Vance's *Dying Earth* series. It's crazy, but an author of Vance's caliber was, in effect, *obscure* during the eighties…!

You see, by the time most people had stumbled into tabletop role-playing games, most of the books that had inspired the games were long gone. When we were watching, you know, *actual music videos* on MTV, those books would have seemed downright old. As old as the Beatles, even, who would have been considered to be ancient history by the average teen at the time even if they did happen to own *The White Album* and *Abbey Road* on compact disc. Classic pulpy fiction was from another era, and if our parents had ever gotten into that sort of thing, they were liable to have treated their magazines like the disposable entertainment that they really were. (One is reminded of the time when Jack McDevitt's aunt helpfully cut out all the naughty pictures from his pulp magazines as a favor to him![5])

There was no Internet. There was no Amazon. For a lot of people, if it wasn't on the bookstore shelf, they didn't know about it. Most of us didn't even *know* that we didn't know about it. Of course, picking up a copy of *Space Gamer* magazine, you could even then have seen Lewis Pulsipher opining on Appendix N literature in almost exactly the same fashion as the game bloggers of today.[6] Even so, the consequences of someone being fluent in golden age literature would have completely escaped most peoples' notice at the time.

It's obvious now in retrospect—at least it is when you read something like Marc Miller's review of the classic *Traveller* adventure "Leviathan."[7] Even though he had done almost no preparation for the game session, he was able to immediately improvise an adventure on the spot with only two paragraphs of world description to guide him. His secret? He just so happened to remember an old Fritz Lieber story that was a perfect fit for the situation! Gaming challenges that would stymie novice game masters for decades crumble away in the face of that particular brand of literacy.

While the games were designed by people with that level of fluency, they would ultimately get played by people who lacked even a cursory familiarity with anything less popular than Middle Earth or Narnia. And the people digging through esoteric articles in the game magazines were not, in fact, the ones that set the course of gaming history. It wasn't even the dedicated Dungeon Masters that organized and mediated the games that did that. You see, the rules that most influence actual play about eighty percent of the time are the sections dealing with character generation. More than anything else, it is the players who set the tone for the game, and they make almost all of their decisions based on what they see on the character sheets and the sections that explain how to fill them out. You can tell this is true because character-oriented rules that don't appear integrated with this particular portion of the rules are largely ignored in practice!

It's an open secret that Dungeon Masters don't actually need rules to run a game.[8] (The impression of rules is sufficient. Everything else is theater.) Eighty percent of the rules they care about deal with adjudicating combat, and the rest pretty well boils down to general advice on more or less *making stuff up*. Indeed, it doesn't take all that much to entertain players. With just nine pages of adventure information, "G1 Steading of the Hill Giant Chief" can easily keep a group gaming for fifteen hours or more. Something like "B2 Keep on the Borderlands" can keep a party engaged over the course of a year of game sessions if the Dungeon Master is willing to let player-characters die while also restocking portions of the dungeon occasionally.

You can run entire sessions built around a single very simple monster encounter. By the time the players get their equipment, gather rumors, make their plans, and figure out how they want to handle it, a couple of hours or more are liable to be gone. When I make up my own adventure material, I usually have to omit the most complicated aspects of my outlines and generally end up trying to make up a game on the spot about whatever it is that the players actually grasp of the situation. You generally don't want to put anything into an adventure that is hard to explain because it can bring play to a halt and snap players out of their sense of immersion. When running games regularly, you quickly find that clichés and common tropes are essential if you want to keep things moving. At the same time, nothing is harder on player engagement than the times when they simply don't know what to do. But give them a straight-ahead dungeon crawl with standard monsters and typical delving equipment, and the players immediately start developing elaborate plans to maximize every asset at their disposal. While this turns out to be a severe limiting factor for adventure designers, it must be noted that the constraints increase geometrically when the form transitions to the computer.

In a sense, the entire hobby recapitulates Darwin's *Descent of Man* in reverse. The type of literature that inspired role-playing games was already obscure when the games were achieving their first big wave of popularity. That literature was itself looted for ideas that could translate to the tabletop environment. The wilder and more imaginative stuff was simply left out because it couldn't make the transition. But then another set of cuts were made: anything that didn't make sense to the gamers (and there was a lot of that) did not get used in actual play. The sieving process was complete when role-playing transitioned to computers, where the improvisational aspects of the hobby could not be effected at all. In the new medium, there was no way to make up new situations, locations, and objects in direct response to the group's particular approach to gaming. There was no way to reframe the tone of the campaign in direct response to unpredictable events at the table. There was no way to modify the rules in the course of play. The attitudes and assumptions of computer gaming were then folded back into a new generation of tabletop games which were far more procedural and far more like board games than anything extant at the dawn of the hobby.

Combined with the narrowing[9] of fantasy in general, these trends mean that reading the literary antecedents of *Dungeons & Dragons* is almost always going to be disproportionately astounding today. It's like being able to get your fantasy straight rather than in some kind of slurry with a little paper umbrella sticking out. In the case of Jack Vance's *The Eyes of the Overworld*, you can see many things that clearly inspired various aspects of the old games, but which are now in unnerving opposition to our more current tastes and expectations.

Behold:

Cugel strode down a sweep of circular stairs into a great hall. He stood enthralled, paying Iucounu the tribute of unstinted wonder. But his time was limited; he must rob swiftly and be on his way. Out came his sack; he roved the hall, fastidiously selecting those objects of small bulk and great value: a small pot with antlers, which emitted clouds of remarkable gasses when the prongs were tweaked; an ivory horn through which sounded voices from the past; a small stage where costumed imps stood ready to perform comic antics; an object like a cluster of crystal grapes, each affording a blurred view into one of the demon-worlds; a baton sprouting sweetmeats of assorted flavour; an ancient ring engraved with runes; a black stone surrounded by nine zones of impalpable color. He passed by hundreds of jars of powders and liquids, likewise forebore from the vessels containing preserved heads. Now he came to shelves stacked with volumes, folios and librams, where he selected with care, taking for preference those bound in purple velvet, Phandaal's characteristic color. He likewise selected folios of drawings and ancient maps, and the disturbed leather exuded a musty odor. (p 9-10)

In all my years of gaming, I have never seen a treasure haul that could compete with *this*. It's reminiscent of how James Raggi made this point in his particular take on the original fantasy game: "Because monsters should be unnatural and hopefully a little terrifying, using stock examples goes against the purpose of using monsters to begin with."[10] This is no doubt in response to how the nature of tabletop gaming is impacted by players having memorized the *Monster Manual*, but in the above passage, Jack Vance makes the same case with regard to magic items. There are no swords +1 or wands of fireballs in his world; everything is unique. Sometimes frighteningly so.

> *Cugel proceeded along the beach, well pleased with the events of the morning. He examined the amulet at length: it exuded a rich sense of magic, and in addition was an object of no small beauty. The runes, incised with great skill and delicacy, unfortunately were beyond his capacity to decipher. He gingerly slipped the bracelet on his wrist, and in so doing pressed one of the carbuncles. From somewhere came an abysmal groan, a sound of the deepest anguish. Cugel stopped short, and looked up and down the beach. Gray sea, pallid beach, foreshore with clumps of spinifex. Benbadge Stull to the west, Cil to the east, gray sky above. He was alone. Whence had come the great groan? Cautiously Cugel touched the carbuncle again, and again evoked the stricken protest. In fascination Cugel pressed another of the carbuncles, this time bringing forth a wail of piteous despair in a different voice. Cugel was puzzled. Who along this sullen shore manifested so frivolous a disposition? Each carbuncle in turn he pressed and caused to be produced a whole concert of outcries, ranging the gamut of anguish and pain. Cugel examined the amulet critically. Beyond the evocation of groans and sobs it displayed no obvious power and Cugel presently tired of the occupation. (p 46)*

While Gary Gygax did include a section on artifacts in his 1979 *AD&D Dungeon Masters Guide*, there's really nothing in there like *this*. It's not mentioned above, but possession of that artifact automatically gives you the status of rule in a nearby town. The only thing in gaming that I've seen that is even remotely close to this in deviousness is in Infocom's *Enchanter*. Indeed, this passage (and the many passages mentioning grues in passing) indicates that the renowned implementors of the iconic interactive fiction company were directly inspired by Jack Vance rather than just the tabletop games themselves.

> *Pharesm made a peremptory gesture. Cugel fell silent. Pharesm drew a deep breath. 'You fail to understand the calamity you have visited upon me. I will*

*explain, so that you may not be astounded by the rigors which await you. As
I have adumbrated, the arrival of the creature was the culmination of my
great effort. I determined its nature through a perusal of forty-two thousand
librams, all written in cryptic language: a task requiring a hundred years.
During a second hundred years I evolved a pattern to draw it in upon itself
and prepared exact specification. Next I assembled stone-cutters, and across
a period of three hundred years gave solid form to my pattern. Since like
subsumes like, the variates and intercongeles create a suprapullulation of all
areas, qualities and intervals into a crystorrhoid whorl, eventually exciting
the ponentiation of a pro-ubietal chute. Today occurred the concatenation;
the "creature" as you call it, pervolved upon itself; in your idiotic malice you
devoured it.' (p 116-117)*

Have players in your games ever encountered wizards that were undertaking
centuries-long projects? I haven't seen much if anything in that vein. This
particular bit is relevant to one of those things that were in the original rules
of *Dungeons & Dragons* but which got culled from later iterations. In the
AD&D wilderness rules there were castles placed wherever there were pools
on Avalon Hill's *Outdoor Survival* map. (Yes, the original rules assumed you
would have access to two other games that a lot of people would not have
even heard of at the time. You could not even understand the combat rules
without one of them!) Anyway, you'd roll to see what type of person occupied
the castles, and one of the results was some shade of magic-user. The notes
on handling these domains are quite terse, but after reading Jack Vance, you'll
understand exactly what these guys are up to, what could go wrong if you
encounter one, and what sort of quests they'll send you on if they happen
to geas your party! This sort of thing can make your game world far more
paranoid and inscrutable than the typical eighties-era fantasy milieu.

*Passing through a portal, the travelers entered an office overlooking the central
yard, where pens, cages and stockades held beasts of so great variety as to
astound Cugel.... Garstang, who had been surveying the compound, shook
his head ruefully. 'I confess to puzzlement. Each beast is of a different sort,
and none seem to fit any well-defined categories.' The keeper admitted that
such was the case. 'If you care to listen, I can explain all. The tale is of
a continuing fascination, and will assist you in the management of your
beasts.... In a past eon Mad King Kutt ordained a menagerie like none*

*before, for his private amazement and the stupefaction of the world. His
wizard, Follinense, therefore produced a group of beasts and teratoids unique,
combining the wildest variety of plasms; to the result you see…. [Mad King
Kutt] loosed the entire assemblage upon the general countryside, to the general
disturbance. The creatures, endowed with an eclectic fecundity, became more
rather than less bizarre, and now they roam the Plain of Oparona and
Blanwalt Forest in great numbers.' (p 164-166)*

Is there anything on your campaign's wilderness map that is the result of
some crazy magician's mucking around eons ago? Does it impact not only the
wandering monsters tables but also the local economy in terms of what sorts
of things are available? Is it mind-numbingly strange and almost painfully
bizarre? In most peoples' games, the answer is going to be "no" for most
of those questions. They've traded in the vibrancy of uniqueness for the
blandness of accessibility and consistency… *and that's okay.* As a game master,
you're responsible for creating a playing field that allows the players maximum
latitude to set their own course and to become the stars of the show. If you
want to create a world chock full of stuff this crazy, you need to just become
a novelist and have done with it, right?

But then there's this:

*The spell known as the Inside Out and Over was of derivation so remote
as to be forgotten. An unknown Cloud-rider of the Twenty-first Eon had
constructed an archaic version; the half-legendary Basile Blackweb had refined its contours, a process continued by Veronifer the Bland, who added
a reinforcing resonance. Archemand of Glaere had annotated fourteen of
its pervulsions: Phandaal had listed it in the "A," or "Perfected," category
of his monumental catalog. In this fashion it had reached the workbook of
Zaraides the Sage, where Cugel, immured under a hillock, had found it and
spoken it forth. (p 198)*

While there are rules for spell research going back at least as far back as first
edition *AD&D*, you certainly don't hear of players contributing to anything
like this particular chain of development. And while you do see spells like
"Tenser's Floating Disc" or "Bigby's Grasping Hand," you certainly don't see
elaborate backgrounds like this for any of the canonical spells of the game.
Spell research is not something players tend to mess with because the rules

on it are tucked away in the back of the *Dungeon Masters Guide* or in an odd corner of the Expert Rulebook. Dungeon Masters do not tend to incorporate the rules into their adventure or setting design because it's not something that players expect or clamor for. Without a lot of initiative and effort, the rules are not much more than cruft for most gamers.

> *Days went by and Iucounus's trap, if such existed, remained unsprung, and Cugel at last came to believe that none existed. During this time he applied himself to Iucounu's tomes and folios, but with disappointing results. Certain of the tomes were written in archaic tongues, indecipherable script or arcane terminology; others described phenomena beyond his comprehension; others exuded a waft of such urgent danger that Cugel instantly clamped shut the covers. One or two of the work-books he found susceptible to his understanding. These he studied with great diligence, cramming syllable after wrenching syllable into his mind, where they rolled and pressed and distended his temples. Presently he was able to encompass a few of the most simple and primitive spells, certain of which he tested upon Iucounu: notably Lugwiler's Dismal Itch. But by and large Cugel was disappointed by what seemed a lack of innate competence. Accomplished magicians could encompass three or even four of the most powerful effectuants; for Cugel, attaining even a single spell was a task of extraordinary difficulty. (p 214)*

This passage is of interest because Cugel the Clever is not actually a magic-user. He's more of a dashing rogue *without* a heart of gold. While you don't see a character class like this show up in any of the older *D&D* rule sets, he does in fact turn up in the earliest versions of *Tunnels & Trolls*, where "rogues can both fight and use magic, but they don't know any spells to start with and they must be taught each spell they learn separately by a magic-user."[11] They have the "innate ability to be magic-users, but never got the training."[12] As a consequence, they cannot create new spells of their own devising; they just don't grasp things well enough to do that. In contrast, *Tunnels & Trolls* magic-users start with all of the first-level spells from that game and may purchase higher-level spells from their guild when they are able to cast them. While this is a more freewheeling take on thieves and magic-users than is normal in *D&D* circles, it's clear that Ken St. Andre took at least some inspiration from Jack Vance for his rogue class from Jack Vance.

Consulting the work-book, he encompassed the spell; then, pointing and naming Fianosther, he spoke the dreadful syllables. But Fianosther, rather than sinking into the earth, crouched as before. Cugel hastily consulted the work-book and saw that in error he had transposed a pair of pervulsions, thereby reversing the quality of the spell. Indeed, even as he understood the mistake, to all sides there were small sounds, and previous victims across the eons were now erupted from a depth of forty-five miles, and discharged upon the surface. Here they lay, blinking in glazed astonishment; though a few lay rigid, too sluggish to react. Their garments had fallen to dust, though the more recently encysted still wore a rag or two. Presently all but the most dazed and rigid made tentative motions, feeling the air, groping at the sky, marveling at the sun. (p 218)

From the standpoint of the raw design of the early role-playing games, this passage is probably the most surprising of all. This is perhaps the original source for the concept of reversing spells that is a common trope in the old games. I doubt that designers were overly concerned with the implications of making it easy to do this. Rule books were spartan at the dawn of the hobby, and it would have simply been convenient to be able to create a quick-and-dirty necromancer type that could cast "Cause Light Wounds" without having to make up new spells or class details. The real surprise here is that the spell reversal here was accidental; it was a result of a rogue attempting to cast a spell that was beyond his ability! Critical failure tables with results like this would have been a common modification by the time Steve Jackson incorporated one into his first edition of *GURPS Fantasy* in the mid-eighties, but while such an approach was natural and obvious to a certain type of gamer then, it was not in line with the design choices of Gary Gygax and Ken St. Andre in the first two role-playing games. Skill checks and critical failure effects are simply not a part of how they set things up at the ground level of the hobby.

But take another look at that last passage. Everyone in a very large area that had ever been put away by the Spell of Forlorn Encystment and imprisoned deep in the earth was suddenly set free. Who knows what things they would remember that had been long forgotten by the people of the dying earth! What if they remembered spells that were otherwise lost? Would they be able to transcribe them into spell books from memory? What would happen to all those people? *What happens next?* I can barely even begin to guess about that, but I can surely say that I've never seen anything even close to that awesome happen as a side effect of some game's magic system.[13]

It's not just that Jack Vance was ahead of his time; game designers simply haven't gotten around to catching up to him yet.

Notes

1. This is from the James M. Ward interview in Fight On! #12.

2. This insight is original to designer S. John Ross.

3. This is from *Dragon Magazine #52* where J. Eric Holmes reviewed the new Moldvay Basic D&D set and compared it to his edition.

4. "A Game as Literary Tutorial," *The New York Times*, July 13, 2014

5. See my post "Jack McDevitt on John Carter, Pulp Artwork, and NASA" for details, but alas… it looks like his journals are gone now.

6. "Notes for Novice Dungeon Masters" by Lewis Pulsipher appeared in *Space Gamer #35*. (And by the way, based on this article, it looks like Dr. Pulsipher was aware back then that Michael Moorcock was merely the *popularizer* of the idea of the struggle between Law and Chaos.)

7. "Aboard the Leviathan" by Marc Miller appeared in *Space Gamer #40*.

8. My own session report "A Role-Playing Game… with Imaginary Rules and Dice" illustrates this.

9. See "The narrowing of fantasy" at the Castalia House Blog for more on this.

10. *Legends of the Flame Princess* ref book, page 48.

11. *Tunnels & Trolls* fourth edition, page 9.

12. *Tunnels & Trolls* fourth edition, page 30.

13. Jeff Rients's treatise on "Fireballs and Dragonbreath" is still pretty cool though.

A Princess of Mars
by Edgar Rice Burroughs

Even as a kid, I always understood that there was something portentous about the *Barsoom* series paperbacks on the shelf at the library. Nevertheless, I'd always passed them over for books by authors that got more credit as being "grandmasters" of science fiction. I just couldn't take Edgar Rice Burroughs's books seriously at the time. That's a shame, really, because, without at least some familiarity with his work, it's hard to truly grasp what's happened in the past hundred years of science fiction.

He casts an imposing shadow. Not only did he originate the "sword and planet" genre, but he was also a direct influence on creators ranging from Ray Bradbury to James Cameron. And though the way John Carter jumps around might be somewhat underwhelming by today's standards, it was serious business back when Jerry Siegel was developing a character that could *leap tall buildings with a single bound*.[1]

There is a similar connection to the iconic *Star Wars* movie poster by Tom Jung. I'm sure you recall it. Luke is raising his lightsaber in a combination of triumph and rage, his robes spilling open to reveal a perfectly chiseled chest, his left foot on the top of a hill of some alien Iwo Jima, a maelstrom of space battle erupting in the sky above him. The two robots practically cower behind him. Leia cocks her chest to one side affording a more pronounced view of her cleavage, one hand on her hip and with a slit going up her dress that will *not quit*. There is a brazenness to her pose, to be sure, but also something else. I think every great gangster knows this on some level, but her standing with Luke, aligning herself with him like that, and being as alluring and provocative as she is, she multiplies Luke's intimidation factor even as she subtly upstages him. It is a dynamite combination that positively sizzles.

Unfortunately, it presents a forceful, epic tone that is not at all to be found in the movie itself. You see, it wasn't until George Lucas realized that he couldn't do Flash Gordon that he even cast his gaze upon Burroughs's influential Mars series. When he finally came across them, he was so smitten with the Frank Frazetta covers that he actually wanted to hire him to make the poster. The resemblance is no accident, and it invites comparison. In a sense, *Star Wars* comes in the exact same packaging as the John Carter series, but it's clear that Lucas was unable to fully translate the content of those books into cinematic form.

Consider this:

> *And the sight which met my eyes was that of a slender, girlish figure, similar in every detail to the earthly women of my past life. She did not see me at first, but just as she was disappearing through the portal of the building which was to be her prison she turned, and her eyes met mine. Her face was oval and beautiful in the extreme, her every feature was finely chiseled and exquisite, her eyes large and lustrous and her head surmounted by a mass of coal black, waving hair, caught loosely into a strange yet becoming coiffure. Her skin was of a light reddish copper color, against which the crimson glow of her cheeks and the ruby of her beautifully molded lips shone with a strangely enhancing effect. She was as destitute of clothes as the green Martians who accompanied her; indeed, save for her highly wrought ornaments she was entirely naked, nor could any apparel have enhanced the beauty of her perfect and symmetrical figure. (Chapter VIII)*

Star Wars fans got to see Princess Leia in a slave girl costume for a grand total of 150 seconds in *Return of the Jedi*. The absence of that sort of thing in the first two films was a glaring omission, and the outfit inspired by Frank Frazetta's depictions of Dejah Thoris was perhaps an inevitable development.[2] It so captured the imagination of fandom that it has made a mark on every major comic book and gaming convention since. But why settle for a fleeting glimpse of space princess majesty when you can have Dejah Thoris in an even skimpier outfit for a dozen book-length adventures? The battered old paperbacks are a much better deal....

Then there's the fact that Leia is sort of a princess in name only. We find out later that she must have been adopted when she is retconned into being Luke's sister. Eh, she was always more of the sassy space senator type to begin with, but Dejah Thoris is no counterfeit: she's "the daughter of ten thousand jeddaks" and can trace her "ancestry straight back without a break to the builder of the first great waterway." (Chapter XIII)

Consider how the hero and heroine first encounter each other in *A Princess of Mars*:

> *As her gaze rested on me her eyes opened wide in astonishment, and she made a little sign with her free hand; a sign which I did not, of course, understand. Just a moment we gazed upon each other, and then the look of hope and renewed courage which had glorified her face as she discovered me, faded into one of utter dejection, mingled with loathing and contempt. I realized I had not answered her signal, and ignorant as I was of Martian customs, I intuitively felt that she had made an appeal for succor and protection which my unfortunate ignorance had prevented me from answering. And then she was dragged out of my sight into the depths of the deserted edifice. (Chapter IX)*

I call this the "Darcy effect" after the leading man of *Pride and Prejudice*. When that icon of vintage romance novels first enters the scene, it is with an incredible insult to the effect that none of the local girls is worth dancing with. While this makes him look like an arrogant jerk to everyone in earshot, it all too predictably rockets him into Elizabeth's attention. It's yet another testament to the fact that nice guys finish last, but it's nevertheless a classic opening gambit. Burroughs takes a similar tack in his tale but ups the ante by putting Dejah Thoris in a significant amount of danger as a direct consequence of John Carter's initial snub. And unlike Mr. Darcy, John Carter retains his likability as a character because all of this is accidental, a consequence of his unfamiliarity with Barsoom's cultures.

Compare that to Luke and Leia. Luke is smitten with a pint-sized hologram of Leia. It's kind of sappy for him to want to play her message over and over just so he can keep on ogling her. When Luke risks incomprehensible levels of danger to save her from her scheduled execution, her first words to him are a sarcastic put down: *Aren't you a little short for a stormtrooper?* This is not the sort of situation that any young man would seriously aspire to be in. I've always identified with Luke and even wanted to be Luke when I was a kid, but he retains his "best buddy" status for the duration of the film franchise and never truly graduates to anything resembling a true leading man. Maybe

I could never quite put my finger on the problem back in the day, but this really is frustrating.

Granted, Lucas put together a fantastic cast that had great chemistry together, and whoever did the editing made sure everything ended up punchy and entertaining, but Burroughs knew how much more credible a romantic arc can be if it's established early on that the hero has passed over plenty of chances to settle down:

> *So this was love! I had escaped it for all the years I had roamed the five continents and their encircling seas; in spite of beautiful women and urging opportunity; in spite of a half-desire for love and a constant search for my ideal, it had remained for me to fall furiously and hopelessly in love with a creature from another world, of a species similar possibly, yet not identical with mine. A woman who was hatched from an egg, and whose span of life might cover a thousand years; whose people had strange customs and ideas; a woman whose hopes, whose pleasures, whose standards of virtue and of right and wrong might vary as greatly from mine as did those of the green Martians. (Chapter XIV)*

While it's perfectly reasonable for a farm boy on a backwater world to be smitten with the first space princess to come along, the whole scenario in the film is decidedly less awe-inspiring than what's implied by the movie posters. Edgar Rice Burroughs again provides the better deal. He doesn't drop the ball as the romantic stakes grow ever higher, either. After John Carter's close shave with death, the space princess inadvertently reveals her true feelings for him:

> *"Is she injured?" I asked of Sola, indicating Dejah Thoris by an inclination of my head. "No," she answered, "she thinks that you are dead." "And that her grandmother's cat may now have no one to polish its teeth?" I queried, smiling. "I think you wrong her, John Carter," said Sola. "I do not understand either her ways or yours, but I am sure the granddaughter of ten thousand jeddaks would never grieve like this over any who held but the highest claim upon her affections. They are a proud race, but they are just, as are all Barsoomians, and you must have hurt or wronged her grievously that she will not admit your existence living, though she mourns you dead. (Chapter XV)*

As Robert E. Lee famously said, it is "the forbearing use of power does not only form a touchstone, but the manner in which an individual enjoys certain advantages over others is a test of a true gentleman." With the sure knowledge that he has Dejah Thoris's heart in the palm of his hand, John Carter demonstrates the kind of forbearance that fully establishes his character as the quintessential gentleman of Virgina. You can respect these characters and their relationship in a way that just doesn't seem to happen very often in more recent space opera.

But the story was just getting warmed up at that point. There were desperate treks across the wilderness to fulfill, deadly arena combats to fight, an epic air war in the martian skies that could rival the Battle of Yavin, sieges to break, and disastrously arranged marriages that had to be foiled at the last second. There's plenty for movie makers to plunder, and it happens to this day, but there is one thing that this book does that highlights the most glaring deficiency in the *Star Wars* franchise. There just really isn't that big of a payoff in comparison to this:

"I have done many strange things in my life, many things that wiser men would not have dared, but never in my wildest fancies have I dreamed of winning a Dejah Thoris for myself—for never had I dreamed that in all the universe dwelt such a woman as the Princess of Helium. That you are a princess does not abash me, but that you are you is enough to make me doubt my sanity as I ask you, my princess, to be mine." "He does not need to be abashed who so well knew the answer to his plea before the plea were made," she replied, rising and placing her dear hands upon my shoulders, and so I took her in my arms and kissed her. (Chapter XXV)

I admit, I do wonder if the "Princess of Helium" talks in a high-pitched cartoon voice. And I'm completely at a loss to explain how a human and a Red Martian can procreate when the women on Mars all lay eggs. But it's clear that John Carter's military and diplomatic accomplishments rival those of Tolkien's Aragorn: *Never before had an armed body of green warriors entered the gates of Helium, and that they came now as friends and allies filled the red men with rejoicing.* (Chapter XXVI) That really nails down why *Star Wars* pales in comparison to this science-fiction classic. Edgar Rice Burroughs not only gives us a space princess of unsurpassed quality, but he also shows us a man that is worthy of her. Lucas either fails to grasp the concept or else doesn't even try.

Now I love *Star Wars*, I really do. I grew up with the movies and treasured my Kenner action figures and their Darth Vader carrying case as much as any other boy my age. But I would have been much better served had some kindhearted adult known to introduce me to the John Carter series at some point. And I have to confess I'd probably feel somewhat more kindly toward the massively popular film franchise if not for the appropriation of Frank Frazetta's style and the many people making strongly worded claims of its mythic potency.

Seriously, though: what kind of epic myth is it where the guy doesn't get the girl in the end? Much better, in my opinion, is *The Lord of The Rings*, in which not only does Arwen Evenstar give up her immortality for a man of renown, but even the humble Samwise Hamfast can settle down in Hobbiton as mayor-for-life with Rosie to keep him company and Elanor to sit on his knee. Edgar Rice Burroughs is practically on the same page as J. R. R. Tolkien here, and as far as happy endings go, they're light years ahead of a big party with the Ewoks. Honestly, I don't know what my expectations were going in here, but I'm fairly certain that *Star Wars* has lost more than a little of its luster for me as a result of my having read *A Princess of Mars*.

Notes

1. See Michael Sellers's "Jerry Siegel Cites Both Tarzan and John Carter as Key Influences in Creating Superman" for more on this.

2. "Frank Frazetta: Fantasy Legend" by Charles Moffat is online at *Art History Archive*.

Jack of Shadows
by Roger Zelazny

This book is so flawed it's shocking. It's a shame since it's otherwise full of great imagery delivered at a brisk tempo. Every chapter seems to have a new shade or tone that contrasts with the previous one, but it ultimately falls apart. I'm impressed that Zelazny could whip up something like this in a single draft, but the lack of serious effort on this one is evident.

I suspect that the main reason that this particular title was singled out in Gary Gygax's Appendix N reading list is that the author at least had the sense to *want* to make something derivative of *The Eyes of the Overworld*. That is exactly the sort of thing I would want to see more of at any rate. And given that not everyone can acquire a taste for Jack Vance's prose, it's probably a good thing that someone tried to make a toned-down version of that particular oeuvre. Unfortunately, not even an author of Zelazny's caliber was up to the task of emulating Vance.

But that's not to say that this book didn't have an impact. Old school *Dungeons & Dragons* in all probability has "Hide in Shadows" set apart as a specific ability of the thief because of this book.[1] The title character here has the ability not only to vanish into shadows but also to travel through them instantaneously. If he stands even partially within any sort of shadow, he becomes invulnerable and can even reflect special attacks, such as level drains and breath attacks, back at his attackers.[2] More intriguingly, the Jack of Shadows can actually even hear when his name is spoken in shadows. He can't always tell who is saying it, but he can tell the general direction and distance from which it happened.

I've long wondered why *D&D* thieves could so easily "Climb Steep Surfaces" even at low level. Well, in this book, the thief can literally walk up even a vertical face as long as there are shadows on it. And if you ever wonder why thief and rogue characters on old games often have a surprising degree of magical ability, Zelazny's Jack of Shadows and Vance's Cugel the Clever have about equal shares in helping establish this once-common trope. Jack of Shadows is actually the top magic-user on his side of the world; he's nearly Sauron-like in his level of accomplishment and dominion. But purists that are looking for more reasons to object to the addition of the thief class to the original fantasy role-playing game will be glad to know that he acquires his title of "thief" because what he *does*, not because of what his exact skill set is.

The setting of the book is completely off the wall though. The earth in it is tide locked, but science only works on the light side while magic only works on the dark side. In the first place, this doesn't make any sense; and yes, the laws of physics and even the nature of reality seem to change from one side to the other. But this is just a terrible premise for a game. I mean, if you have swords and sorcery in a setting, then everyone will want to know which is better, just like people want to know who would win if Superman and Batman got into a fight.[3] Steve Jackson knew that, which is why when you put his two classic MicroGames *Melee* and *Wizard* together, you really could find out if an iconic barbarian could win against a devious spell-caster. In a similar vein, I really wanted to see science and magic go mano-a-mano in this work… or maybe even battle at a strategic level.[4] Alas, the world in this setting just isn't there to be toyed with in that manner. Indeed, it's there to make some sort of literary point.[5]

You see, there's this big mysterious demon-looking guy that's merged some-how into part of a mountain in the twilight zone between the worlds of magic and science. It is the only real friend that Jack of Shadows has, and Jack drops by every now and then to give it wine and discuss the deep questions of the universe. If it isn't clear that you're supposed to be moved and impressed by the inherent wisdom of this creature, then the fact that it is essentially confirmed to have oracular powers later on should give it some credibility by the time you're finished with the book. Here's a section of their dialog:

> *"I have heard daysiders say that the core of the world is a molten demon, that the temperature increases as one descends toward it, that if the crust of the world is pierced then fires leap forth and melted minerals build volcanoes. Yet I know that volcanoes are the doings of fire elementals who, if disturbed, melt the ground about them and hurl it upward. They exist in small pockets. One*

may descend far past them without the temperature increasing. Travelling far enough, one comes to the center of the world, which is not molten— which contains the Machine, with great springs, as in a clock, and gears and pulleys and counterbalances. I know this to be true, for I have journeyed that way and been near to the Machine itself. Still, the daysiders have ways of demonstrating that their view is the correct one. I was almost convinced by the way one man explained it, though I knew better. How can this be?" "You were both correct," said Morningstar. "It is the same thing that you describe, although neither of you sees it as it really is. Each of you colors reality in keeping with your means of controlling it. For if it is uncontrollable, you fear it. Sometimes then, you color it incomprehensible. In your case, machine; in theirs, a demon." "The stars I know to be the houses of spirits and deities— some friendly, some unfriendly and many not caring. All are near at hand and can be reached. They will respond when properly invoked. Yet the daysiders say that they are vast distances away and that there is no intelligence there. Again?" "It is again but two ways of regarding reality, both of them correct." "If there can be two ways, may there not be a third? Or a fourth? Or as many as there are people for that matter?" "Yes," said Morningstar. "Then which one is correct?" "They all are."

This is just about the dumbest thing—bar none—that I can remember reading in any science-fiction or fantasy story. I want to say that the author is well aware that he's on shaky ground with this and that he follows through by developing the consequences of this premise. And he tries to some extent. But this idea that each person has his own individual truth is not a premise at all. It's an anti-premise, an idea that pretty much refutes itself. *There are no consequences to such an idea, and nothing follows from it logically.*

Maybe the author was aware of this: after all, the assertion is presented by a character that hasn't got a leg to stand on! But why would he try to pawn this off on the reader if he actually understood how idiotic it was? If that was the case, then he'd have to be pretty cynical to think he could get away with it. "I can put anything in here, and my stupid fans will just swill it up, ha ha ha!" No, I expect that Roger Zelazny really was clueless enough to think that this was both daring and inspiring. He would, of course, have fit right in with his times: John Lennon's "Imagine," which was released the same year, is essentially a hymn to this sort of non-thought.

I suspect the author had to make this a central pillar of his tale because he chose to go whole hog into making a basically evil protagonist. He knew he had a lot of work to do to sell this to his readers, so he knocked down anything that would get in the way of their ability to identify with him. What's interesting about this is just how far down this particular rabbit hole Zelazny actually ends up going:

> *"Why is it," he asked, "that the Fallen Star who brought us knowledge of the Art, did not extend it to the daysiders as well?" "Perhaps," said Morningstar, "the more theologically inclined among the lightlanders ask why he did not grant the boon of science to the darksiders. What difference does it make? I have heard the story that neither was the gift of the Fallen One, but both the inventions of man; that his gift, rather, was that of consciousness, which creates its own systems."*

What difference does anything make at this point, eh?[6] Yeah, this really is in there: pretty much "what's true for them is not true for you... and oh, by the way... not only is Satan a misunderstood Prometheus, but he is also responsible for giving mankind consciousness and the ability to think so that we can each make up our own individual truths that don't have anything to do with anything else." Something like that. It's incredible, really, that anyone would so quickly jump to strongly stated theological assertions right after attempting to destroy the foundations of logic. I'd actually be surprised if it wasn't par for the course. It's only the audacity of the purveyors of this nonsense that shocks me anymore. Why would anyone need cater to your opinions once you've declared truth to be relative anyway? Who's listening at that point?

These are the lengths that the author necessarily had to go in order to give the impression that Jack of Shadows isn't such a bad guy for being such a bad guy. And I suppose it even makes sense that the story ends on a cliffhanger; I mean, what else can be concluded once you've concluded that there can't be any conclusions? I'm not sure what else there is to say about this, but I have to say... if you have to recast the Devil as a misunderstood force for good in order to make your lead character seem even marginally sympathetic, then you may not have a strong-enough story concept to really work for much of anything. Much more entertaining, in my opinion, is seeing Cugel the Clever swindle people who are less trustworthy than himself. Jack Vance, at the very least, understood just how satisfying it was to see a brazenly greedy conman get a devastating comeuppance in the end.

Notes

1. Usually the "Hide in Shadows" and "Move Silently" are combined into a more generic "Stealth" skill in more recent games.

2. I haven't seen this ability creep into anyone's thief or rogue archetypes. I like it though!

3. Batman would totally beat up Superman, by the way.

4. Why not just have magic not work on the light side and then see where that leads?

5. Which is why literary fiction is pretty well useless as an inspiration for game design. The latter is about doing something *for* somebody while the former is too often about doing something *to* a person.

6. This phrase is not exactly the touchstone of honesty and intellectual rigor.

At the Earth's Core
by Edgar Rice Burroughs

When a Connecticut-born mining operator goes to visit his dilettante paleon-tologist friend that has constructed a "mechanical subterranean prospector," an "iron mole" with "a mighty revolving drill" capable of tunneling through the earth at unparalleled speed, things quickly go off the rails. Not five para-graphs into the story, the two are on board the hundred-foot-long machine burrowing down into the earth. Predictably, the machine ends up going straight down with the steering controls locked. They avoid burning up in the intense heat, they nearly die when the oxygen tanks run out, and everything seems lost, but then the machine breaks through the surface. For a moment, it appears that they might have turned around while inside an ice strata at some point, causing them to resurface in a random location, but then they notice that things are not as they seem:

> As I looked I began to appreciate the reason for the strangeness of the landscape that had haunted me from the first with an illusive suggestion of the bizarre and unnatural—THERE WAS NO HORIZON! As far as the eye could reach out the sea continued and upon its bosom floated tiny islands, those in the distance reduced to mere specks; but ever beyond them was the sea, until the impression became quite real that one was LOOKING UP at the most distant point that the eyes could fathom—the distance was lost in the distance. That was all—there was no clear-cut horizontal line marking the dip of the globe below the line of vision.... I glanced up to find the great orb still motionless in the center of the heaven. And such a sun! I had scarcely noticed it before. Fully thrice the size of the sun I had known throughout my life, and apparently so near that the sight of it carried the conviction that one might almost reach up and touch it. (Chapter 2)

After some encounters with the local fauna, the two travelers realize that there is some sort of new world on the *inside* of the earth. Now, a hollow earth is one thing, and the whole idea of a lost world is great, but Edgar Rice Burroughs has gone to an inconceivably fantastic level by having a sun inside the earth to light this strange domain. The nutty professor type character explains how it can be:

> "*The earth was once a nebulous mass. It cooled, and as it cooled it shrank. At length a thin crust of solid matter formed upon its outer surface—a sort of shell; but within it was partially molten matter and highly expanded gases. As it continued to cool, what happened? Centrifugal force hurled the particles of the nebulous center toward the crust as rapidly as they approached a solid state. You have seen the same principle practically applied in the modern cream separator. Presently there was only a small super-heated core of gaseous matter remaining within a huge vacant interior left by the contraction of the cooling gases. The equal attraction of the solid crust from all directions maintained this luminous core in the exact center of the hollow globe. What remains of it is the sun you saw today—a relatively tiny thing at the exact center of the earth. Equally to every part of this inner world it diffuses its perpetual noonday light and torrid heat.*" *This inner world must have cooled sufficiently to support animal life long ages after life appeared upon the outer crust, but that the same agencies were at work here is evident from the similar forms of both animal and vegetable creation which we have already seen. Take the great beast which attacked us, for example. Unquestionably a counterpart of the Megatherium of the post-Pliocene period of the outer crust, whose fossilized skeleton has been found in South America.*" "*But the grotesque inhabitants of this forest?*" *I urged. "Surely they have no counterpart in the earth's history." "Who can tell?" he rejoined. "They may constitute the link between ape and man, all traces of which have been swallowed by the countless convulsions which have racked the outer crust, or they may be merely the result of evolution along slightly different lines—either is quite possible.*" (Chapter 3)

With the help of a library in an underground city, they discover more about the geography of this strange place:

> "*Look,*" *he cried, pointing to it, "this is evidently water, and all this land.*

Do you notice the general configuration of the two areas? Where the oceans are upon the outer crust, is land here. These relatively small areas of ocean follow the general lines of the continents of the outer world." We know that the crust of the globe is 500 miles in thickness; then the inside diameter of Pellucidar must be 7,000 miles, and the superficial area 165,480,000 square miles. Three-fourths of this is land. Think of it! A land area of 124,110,000 square miles! Our own world contains but 53,000,000 square miles of land, the balance of its surface being covered by water. Just as we often compare nations by their relative land areas, so if we compare these two worlds in the same way we have the strange anomaly of a larger world within a smaller one! (Chapter 5)

And finally, almost as an afterthought, Burroughs introduces one more mind-blowing element to his inner world:

"What is the Land of Awful Shadow?" I asked. "It is the land which lies beneath the Dead World," replied Dian; "the Dead World which hangs forever between the sun and Pellucidar above the Land of Awful Shadow. It is the Dead World which makes the great shadow upon this portion of Pellucidar." I did not fully understand what she meant, nor am I sure that I do yet, for I have never been to that part of Pellucidar from which the Dead World is visible; but Perry says that it is the moon of Pellucidar—a tiny planet within a planet—and that it revolves around the earth's axis coincidently with the earth, and thus is always above the same spot within Pellucidar. (Chapter 15)

Taken together, this is so audacious as to be utterly confounding. It's the little things that make it seem real though. With no stars and no day or night, the inner world becomes strangely timeless, and navigation is impossible. The paleontology is, of course, dated. There are an awful lot of goofy coincidences holding the plot together, too. But reading this, it becomes pretty clear that our baseline concepts of romance are essentially medieval in origin. The stock love interest arc developed in *Princess of Mars* is completely out of place when it is transposed onto some kind of prehistoric milieu. Dian the Beautiful might be a fine specimen, but she pales in comparison to the daughter of a thousand jeddaks. Plus, the way she screams, "I hate you!" at the hero throughout the book gets old after a while.

It's the casual way in which the protagonists initiate a combination of uplift, revolution, and missionary work that is especially striking today:

> *"Why, Perry," I exclaimed, "you and I may reclaim a whole world! Together we can lead the races of men out of the darkness of ignorance into the light of advancement and civilization. At one step we may carry them from the Age of Stone to the twentieth century. It's marvelous—absolutely marvelous just to think about it." "David," said the old man, "I believe that God sent us here for just that purpose—it shall be my life work to teach them His word— to lead them into the light of His mercy while we are training their hearts and hands in the ways of culture and civilization." "You are right, Perry," I said, "and while you are teaching them to pray I'll be teaching them to fight, and between us we'll make a race of men that will be an honor to us both."*
> *(Chapter 5)*

Fortunately, the book never really devolves into some kind of paper-thin morality play. The peoples of Pellucidar are their own thing... not stand-ins for real-world nations or people groups. The ape-men with prehensile tales are the minions of the dominant species of the underworld: winged lizard people with strange telepathic powers. The ape-men capture the human-like cave men and cave women and force them to work as slaves for their overlords. Meanwhile, other groups of cave people have cut a deal with the lizard folk: they will capture people from enemy tribes and deliver them to temples, where they will be eaten in diabolical rituals. Evidently, this latter activity would be offensive to the ape-man minions if they knew of it, so it has to occur in locations remote from the core of the lizard peoples' civilization.

It isn't immediately obvious what the right thing to do with this situation is, but it's rich enough (and straightforward enough) that it would be interesting to see how tabletop role-playing gamers respond to it. Usually in games, the good guys and bad guys are clearly demarcated, and the scenario objectives are generally pretty clear. A lot of adventuring boils down to a combination of investigation and exploration that just so happens to end with a climatic "boss" encounter or some kind of puzzle. That style of play is so easy to run that even a computer can do it! While the classic module "The Island of Dread" does introduce a number of factions that is comparable to what is seen here, it does not delve overmuch into the possibilities of how the players can alter the status quo of the balance of power the way Burroughs does here.

I think the thing that actually got translated from this book into early *D&D* culture is a willingness to put an epic payoff in the strangest places. You can see this in the iconic Stone Mountain dungeon from the first *Basic Set* edited by J. Eric Holmes, where there is an entire domed city on the seventh level on an island in an underground lake. In Tom Moldvay's "The Lost City," the titular metropolis turns out to be deep in the earth in a vast underground far below the well-trod levels of the ziggurat. I always thought this was pretty ambitious stuff, but compared to Edgar Rice Burroughs, this is actually pretty tame. But these underground cities are like the inner world of Pellucidar in that they require something more than the usual dungeon crawling premise to translate them into actual gameplay.

What exactly is to be done with those cities is something that is only hinted at rather than explicitly worked out in rule sets or adventure modules. Burroughs's solution to this design problem is actually rather innovative:

> *Ghak and Dacor reached a very amicable arrangement, and it was at a council of the head men of the various tribes of the Sari that the eventual form of government was tentatively agreed upon. Roughly, the various kingdoms were to remain virtually independent, but there was to be one great overlord, or emperor. It was decided that I should be the first of the dynasty of the emperors of Pellucidar. We set about teaching the women how to make bows and arrows, and poison pouches. The young men hunted the vipers which provided the virus, and it was they who mined the iron ore, and fashioned the swords under Perry's direction. Rapidly the fever spread from one tribe to another until representatives from nations so far distant that the Sarians had never even heard of them came in to take the oath of allegiance which we required, and to learn the art of making the new weapons and using them. We sent our young men out as instructors to every nation of the federation, and the movement had reached colossal proportions before the Mahars discovered it. The first intimation they had was when three of their great slave caravans were annihilated in rapid succession. They could not comprehend that the lower orders had suddenly developed a power which rendered them really formidable. (Chapter 15)*

The crucial element in the action here lies in how the characters form alliances and play different groups off of each other. This is echoed in how the players are expected to engage with the various monster tribes of Gary

Gygax's "Keep on the Borderlands." People rarely played the game in that manner because there is little in the rules to assist the novice Dungeon Master: so many of the rulings that will have to be made should the players attempt something along those lines come down to little more than judgment calls. The fact that large swaths of play end up taking place outside the scope of the rules is exactly what makes it fun. However, if you want to transition into something closer to this type of domain level play early on, you're going to have to be comfortable in allowing for diplomacy rather than simply expecting the players to be able to systematically "clean out" the adventure location with only their own resources. Indeed, current notions of encounter balance have to go out the window in order to force the players to start getting creative.

Violence isn't the answer to this one. Not initially anyway.... Not that there isn't furious action and a large set-piece battle in the book, but with Edgar Rice Burroughs, when you delve deep enough into the earth, you end up in a *Foundation*-type scenario, a 4X strategy game along the lines of Sid Meier's *Civilization*. As Ryan Harvey said over at *Black Gate*, Burroughs "re-shaped popular fiction, helped change the United States into a nation of readers, and created the professional fiction writer." His contributions to fiction are enormous, but his contribution to gaming included what can only be the biggest dungeon ever conceived. It's awe inspiring; it's epic in its scope... and loaded with possibilities.

The Pirates of Venus
by Edgar Rice Burroughs

At least three of Edgar Rice Burroughs's series are part of the same continuity: both *Tarzan* and events from the *Pellucidar* series are mentioned in this first novel in the Venus series. The Mars series *could* have been brought in here as well as the protagonist fully intended to go there. Alas, his calculations for his trajectory failed to account for the gravitational pull of the moon. He resigns himself to a slow, ignoble death in the depths of interstellar space, but then he miraculously finds himself hurtling toward Venus instead. "I had aimed at Mars and was about to hit Venus," Carson Napier admits, "unquestionably the all-time cosmic record for poor shots."

It gets better though. Not only does Carson Napier survive his unexpected planetfall, but he also discovers an inhabitable world populated by the humanoid Vepagans, which mankind could presumably interbreed with. There are vast stretches of wilderness full of incredible creatures to fight. And though the local civilization has a variety of devastating ray guns, they are in short-enough supply that there is still plenty of cause for nearly everyone to carry a sword. That's right; in another incredible coincidence, Mars, the Earth's Core, and Venus all turn out to have exactly the right conditions for epic romance and adventure. And by a sort of comic book logic, the ramifications of this appear not at all to infringe upon the ongoing developments back in the "real" world.

Further compounding on the preceding coincidences, the recent history of Venus is *strangely familiar*:

> *Vepaja was prosperous and happy, yet there were malcontents. These were the lazy and incompetent. Many of them were of the criminal class. They were envious of those who had won to positions which they were not mentally equipped to attain. Over a long period of time they were responsible for*

minor discord and dissension, but the people either paid no attention to them or laughed them down. Then they found a leader. He was a laborer named Thor, a man with a criminal record.

This man founded a secret order known as Thorists and preached a gospel of class hatred called Thorism. By means of lying propaganda he gained a large following, and as all his energies were directed against a single class, he had all the vast millions of the other three classes to draw from, though naturally he found few converts among the merchants and employers which also included the agrarian class.

The sole end of the Thorist leaders was personal power and aggrandizement; their aims were wholly selfish, yet, because they worked solely among the ignorant masses, they had little difficulty in deceiving their dupes, who finally rose under their false leaders in a bloody revolution that sounded the doom of the civilization and advancement of a world.

Their purpose was the absolute destruction of the cultured class. Those of the other classes who opposed them were to be subjugated or destroyed; the jong and his family were to be killed. These things accomplished, the people would enjoy absolute freedom; there would be no masters, no taxes, no laws. They succeeded in killing most of us and a large proportion of the merchant class; then the people discovered what the agitators already knew, that someone must rule, and the leaders of Thorism were ready to take over the reins of government. The people had exchanged the beneficent rule of an experienced and cultured class for that of greedy incompetents and theorists. Now they are all reduced to virtual slavery. An army of spies watches over them, and an army of warriors keeps them from turning against their masters; they are miserable, helpless, and hopeless. (Chapter 5)

Keep in mind that this was published in 1934, two years after Walter Duranty received a Pulitzer Prize for his coverage of the Soviet Union and seventeen years after the Bolsheviks had seized power. When Carson Napier encounters people from the Thorist country later on, it's clear that the revolution had occurred in their lifetimes just as the October Revolution had occurred in Burroughs's. In his estimation, it's clear that "the former free men among them had long since come to the realization that they had exchanged this freedom, and their status of wage earners, for slavery to the state, that could no longer be hidden by a nominal equality." One guy that had been a slave under the old regime admits that he was better off before he got set free by the Thorists: "Then, I had one master; now I have as many masters as there are government officials, spies, and soldiers, none of whom cares anything about me, while my old master was kind to me and looked after my welfare."

This panoply of impossible parallels is engineered with a single aim in mind: to provide a backdrop for nonstop action. And there is plenty of action here. There are sword fights, ambushes, monsters, winged bird-men, mutinies, boarding actions, and ship-to-ship battles. This book is loaded, and the author does not hold back for a second. The approach to setting and plot here is comparable to those of role-playing games where ragtag groups of adventurers that have no real reason to cooperate just so happen to run into each other at a tavern where an old man has a perfectly brilliant adventure opportunity. It's not unlike the iconic Traveller adventure "Shadows," which begins with a random earthquake uncovering ancient pyramids just as the players' ship is taking off from the planet. When the players investigate, they discover that they cannot leave until they disable the installation's defense lasers. The players have no choice but to explore this mysterious locale! While it wouldn't take too much for the average know-it-all to poop this kind of party, most people are willing enough to play the game that is set before them.

However, Burroughs goes far beyond the confines of the typical adventure game scenario. The key difference is that when his heroes are dropped into an alien world, they generally end up naked. There isn't any time spent haggling over how they're going to spend their 3d6x10 gold pieces. No, they're lucky to get a loincloth most of the time. The other thing that happens is that they immediately pick a faction, form alliances, and set themselves to the task of reordering the status quo according to their own vision and ideals. There are no angst, no hand-wringing, no self-doubt, and not even a quiet desire to just live and let live. The idea of some kind of prime directive where it somehow makes sense for other cultures to learn everything the hard way never crosses the mind of the hero.

The third thing in a Burroughs-style scenario that is utterly contrary to how things are typically done in tabletop role-playing games is the romantic element. No matter how alien the world is, there is always a match for the hero out there among its peoples. Coincidence often thrusts them together; social convention would keep them apart, but there's always something more to the hero's feminine counterpart than mere animal attraction. She's pretty to look at, sure, but she's more than just a pretty face. In the Venus series she's also the last best hope of a world in crisis:

I was still meditating on names in an effort to forget Duare, when Kamlot joined me, and I decided to take the opportunity to ask him some questions concerning certain Amtorian customs that regulated the social intercourse between men and maids. He opened a way to the subject by asking me if I had seen Duare since she sent for me. "I saw her," I replied, "but I do not understand her attitude, which suggested that it was almost a crime for me to look at her." "It would be under ordinary circumstances," he told me, "but of course, as I explained to you before, what she and we have passed through has temporarily at least minimized the importance of certain time-honored Vepajan laws and customs. Vepajan girls attain their majority at the age of twenty; prior to that they may not form a union with a man. The custom, which has almost the force of a law, places even greater restrictions upon the daughters of a jong. They may not even see or speak to any man other than their blood relatives and a few well-chosen retainers until after they have reached their twentieth birthday. Should they transgress, it would mean disgrace for them and death for the man." "What a fool law!" I ejaculated, but I realized at last how heinous my transgression must have appeared in the eyes of Duare. Kamlot shrugged. "It may be a fool law," he said, "but it is still the law; and in the case of Duare its enforcement means much to Vepaja, for she is the hope of Vepaja." I had heard that title conferred upon her before, but it was meaningless to me. "Just what do you mean by saying that she is the hope of Vepaja?" I asked. "She is Mintep's only child. He has never had a son, though a hundred women have sought to bear him one. The life of the dynasty ends if Duare bears no son; and if she is to bear a son, then it is essential that the father of that son be one fitted to be the father of a jong." "Have they selected the father of her children yet?" I asked. "Of course not," replied Kamlot. "The matter will not even be broached until after Duare has passed her twentieth birthday."

I was greatly impressed by Dejah Thoris in *A Princess of Mars* when she was willing to marry an enemy prince just to end the war and to save her own people from destruction. The book presented almost exactly the same premise as *The Princess Bride*, but John Carter's love interest *does something* to actually show her character in a good light when she presumes the leading man to be dead. While Duare might do something along those lines in a later sequel, we do not get to see it here in the first installment. Instead, the hero falls in love with her practically at first sight and pursues her relentlessly and arbitrarily. He ends up rescuing her from terrible danger no less than three times: once from violent swordsmen, another time from imprisonment on an enemy ship, and once again from the midst of an ambush by "a dozen hairy, manlike creatures hurling rocks from slings" and firing "crude arrows from still cruder bows."

The persistence and repetitiveness of that particular trope are reminiscent of the "plot" of *Donkey Kong*. To the book's credit, it never descends into self-conscious parody the way that *Dragon Slayer* did. The funny thing is, the much maligned "rescue the princess" theme is not something that gets dealt with in the classic tabletop role-playing adventure games. Oh, it was right there, hard coded into the role-playing elements of *Warriors of Mars*. But that merely establishes how Gary Gygax was fully aware of the potential of using this sort of thing even as he passed it over later on in more significant works.

You can see a similar thing happening with the idea of "extra lives" and explicit "respawning locations" that were a fundamental part of Roger Zelazny's *Jack of Shadows*. The first text adventures implemented this sort of thing right away, and it became an integral part of the later first person shooter games, but in tabletop role-playing games it's not directly addressed as an explicit part of the rules. You see, how players create new characters and re-enter an existing campaign is a matter left entirely to consensus and the game master's discretion. The players will not object no matter how unlikely it is that this new character would just so happen be on hand to join the party's expedition. Heck, I've had people beg to have replacement characters randomly parachuted into odd corners of "The Isle of Dread," not unlike the way that Carson Napier was introduced into Venus!

Groups of role-players just tend not to have "hooking up with a princess" on their bucket lists. It's just not what they're looking to do when they sit down to throw some dice and eat junk food. Oh sure, someone will always say something indecent to the lusty serving wench. But the stock romantic arc does not mesh well with the needs of a party of adventurers. Superheroes, for example, typically gain a non-powered supporting cast in their individual titles. Spider-man has to choose between Gwen Stacy and Mary Jane. In contrast, Pepper Potts has a major role in *Iron Man*, but she isn't generally going to come up in the typical *Avengers*. A romantic interaction that can't be boiled down to single die roll is just off topic for the typical role-playing game. People who demand that sort of thing are like the thief player that wants to *by himself* implement outrageously elaborate heists in town when everyone else just wants to get on with the dungeon crawling.

In a similar vein, the default role-playing adventurer is simply not cut from the same cloth as one of Edgar Rice Burroughs's heroes. They are usually brazenly self-aggrandizing, greedy, and cunning—enough so that it is hard to feel bad for them when they come to a bad end. As dashing as they might be, they are ultimately little more than glorified orcs and brigands themselves. Those who play them tend to have no concept of domain-level play and therefore find gold and magic items to be far more enticing than any sort of princess. They are generally too fatalistic to think that their actions can have an impact on the game's worlds or nations.

But the space princess was an integral part of the pulp literature that inspired games like *Dungeons & Dragons*. Indeed, if game designers needed a generic MacGuffin for the players to rescue in some wizard's tower or dark dungeon, they were all happy to swap in an Amulet of Yendor or some such in her place. That sort of thing is easier to transport and requires less improvised dialog, after all. While there might be plenty of reasons that make this quiet omission a good idea, revisiting this particular trope could open up a lot of possibilities at the domain level.

Nine Princes in Amber

by Roger Zelazny

Imagine the ultimate city, the greatest one that could ever exist: a city so awesome that every other city on every other plane of existence is nothing but a shadow in comparison. Imagine that being king of this city is a very big deal and that this position is contested by nine brothers, all of whom are essentially playing the most titanic game of *Diplomacy* in the history of the multiverse as they vie for it. All of them have the power to travel to other universes. All of them could effectively even create their own parallel universe that is almost exactly like the one that contains this perfect city, but none of them would settle for that. They all have powers ranging from weather control to healing factors, and they can all recruit vast armies gathered from any conceivable reality. Their warriors could have almost any attribute imaginable and are hand picked because their respective cultures idolize these nine princes in their mythologies and believe that fighting in their wars is their ultimate destiny.

Now imagine that you are one of these brothers. You've formed your alliances as best as you can, and the odds are completely stacked against you, but you've chosen to fight for control of this utterly fantastic city. Your men have died in droves, you've fought one incredible sword fight after another, and you come close, so very close to victory, but in the end you are beaten, your eyes are put out, and you are thrown into prison deep in the dungeons beneath city which you desired to rule. And in that dungeon, a friend of yours remembers you and secretly brings to you a care package of food and wine and… something more—something precious beyond all imagining: the only thing that could possibly make your plight at all bearable. Your friend, you see, has brought you… a *carton of Salems*.

And that pretty well sums up how this novel completely captures the zeit-geist of the year of its release, 1970. The characters drink and chain-smoke their way through practically every scene. The protagonist uses the word "dig" as a synonym for either understanding or finding something to be agreeable. And the princes and princesses of Amber all sound so wonderfully good looking that they could all be models for the sort of cigarette advertisements that don't exist anymore. When they have a meal together, I can only assume they do so without the knowledge that salt, butter, and eggs pose some sort of mortal threat to their health. I feel vaguely guilty just reading it. That this book presents what were essentially gods and goddesses charting their destinies across a staggering array of parallel universes that cascade in a mind-blowing psychedelic manner as they traverse between them is one thing. In this day and age, it's probably more startling that they can eat, drink, and smoke without someone hectoring them about it.

Though I'm being somewhat hard on it, I actually quite enjoyed the book. It's dated, sure, but I did not want to stop reading this series in order to write this post. Over at *Tor.com*, Michael R. Underwood has recently asserted that "we cannot keep pointing people at Heinlein, Asimov, Brooks, and Tolkien forever and expect those works to resonate as strongly with people born fifty years after the books were written."[1] I disagree completely as *Starship Troopers*, *The Foundation Trilogy*, and *The Lord of the Rings* were all quite old when they first captured my imagination. They aren't going to stop being landmark works anytime soon. Similarly, Zelazny's Amber stories are as compulsively readable today as when they were first published. Although they were written at a time when every conceivable rule was being challenged in the name of high artistry, these short novels still had to meet the same sort of editorial standards that Jack Vance's work had to meet just a few years before.

But there's something else to it as well, some dim reflection the earlier pulp heroes still manifest in it. The characters are just so darned pretty, after all. Try as I might, I just can't find any sort of heavy-handed message in Zelazny's kickoff to his magnum opus. In comparison, I recently had to set aside the much more recent *Game of Thrones* after gradually figuring out that the superstars of the book consist of a bastard, a dwarf, a cripple, and a carbon copy of that girl from Disney's *Brave*. (It's gripping enough that I might have gone on anyway—the writing is solid after all—but when a thoroughly repugnant character like the Hound had to be given a rather touching origin story that explains why he turned out to be such rough guy, I was done. Ugh.) No, I don't see how anything but a freak show can result if you turn a bunch of people loose in some sort of Dung Age world, each of them with the equivalent of a hundred points or more in *GURPS* disadvantages. If I want to see a freak show, all I have to do is look out my window. If I'm reading fantasy, I'd rather read about a bunch of people with a particularly interesting world-jumping ability who are set loose to fight a war across countless alternate realities. That's just cool:

> *Now, it is written that only a prince of Amber may walk among Shadows, though of course he may lead or direct as many as he chooses along such courses. We led our troops and saw them die, but of Shadow I have this to say: there is Shadow and there is Substance, and this is the root of all things. Of Substance, there is only Amber, the real city, upon the real Earth, which contains everything. Of Shadow, there is an infinitude of things. Every possibility exists somewhere as a Shadow of the real. Amber, by its very existence, has cast such in all directions. And what may one say of it beyond? Shadow extends from Amber to Chaos, and all things are possible within it. There are only three ways of traversing it, and each of them is difficult. If one is a prince or princess of the blood, then one may walk, crossing through Shadows, forcing one's environment to change as one passes, until it is finally in precisely the shape one desires it, and there stop. That Shadow world is then one's own save for family intrusions, to do with as one would. In such a place had I dwelled for centuries. (page 99-100)*

Dig it. It would take a long time before games could catch up to this level of epic fantasy: Tom Moldvay's *Lords of Creation*, for instance, and the *GURPS Infinite Worlds* setting from Steve Jackson Games. Although the original edition of *AD&D* included strange planes of existence as a core part of its default milieu, it really doesn't contain anything quite like *this*. The closest you could get to this sort of tone would be if you attack all of Hell with an army of Modrons in an attempt to depose Beezelbub to take his throne for yourself. This book is a wonderful example of just how diverse the books of Gary Gygax's Appendix N list are from one another. For anyone that is only familiar with the watered-down Tolkien ripoffs of the eighties, this book, and others like it, will be an engaging surprise.

One odd corner of classic *AD&D* that this book sheds light on is how for some classes, there are only a limited number of high-level positions available for the players. There are only nine ninth-level druids in the default campaign setting, nine tenth-level druids, and at the eleventh level, there can be only one *Great Druid*. Now, I'm not saying that this book necessarily inspired this sort of thing directly, but I will say that it can provide some pretty good inspiration for how to actually run with it.

Here's one particularly involved example from the Monk class:

There can be only a limited number of monks above 7th level (Superior Master). There are three 8th level (Master of Dragons) and but one of each higher level. When a player-character monk gains sufficient experience points to qualify him or her for 8th level, the commensurate abilities are attained only temporarily. The monk must find and defeat in single combat, hand-to-hand, without weapons or magic items, one of the 8th level monks - the White, the Green, or the Red. The same must be done at the ninth and higher levels. The loser of these combats loses enough experience points to place him or her at the lowest number possible to attain the level just beneath the new level. The monk character will know where to locate the higher level monks; and he or she must proceed immediately to do combat or else lose experience points equal to the number which will place him or her at the lowest number possible to have attained the level just beneath that of the monk he or she should have sought out but did not. That is, the player-character drops to 7th level in the above case and must then work upwards once again.

This stuff is crazy for a lot of reasons. In the first place, few adventuring groups are going to play long enough to get to this stage of the game, so why bother laying all of this stuff out in such careful detail? Secondly, it may even be unreasonable to assume that there are that many high-level characters in the campaign setting at all.[2] Third, while other players are setting up their domains or running off the enemy thieves guild of some decadent metropolis, these other classes are assumed to be spending their end game competing for slots in some sort of oddball fantasy bureaucracy. Honestly, is that really what epic "immortal-level" gaming should look like?

Finally, if there's one thing that players of these sorts of games would tend to expect, it's that if they bust their tails to earn experience points session after session, then they are just entitled to level up when the time comes. Okay, they might go along with training costs that have to be paid, sure, but for someone to be demoted a level because he failed to win some kind of hokey staged single combat? If he loses, I can't imagine any other outcome but for the player to flip the table over, storm away, and never come back.

But hey, maybe gamers were made of sterner stuff back in the seventies when these rules were being composed. Or maybe the game masters were well-read enough that they would have instinctively known how to make this awesome anyway. Books like *Nine Princes in Amber* and *Game of Thrones* indicate that whoever takes charge of these sorts of limited high-level positions would be a very big deal. Players who are not in the running will have a vested interest in backing a particular candidate. This support, of course, will be provided in return for favors and titles and cushy political offices that will presumably be doled out later on.

The side-effects of this sort of this sort of endgame should be felt and observed long before the players themselves reach the upper levels of power. When someone reflects sunlight into your character's eyes during a pivotal moment of his duel, it's not going to be a huge surprise as to who is behind it. But why would those powerful nonplayer-characters wait until *then* to act? It's not like they don't have an interest in seeing potential rivals fail to come back when they go off adventuring to gain enough experience points to be able to challenge them....

There's something inherently "busy" and cosmopolitan about this type of situation that may not be for everyone, and in that case, *Nine Princes in Amber* again provides a clue for campaign designers. You don't have to muddy up the mundane world with these sorts of rivalries and political maneuvers, but these sorts of design elements might be the perfect fit for explaining what all is going on at the god-like level of play. Those gold boxed *Immortals Rules* sets for the Frank Mentzer iteration of *D&D* were a must-have item that ultimately saw very little actual play by its purchasers. Indeed, the concept of a wide open wilderness sandbox would have been quite enough for the typical preteen Dungeon Master of the time, but who knows what sort of epic games might have happened had more of them been familiar with this highly entertaining fantasy classic.

Notes

1. See "Science Fiction and Fantasy 101: Thinking Academically About Genre" for the whole thing.

2. See Lewis Pulsipher's classic article, "Fantasy Demography" in *The Space Gamer #44*: "These figures should astonish those referees who customarily sprinkle across the landscape characters of double figure levels. Even at the most favorable rate, high level adventurers are extremely rare birds."

Conan of Cimmeria
by Robert E. Howard

When most people think of Conan, they tend to think of a wild, black-haired man running around with very little in the way of clothing or armor. Just as Sherlock Holmes is now indelibly linked to his iconic deerstalker, so too is the original fantasy swordsman now wedded in our collective imaginations to Arnold's Schwarzenegger's atrocious accent. In spite of this muddying of the waters, the iconic helmet and cloak of the character should still be immediately recognizable even to the more casual fantasy fan:

> He saw a tall powerfully built figure in a black scale-mail hauberk, burnished greaves and a blue-steel helmet from which jutted bull's horns highly polished. From the mailed shoulders fell the scarlet cloak, blowing in the sea-wind. A broad shagreen belt with a golden buckle held the scabbard of the broadsword he wore. Under the horned helmet a square-cut black mane contrasted with smoldering blue eyes. (page 122)

But even that is just a snapshot of a single phase of the character's career. Conan did just about everything and he was rarely "just" a barbarian. He was a mercenary, adventurer, thief, and pirate. He led armies into battle and tribesmen on raids; he captained ships and even became a king:

> When King Numedides lay dead at my feet and I tore the crown from his gory head and set it on my own, I had reached the ultimate border of my dreams. I had prepared myself to take the crown, not to hold it. In the old free days all I wanted was a sharp sword and a straight path to my enemies. Now no paths are straight and my sword is useless.... When I led her armies to victory as a mercenary, Aquilonia overlooked the fact that I was a foreigner, but now she can not forgive me. (page 11)

Robert E. Howard's Conan stories are marked not just by the breadth and height of the hero's adventures, but range even beyond the boundaries of what we now call swords and sorcery. Many of the early Conan tales would be more rightly termed as being "swords and Lovecraftian horror" or even "swords and evolution." The backdrop of Conan's world is thus starkly nihilistic. Conan's god Crom is a gloomy and savage entity that hates weaklings. His only redeeming quality is the fact that he gives men courage and the will and might to kill their enemies. But in spite of Conan's straightforward brutality and simplicity[1], he shows more than a few traditional virtues. For starters, he is intensely loyal regardless of the consequences:

> *Well, last night in a tavern, a captain in the king's guard offered violence to the sweetheart of a young soldier, who naturally ran him through. But it seems there is some cursed law against killing guardsmen, and the boy and his girl fled away. It was bruited about that I was seen with them, and so today I was hauled into court, and a judge asked me where the lad had gone. I replied that since he was a friend of mine, I could not betray him. Then the court waxed wroth, and the judge talked a great deal about my duty to the state, and society, and other things I did not understand, and bade me tell where my friend had flown. By this time I was becoming wrathful myself, for I had explained my position. But I choked my ire and held my peace, and the judge squalled that I had shown contempt for the court, and that I should be hurled into a dungeon until I betrayed my friend. So then, seeing they were all mad, I drew my sword and cleft the judge's skull; then I cut my way out of the court.... (page 123)*

Conan's faithfulness does not change regardless of how high he climbs in stature or authority. He can't be bought even to save his own life[2]:

"His captors had no reason to spare him. He had been placed in these pits for a definite doom. He cursed himself for his refusal of their offer, even while his stubborn manhood revolted at the thought, and he knew that were he taken forth and given another chance, his reply would be the same. He would not sell his subjects to the butcher. And yet it had been with no thought of anyone's gain but his own that he had seized the kingdom originally. Thus subtly does the instinct of sovereign responsibility enter even a red-handed plunderer sometimes." (page 94)

Even when no one could know of his actions, he does the right thing. He reciprocates and fulfills his end of a bargain[3] when just about anyone else in the same situation would be willing to walk away. Technicalities or ambiguities are not reason enough for him back out of a deal:

> It occurred to him that since he had escaped through his own actions, he owed nothing to Murilo; yet it had been the young nobleman who had removed his chains and had the food sent to him, without either of which his escape would have been impossible. Conan decided that he was indebted to Murilo, and, since he was a man who discharged his obligations eventually, he determined to carry out his promise to the young aristocrat. (page 284)

And though on an individual level he cares for little else than killing and drinking, when he is responsible for a state, his reign is marked by a striking combination of fiscal restraint and concern for the weak:

> "I found Aquilonia in the grip of a pig like you—one who traced his genealogy for a thousand years. The land was torn with the wars of the barons, and the people cried out under oppression and taxation. Today no Aquilonian noble dares maltreat the humblest of my subjects, and the taxes of the people are lighter than anywhere else in the world. What of you? Your brother, Amalrus, holds the eastern half of your kingdom and defies you. And you, Strabonus, your soldiers are even now besieging castles of a dozen or more rebellious barons. The people of both your kingdoms are crushed into the earth by tyrannous taxes and levies. And you would loot mine—ha! Free my hands and I'll varnish this floor with your brains!" (page 91)

Time and again, Conan shows that he has nothing but contempt for the partiality[4] that is endemic to more civilized places:

> "If what he says is true, my lord," said the Inquisitor, "it clears him of the murder, and we can easily hush up the matter of attempted theft. He is due ten years at hard labor for house-breaking, but if you say the word, we'll arrange for him to escape and none but us will ever know anything about it. I understand—you wouldn't be the first nobleman who had to resort to such things to pay gambling debts and the like. You can rely on our discretion." (page 56)

And in spite of his humble simplicity and the distant nature of his god, Conan takes a very dim view of both the fatalism and human sacrifice endemic in more "advanced" cultures:

> *"When I was a child in Stygia the people lived under the shadow of the priests. None ever knew when he or she would be seized and dragged to the altar. What difference whether the priests give a victim to the gods, or the god comes for his own victim?" "Such is not the custom of my people," Conan growled, "nor of Natala's either. The Hyborians do not sacrifice humans to their god, Mitra, and as for my people—by Crom, I'd like to see a priest try to drag a Cimmerian to the altar! There'd be blood spilt, but not as the priest intended." (page 231)*

The people of Conan's Cimmeria appear to be little more than rough living rednecks that are adept at climbing, but they hold fast to an admirable degree of decency, a code of honor that enshrines a sense of human dignity even as they cut down their foes with the sword. For instance, Conan reacts with disdain towards the Hykranian practice of selling their children. In contrast, the nation of Stygia stands as a manifestation of pure, unmitigated evil:

> *From where the thief stood he could see the ruins of the great hall wherein chained captives had knelt by the hundreds during festivals to have their heads hacked off by the priest-king in honor of Set, the Serpent-god of Stygia. Somewhere nearby there had been a pit, dark and awful, wherein screaming victims were fed to a nameless amorphic monstrosity which came up out of a deeper, more hellish cavern. Legend made Thugra Khotan more than human; his worship yet lingered in a mongrel degraded cult, whose votaries stamped his likeness on coins to pay the way of their dead over the great river of darkness of which Styx was but the material shadow. (page 155)*

To them, women are merely bait to be used to bring men to their destruction[5]:

> *Ships did not put unasked into this port, where dusky sorcerers wove awful spells in the murk of sacrificial smoke mounting eternally from bloodstained altars where naked women screamed, and where Set, the Old Serpent, archdemon of the Hyborians but god of the Stygians, was said to writhe his shining*

coils among his worshipers. Master Tito gave that dreamy glass-floored bay a wide berth, even when a serpent-prowed gondola shot from behind a castellated point of land, and naked dusky women, with great red blossoms in their hair, stood and called to his sailors, and posed and postured brazenly.

Conan's behavior, in contrast, borders almost on chivalry. Sure, if a wench betrays him, he's liable to throw her over his shoulder and unceremoniously dump her into a cesspool. And even under less than dire circumstances, he suffers no shortage of attention from women. Yet he never takes undue advantage of the women that end up dependent upon him. Whatever sense of morality it is that pushes him to extraordinary levels of honesty in business deals and offices of state is also at work in his dealings with women:

"It was a foul bargain I made. I do not regret that black dog Bajujh, but you are no wench to be bought and sold. The ways of men vary in different lands, but a man need not be a swine, wherever he is. After I thought awhile, I saw that to hold you to your bargain would be the same as if I had forced you." (page 316)

Indeed, the "barbarism" of Conan stands out in stark contrast to the norms of more "civilized" peoples[6]:

She had never encountered any civilized man who treated her with kindness unless there were an ulterior motive behind his actions. Conan had shielded her, protected her, and—so far—demanded nothing in return. (page 206)

His romances and dalliances are born from a simmering, mutual passion. Yet with Belit, this burning desire culminates into something profoundly transcendent[7]:

"There is life beyond death, I know, and I know this, too, Conan of Cimmeria"—she rose lithely to her knees and caught him in a pantherish embrace—"my love is stronger than any death! I have lain in your arms, panting with the violence of our love; you have held and crushed and conquered me, drawing my soul to your lips with the fierceness of your bruising kisses. My heart is welded to your heart, my soul is part of your soul! Were I still in death and you fighting for life, I would come back from the abyss to aid you—aye, whether my spirit floated with the purple sails on the crystal

sea of paradise, or writhed in the molten flames of hell! I am yours, and all
the gods and all their eternities shall not sever us." (pages 133-134)

While Conan's fierce loyalty to the women that come under his care often
gets him into trouble, his good deeds can also rebound to his favor. He is not
following some simplistic script where he always gets to be the guy riding
to some damsel's rescue. Belit called all the shots on her pirate ship, for
example. In another instance, he takes charge of a nation's military forces
at the behest of its princess. At other times, the key to Conan's deliverance
from hopeless situations rests upon the fair damsel type taking on terrifying
risks to reciprocate his freely bestowed kindness. But Conan simply doesn't
do the right thing for what he might get out of it. That never seems to enter
his mind. He is so unwavering in his principles, he never bothers to count the
cost when faced with any sort of moral dilemma. Death does not have the
slightest hold on him nor any influence on his decisions:[8]

> *Life was a continual battle, or series of battles; since his birth Death had*
> *been a constant companion. It stalked horrifically at his side; stood at his*
> *shoulder beside the gaming-tables; its bony fingers rattled the wine-cups. It*
> *loomed above him, a hooded and monstrous shadow, where he lay down to*
> *sleep. He minded its presence no more than a king minds the presence of his*
> *cup-bearer. Some day its bony grasp would close; that was all. It was enough*
> *that he lived through the present. (page 170)*

Indeed, his resolve seems only to increase in the face of mounting odds.
Certain death is met with an indomitable insistence on going down fighting.

Conan is a profoundly heroic character. In these early stories, we never
quite get a complete picture of his origins. He seems to spring out of nowhere
as if he were an instrument of divine retribution, an inevitable nemesis burning a wake of wrath and justice through the "perverse secrets of rotting civilizations." His world is fully realized, and the tales about him are diverse, but the
common thread running through them all is the simple and direct manner in
which he embodies courage and loyalty. The alacrity with which he slays and
the gusto with which he drinks is matched only by his honesty. Ultimately,
it is not his brutality that sets him up as a contrast to the civilized, but rather
his integrity.

Notes

1. *And said, Verily I say unto you, Except ye be converted, and become as little children, ye shall not enter into the kingdom of heaven.*—Matthew 18:3

2. *Greater love hath no man than this, that a man lay down his life for his friends.*—John 15:13

3. *Render therefore to all their dues: tribute to whom tribute is due; custom to whom custom; fear to whom fear; honour to whom honour. Owe no man any thing, but to love one another: for he that loveth another hath fulfilled the law.*—Romans 13:7-8

4. *If ye fulfil the royal law according to the scripture, Thou shalt love thy neighbour as thyself, ye do well. But if ye have respect to persons, ye commit sin, and are convinced of the law as transgressors.*—James 2:8-9

5. *For the lips of a strange woman drop as an honeycomb, and her mouth is smoother than oil, but her end is bitter as wormwood, sharp as a two-edged sword.*—Proverbs 5:3-4

6. *Verily I say unto you, inasmuch as ye have done it unto one of the least of these my brethren, ye have done it unto me.*—Matthew 25:40

7. *Wherefore they are no more twain, but one flesh. What therefore God hath joined together, let not man put asunder.*—Matthew 19:6

8. *Fear not them which kill the body, but are not able to kill the soul: but rather fear him which is able to destroy both soul and body in hell.*—Matthew 10:28

Creep, Shadow!

by A. Merritt

This book is loaded. It's got seductive shadow women slowly enticing men to commit suicide. It's got a witch that murders people with her animated dolls. It's got sketchy scientists, femme fatales, world-traveling adventurer types, and even a hard-boiled Depression-era Texan. I don't understand why no one had ever pointed me to this author before now; this is really good stuff!

It's also got ancient rites, strange cults, god-like entities, and ancestral memories. Most other authors would settle for making a novel out of even just a fraction of this material, but Abraham Merritt keeps piling on the details and expanding the scope. At the same time, the suspense rises inexorably, and the pace never seems to slow down. It's gripping, sultry, and spicy, and it never fails to be entertaining. The experience of reading this book seems to transport you inside the world of the old black and white movies. The dialog is crisp and punchy. You can tell that everyone is well dressed, classy, and good looking. And every scene is drenched in a combination of charm and menace.

One of the things I especially enjoy about the older books like this is the incidental things that they let drop about how life really was back then. Sometimes the characters can telephone, but other times they have to send a telegram or a cable, for instance. But more than just the side effects of primitive or unrealized technology, sometimes little things happen that show just how much culture has changed in general. My favorite bit like that is this scene where the protagonist escapes serious trouble by climbing out a window and down the side of a building. He takes a chance and finally enters a room that looks like his best bet for getting away:

> There was a brilliantly lighted room. Four men were playing poker at a table liberally loaded with bottles. I had overturned a big potted bush. I saw the

men stare, at the window. There was nothing to do but walk in and take a chance. I did so. The man at the head of the table was fat, with twinkling little blue eyes and a cigar sticking up out of the corner of his mouth; next to him was one who might have been an old-time banker; a lank and sprawling chap with a humorous mouth, and a melancholy little man with an aspect of indestructible indigestion. The fat man said: "Do you all see what I do? All voting yes will take a drink." They all took a drink and the fat man said: "The ayes have it." The banker said: "If he didn't drop out of an airplane, then he's a human fly." The fat man asked: "Which was it, stranger?" I said: "I climbed." The melancholy man said: "I knew it. I always said this house had no morals." The lanky man stood up and pointed a warning finger at me: "Which way did you climb? Up or down?" "Down," I said. "Well," he said, "if you came down it's all right so far with us." I asked, puzzled: "What difference does it make?" He said: "A hell of a lot of difference. We all live underneath here except the fat man, and we're all married." The melancholy man said: "Let this be a lesson to you, stranger. Put not your trust in the presence of woman nor in the absence of man." The lanky man said: "A sentiment, James, that deserves another round. Pass the rye, Bill."

And in that one short scene, we gain a vivid glimpse into another world. The hero ends up convincing them to let him gamble with them for a decent set of clothing:

I opened, and the lanky man wrote something on a blue chip and showed it to me before he tossed it into the pot. I read: "Half a sock." The others solemnly marked their chips and the game was on. I won and lost. There were many worthy sentiments and many rounds. At four o'clock I had won my outfit and release. Bill's clothes were too big for me, but the others went out and came back with what was needful. They took me downstairs. They put me in a taxi and held their hands over their ears as I told the taxi man where to go. That was a quartette of good scouts if ever there was one. When I was unsteadily undressing at the Club a lot of chips fell out of my pockets. They were marked: "Half a shirt": "One seat of pants": "A pant leg": "One hat brim": and so on and so on.

Yes, it's actually a serious obstacle when the main character ends up in a situation where he might have to hail a cab with torn and disheveled clothing!

But here's the interesting thing about this: it's not that these ordinary men pitch in to help a guy that is in a tight spot but that they do it in a way that would allow him to save some face and to feel like he earned it. At the same time, it appears that they are also taking things slowly so that they can get a feel for his character. These are regular guys that leave their wives at home so that they can stay up until four in the morning drinking and playing poker, but there is a lot of wisdom and savvy in how they conduct themselves. It's remarkable.

Another thing about these older books is that the authors seem to really love invoking *old* stuff. To make something horrific, it appears like they have to go way back in time in order to make it sufficiently inscrutable. Ancient Egypt wasn't usually remote enough. No, they seemed to think they had to dig further back into prehistory in order to get something truly spooky:

> I said: "It would take me days to tell you all the charms, counter-charms, exorcisms and whatnot that man has devised for that sole purpose Cro-Magnons and without doubt the men before them and perhaps even the half-men before them. Sumerians, Egyptians, Phoenicians, the Greeks and the Romans, the Celts, the Gauls and every race under the sun, known and forgotten, put their minds to it. But there is only one way to defeat the shadow sorcery—and that is not to believe in it." He said: "Once I would have agreed with you—and not so long ago. Now the idea seems to me to resemble that of getting rid of a cancer by denying you have it."

Along with that, there was a tendency to play up more rational explanations for the horror elements that the characters come across. It's not so much that the authors are actually going to allow things to culminate into some sort of *Scooby Doo* type ending. But rather, in order for the characters to have credibility, they had to display a certain degree of skepticism as they encounter the supernatural. The way that the *author* gains credibility at the time was to explicitly tie the story elements into a larger, evolutionary picture. This establishes a more scientific tone while creating an epic sweep to the tale:

> "A brilliant Englishman once formulated perfectly the materialistic credo. He said that the existence of man is an accident; his story a brief and transitory episode in the life of the meanest of planets. He pointed out that of the combination of causes which first converted a dead organic compound into

the living progenitors of humanity, science as yet knows nothing. Nor would it matter if science did know. The wet-nurses of famine, disease, and mutual slaughter had gradually evolved creatures with consciousness and intelligence enough to know that they were insignificant. The history of the past was that of blood and tears, stupid acquiescence, helpless blunderings, wild revolt, and empty aspirations. And at last, the energies of our system will decay, the sun be dimmed, the inert and tideless earth be barren. Man will go down into the pit, and all his thoughts will perish. Matter will know itself no longer. Everything will be as though it never had been. And nothing will be either better or worse for all the labor, devotion, pity, love, and suffering of man." I said, the God-like sense of power stronger within me: "It is not true." "It is partly true," he answered. "What is not true is that life is an accident. What we call accident is only a happening of whose causes we are ignorant. Life must have come from life. Not necessarily such life as we know—but from some Thing, acting deliberately, whose essence was— and is—life. It is true that pain, agony, sorrow, hate, and discord are the foundations of humanity. It is true that famine, disease, and slaughter have been our nurses. Yet it is equally true that there are such things as peace, happiness, pity, perception of beauty, wisdom... although these may be only of the thickness of the film on the surface of a woodland pool which mirrors its flowered rim—yet, these things do exist... peace and beauty, happiness and wisdom. They are." "And therefore—" de Keradel's hands were still over his eyes, but through the masking fingers I felt his gaze sharpen upon me, penetrate me "—therefore I hold that these desirable things must be in That which breathed life into the primeval slime. It must be so, since that which is created cannot possess attributes other than those possessed by what creates it." Of course, I knew all that. Why should he waste effort to convince me of the obvious. I said, tolerantly: "It is self-evident." He said: "And therefore it must also be self-evident that since it was the dark, the malevolent, the cruel side of this—Being—which created us, our only approach to It, our only path to Its other self, must be through agony and suffering, cruelty and malevolence." He paused, then said, violently: "Is it not what every religion has taught? That man can approach his Creator only through suffering and sorrow? Sacrifice... Crucifixion!"

Now anyone that actually knows anything about evolution should be face-palming at this passage. The whole idea behind the theory is to demonstrate how things could come to be as they are *without* a supernatural godlike being creating everything. Interpolating one into the chain of events at any point is ludicrous. Even so, when the theory is described, people all too often fall into the habit of anthropomorphizing the process or else talking about how evolution *designed* this or that. Still, such talk is entirely believable coming from these *characters*. This is a common enough error that it's not that unlikely for them to be speaking this way. By not resorting to the third-person omniscient, Merritt sidesteps a problem that many more famous authors failed to avoid.

Probably the most striking difference between this classic tale and how things tend to be done more recently shows up in his handling of Stonehenge and the Druids. Whenever I see people speculating about that iconic monument, they inevitably mumble something about its builders being keen on astronomy. Although some people get into wild theories about space aliens, healing, or ley lines, its actual purpose is generally just regarded as a mystery. Druids are depicted as either zen-like beings with nature manipulation powers or else as kindly old men climbing trees to harvest mistletoe with their sickles. *Creep, Shadow!* is downright metal in comparison:

> I said: "It may be that they were beaten by the waves against the rocks. But it is also true that at Carnac and at Stonehenge the Druid priests beat the breasts of the sacrifices with their mauls of oak and stone and bronze until their ribs were crushed and their hearts were pulp." McCann said, softly: "Jesus!" I said: "The stone-cutter who tried to escape told of men being crushed under the great stones, and of their bodies vanishing. Recently, when they were restoring Stonehenge, they found fragments of human skeletons buried at the base of many of the monoliths. They had been living men when the monoliths were raised. Under the standing stones of Carnac are similar fragments. In ancient times men and women and children were buried under and within the walls of the cities as those walls were built—sometimes slain before they were encased in the mortar and stone, and sometimes encased while alive. The foundations of the temples rested upon such sacrifices. Men and women and children... their souls were fettered there forever... to guard. Such was the ancient belief. Even today there is the superstition that no

bridge can stand unless at least one life is lost in its building. Dig around the monoliths of de Keradel's rockery. I'll stake all I have that you'll discover where those vanished workmen went."

These people in this pre-Christian cult at the dawn of history are not nice, noble savages living close to nature without the corrupting influences of modern civilization. They are brutal and dead set on summoning some kind of horrific elder god no matter the cost in blood. Later writers would revamp witches into kindly "wise women." Vampires would become sparkly, and werewolves would become boyfriend material. But in Merritt's hands, the horrific comes with no chaser whatsoever. Happy earth-goddess people aren't even on the radar. There's an edge to this tale that is very appealing.

Edgar Rice Burroughs might seem crude and formulaic to some readers today. H. P. Lovecraft might be a bit dry. And not everyone is the sort to slog through all of William Hope Hodgson's *The Night Land*. This book by Abraham Merritt is probably a better choice all around for the casual reader that is looking to sample some of the older works. The characters are vividly realized, with human motivations and failings. And the scope of the tale is closer to that of the best science-fiction novels than it is to derivative horror movies. Best of all, the horror is a rare combination of the seductive and the deadly. Merritt's writing is deft and alluring and everything I would expect from the best of the early pulp horror writing.

Notes

While it would be possible to borrow elements of this book in order to embellish the happenings around, say, the Chapel of Evil Chaos from the classic module B2, the events and characters presented here are beyond the scope of a typical *D&D* session. As a scenario for something like *GURPS Horror*, however, this is almost perfect.

There are three major confrontations that would form the adventure structure: the introductory dinner encounter, the seduction encounter, and then the final situation at the shrine. There is plenty of material for combat encounters that could terrorize the players before these events as well. With the players working together to hash out a plan, it actually wouldn't ruin a session if some of these were allowed to play out with mainly just one player in the spotlight. Still, most of the reworking of the various scenes will be to open things up for allowing several players to engage at once, increasing the number of things that the players could research or investigate between the flurries of action, and restructuring situations so that the outcome depends more on what the players can *do* and less on any sort of *deus ex machina*. The tone of the material is far less hopeless than the typical *Call of Cthulhu* adventure, but most of what's in this book should be comprehensible even to more casual role-players. This could be a lot of fun, and the fact that this book is relatively obscure works in its favor for convention play.

The Moon Pool
by A. Merritt

As I read through the Appendix N book list, I am consistently surprised by how good some of this material really is. Edgar Rice Burroughs is superior to his imitators on more than a few points. Roger Zelazny's *Amber* series is one of the most entertaining things I've ever picked up. And Robert E. Howard is such a strong writer that he strikes me as being the American counterpart to J. R. R. Tolkien. Time and again I've kicked myself, wishing I'd read these books sooner and wondering why no one had ever recommended them to me. And I'm often floored when I can't get these books at the library or the bookstore or even as an ebook.

This week's book is, unfortunately, *not* one of those sorts of books. Oh, it's a neat book. It's very influential and has a lot of cool stuff in it. It anticipates the sort of astounding adventure that would be popularized in the old Fantastic Four comic books and in movies like *The Fifth Element*.[1] But Abraham Merritt's *The Moon Pool* is just so hard to slog through, I'm not surprised that it is as obscure as it is now.

It's his first novel, sure… and it came out almost a hundred years ago at the tail end of World War I. But part of the problem is that it was written at a time before typical science-fiction tropes were all nailed down into a common set of conventions. It's like he has to start from scratch when he describes things that we take for granted today. (It takes him five paragraphs to explain what a disintegration ray does, for example.) But the book is just plain ponderous, and the lack of Ernest Hemingway's literary influence is distinctly in evidence as this passage describing the main monster attests:

Nearer and nearer it came, borne on the sparkling waves, and ever thinner shrank the protecting wall of shadow between it and us. Within the mistiness was a core, a nucleus of intenser light—veined, opaline, effulgent, intensely alive. And above it, tangled in the plumes and spirals that throbbed and whirled were seven glowing lights. Through all the incessant but strangely ordered movement of the—thing—these lights held firm and steady. They were seven—like seven little moons. One was of a pearly pink, one of a delicate nacreous blue, one of lambent saffron, one of the emerald you see in the shallow waters of tropic isles; a deathly white; a ghostly amethyst; and one of the silver that is seen only when the flying fish leap beneath the moon.

The premise of this being an eyewitness account is maintained fastidiously. The narrator often launches into long-winded attempts to explain the science behind what he is observing. (He's a respected botanist, so it's in character at least.) Fictional editors occasionally break in to redact sensitive details. As if there's not enough description in the main body of the novel, many of the chapters contain footnotes. And it takes ten chapters just to get past the first door. *Ten chapters!* In the lull between the two big fights in the end, Merritt decides to do two "brain dump" chapters, completely freezing the pace of the storytelling at the worst possible moment. The subsequent chapter actually opens with the narrator saying, "Long had been her tale in the telling, and too long, perhaps, have I been in the repeating." He actually apologizes for it in the text!

We see several of the themes that made his later *Creep, Shadow!* so enjoyable though. Once again, Merritt serves up not one, but *two* space princess-type characters. They're both beautiful, but one is actually an evil priestess with a hidden Gorgon side. (You know the type.) One of the heroes has to flirt with her until he can figure out more of what's going on.[2] The other "space princess" has an army of two hundred thousand frog-man warriors backing her up! The author weaves together threads and themes from Irish mythology, Norse mythology, the "Chamberlain-Moulton theory of a coalescing nebula contracting into the sun and its planets," and even the theory of Panspermia. All of this is then filtered through the narrator's odd blend of skepticism and Christian worldview.[3] The net result is a striking syncretic mash.

From a gaming perspective, the most interesting thing about the book is how Merritt manages to present a credible antecedent for a truly massive dungeon. It's got secret passages, a fantastic underground city replete with grav-cars and rival cults, and even stretches of bizarre alien wilderness. There are a slew of unique artifacts of the Ancients straight out of a good *Traveller* game: *Predator*-style chameleon suits, anti-grav vehicles, age-accelerating contact poisons, powerful healing elixirs, and gravity manipulation rays. Most interesting of all is the way that the puzzles blocking the main entrance which is reminiscent of this common dungeon design technique that Alexis D. Smolensk has identified:

> *My personal experience is that dungeons work best when each 'level' or spreading section has one to three monsters in it. Typically, the main creature plus a supporting creature (goblins with wolves, a wizard with thirty pet owlbears, that sort of thing), and then some sort of vermin for the quiet corners, like spiders, rats, snakes, oozes, etc. This is then separated from the next section by a secret door, a cavern chimney that's difficult to navigate (thus logically keeping the sections separate from one another) or some sort of installed block/barrier where the upper creatures are trying to keep the lower creatures from invading them.*

With this kind of a setup keeping the underground world isolated from the men of 1919, a dangerous game begins when the adventuring party arrives in the underground city. If they cannot successfully shift the balance of power between the rival cults in their favor, they risk unleashing a veritable Armageddon on the war-torn world above!

> *A vision of the Shining One swirling into our world, a monstrous, glorious flaming pillar of incarnate, eternal Evil—of peoples passing through its radiant embrace into that hideous, unearthly life-in-death which I had seen enfold the sacrifices—of armies trembling into dancing atoms of diamond dust beneath the green ray's rhythmic death—of cities rushing out into space upon the wings of that other demoniac force which Olaf had watched at work—of a haunted world through which the assassins of the Dweller's court stole invisible, carrying with them every passion of hell—of the rallying to the Thing of every sinister soul and of the weak and the unbalanced, mystics and carnivores of humanity alike; for well I knew that, once loosed, not any nation could hold this devil-god for long and that swiftly its blight would spread! And then a world that was all colossal reek of cruelty and terror; a welter of lusts, of hatreds and of torment; a chaos of horror in which the*

*Dweller waxing ever stronger, the ghastly hordes of those it had consumed
growing ever greater, wreaked its inhuman will! At the last a ruined planet,
a cosmic plague, spinning through the shuddering heavens; its verdant plains,
its murmuring forests, its meadows and its mountains manned only by a
countless crew of soulless, mindless dead-alive, their shells illumined with
the Dweller's infernal glory—and flaming over this vampirized earth like
a flare from some hell far, infinitely far, beyond the reach of man's farthest
flung imagining—the Dweller!*

These are not the stakes that initially come to mind when novice dungeon
masters look at the megadungeon cross-sections from the Holmes *Basic Set* or
in "The Lost City." This by itself makes the concepts of this book a significant
innovation over Edgar Rice Burroughs's *At the Earth's Core*, where the heroes
not only had a relatively straightforward means of getting back home at the
end but also ended up with a wide-open frontier that was ripe for an almost
leisurely combination of adventure, conquest, and missionary work.

Another thing that's unusual here is that Merritt presents cults that actually
have access to the object of their worship. These are not remote godlike beings
that provide clerical spells in return for prayers. And they are not horrific and
inscrutable in the manner of the alien entities of Lovecraft's work. It's rare
to get to see "the man behind the curtain" to the extent that we do here just
as it's rare that the man turns out to be much more than a man. One of the
god-like beings is a result of hubris on the part of the "good" gods: they've
inadvertently created a monster that is now beyond their control and which
cannot be defeated except through a very specific Achilles heel.

While the "good gods" are shown here to provide both healing and critical
adventure-solving type information, there is one complication with having
them not be so remote:

*She turned his head with one of the long, white hands—and he looked into
the faces of the Three; looked long, was shaken even as had been Olaf and
myself; was swept by that same wave of power and of—of—what can I call
it?—holiness that streamed from them. Then for the first time I saw real
awe mount into his face. Another moment he stared—and dropped upon
one knee and bowed his head before them as would a worshipper before the
shrine of his saint. And—I am not ashamed to tell it—I joined him; and
with us knelt Lakla and Olaf and Rador.*

This passage is surprising now if only because Tolkien was at pains to avoid a scene like *this*. Indeed, the only direct description of religion in *The Lord of the Rings* is the understated and silent prayer of Faramir's men to the West. Religion is only mentioned once when Denethor makes an anachronistic remark about "the heathen kings." His handling of Galadriel arguably borders on this, but Tolkien consciously avoided depicting anything that could be misconstrued as worship. It's just too problematic for a man that takes religion seriously.

If his lack of compunctions on this point is awkward, Abraham Merritt at least doesn't hold back with the payoff. He has an absolutely fantastic battle at the end as a dwarf army battles a much larger number of frog-people. The dwarf side unleashes anti-gravity weapons to good tactical effect at a couple of points, and in the clutch, they even call in an unstoppable army of zombies in order to lay in the final hammer blow. This culminates into a final standoff between the two rival space princess characters and the godlike beings that they each serve. It's awesome.

There is a lot of material here that can provide useful insights into the intent of the early adventure designs. This is certainly a solid premise for how to handle the mysterious domed city on the seventh level of the megadungeon from the Holmes blue book. More subtle is how Merritt can alternate between both scientific and religious explanations of what is going on while he combines science fiction gadgets with traditional mythical creatures in a sprawling underworld. If you've ever wondered why early *D&D* materials are bursting with the sort of chutzpah that would allow designers to randomly insert an honest-to-goodness leprechaun[4] of all things in the middle of something like *this*, it might be because guys like Abraham Merritt paved the way for them.

Notes

1. Some people have argued that this book might have inspired the television series *Lost*. Tim Callahan over at Tor.com says, "*The Moon Pool* is nothing like *Lost*. It has about as much to do with *Lost* as *The Jetsons* has to do with *Star Wars*. And *The Moon Pool* has more imagination in any one chapter than *Lost* had in any ultra-long and tedious season." I did end up watching *Lost* all the way through, and I've got to say that I didn't think of it once while reading this book!

2. The rugged romantic lead actually teaches the femme fatale to sing the hit song from 1900, "A Bird in a Gilded Cage." What a joker!

3. The femme fatale starts speaking after the fashion of Hebrew poetry when things get serious, the character Olaf makes an allusion to Satan offering Christ "power over all the world" in order to describe her spiel, and at the climax, the otherwise skeptical and scientific narrator lets loose with this:

> *The blood rushed from my heart; scientist that I am, essentially, my reason rejected any such solution as this of the activities of the Dweller. Was it not, the thought flashed, a propitiation by the Three out of their own weakness—and as it flashed I looked up to see their eyes, full of sorrow, on mine—and knew they read the thought. Then into the whirling vortex of my mind came steadying reflections—of history changed by the power of hate, of passion, of ambition, and most of all, by love. Was there not actual dynamic energy in these things—was there not a Son of Man who hung upon a cross on Calvary*

4. The leprechaun is about the biggest clue bat that I've ever seen. Here's a particularly striking bit from his short dialog with the hero:

> *" 'It's what I came to tell ye,' says he. 'Don't ye fall for the Bhean-Nimher, the serpent woman wit' the blue eyes; she's a daughter of Ivor, lad—an' don't ye do nothin' to make the brown-haired Coleen ashamed o' ye, Larry O'Keefe. I knew yer great, great grandfather an' his before him, aroon,' says he, 'an' wan o' the O'Keefe failin's is to think their hearts big enough to hold all the wimmen o' the world. A heart's built to hold only wan permanently, Larry,' he says, 'an' I'm warnin' ye a nice girl don't like to move into a place all cluttered up wid another's washin' an' mendin' an' cookin' an' other things pertainin' to general wife work. Not that I think the blue-eyed wan is keen for mendin' an' cookin'!' says he.*

Kothar—Barbarian Swordsman
by Gardner Fox

Kothar the *barbarian*? From *Cumberia*… in the *north*? A rough and extremely strong mercenary that likes cheap wine and cute serving wenches? Swears by *Dwallka of the War Hammer* or other made-up gods when he is angry or startled? Yeah, this is more than a little derivative. He even wears mail that is described in the stories but which somehow fails to end up being depicted in the cover art!

Some of the "innovations" are actually even more grating. Kothar's got a magic sword called Frostfire. He's got his trusty steed Greyling. He's dogged by random visions of Red Lori, a witch he once double-crossed. (If there's nastiness about, Red Lori makes sure Kothar gets in the thick of it.) But there's a wrinkle: even though he's the kind of guy that tackles jobs other adventurers won't do to win all kinds of fabulous treasures, there's a curse on his sword: it can only be carried by someone who has no other wealth! Not only does he have overtones of *The Lone Ranger* and *King Arthur*, but he's also saddled with a magical impediment that Cugel the Clever would have defeated in less than half a chapter.

The addition of a cutesy origin story doesn't do anything to help him, either:

> *He had always loved the sea—he was spawn of the ocean, having come to Cumberia long ago in a boat as a lonely child—and the smell and fragrance was a stimulant to him.*

It sounds almost like a comic book, which shouldn't be surprising given the author here. Gardner Fox is of course the creator of golden age characters ranging from Hawkman to the Flash. (He even had a hand in creating the uber-cool Sandman.) He created the first superhero team, the Justice Society of America. Later on, he got tapped to revamp these properties at the dawn of the Silver Age of comics. He even created the concept of the comic book multiverse when he wrote "The Flash of Two Worlds," a story where the new Flash teams up with his golden age counterpart! This led to the institution of yearly crossovers in the pages of the Justice League of America featuring even more appearances of golden age characters in some truly quintessential tales.

The man is a giant, no doubt. But does anything resembling that awesomeness appear in the pages of his swords and sorcery tales? Actually, yes. But it's tucked away in the introduction of this particular volume:

Ages ago, as the legends say, the race of Man knew those stars and all their planets, named and visited them, and left on those planetary surfaces vast cities, great monuments to mankind's own greatness. Once, uncounted millenia before, an empire of Man was spread throughout the universe. This empire died more than a billion years ago, after which man himself sank into a state of barbarism.... Today, wherever man can be found on the planets of the dying star-suns, the very shape of the continents on which he lives bear little resemblance to those he knew two billion years before. The oceans cover his cities, the desert sands his tombs and temples, while the fierce north wind ruffles vegetation that earlier man had never seen.... And yet—to some men and women who live in the sunset years of the race has been given a power unknown to those men in an earlier age, yet a power famed and feared in the legendry of his people. For there are wizards and warlocks, sorcerers and witches in these days and their spells and incantations are known to work malignant miracles.

The epic nature of this passage is matched only by the disappointment that emerges when the reader slowly realizes that nothing about it impacts anything about the setting or action of the stories. There are no relics of the past, fantastic ruins, or inscrutable artifacts. There isn't even the strange decadence of something like the *Dying Earth* stories. It's just straight ahead swords and sorcery with barely even a nod to the fact that it actually occurs in some Long Night of a sprawling interstellar civilization. Seriously with a setup this cool, I was really hoping to see the freaky alien stuff like what you see in classic Conan stories like "Queen of the Black Coast" or "The Pool of the Black One," but it just isn't there!

Fox does at least provide a brief glimpse into how sorcerers conduct their spell research. It's dimly reminiscent of "The Tower of the Elephant" and is the closest he comes to developing from the really good parts of Conan:

> *"Long have I sat here in this ancient castle, stripping it bit by bit of all its treasure, paying them over to the wizards and warlocks of the interstellar and intergalactic abysses, that they might teach me their spells and cantraips. In a little while I would have been the greatest magician on Yarth! Then nothing could harm me. I have sat here without stirring for these many months. I have studied and learned, and my brain teems with sorceries with which to turn you into a mouse—to drive you mad with unguessable horrors...."*

In Fox's world, magic-users do not automatically gain new spells when they level up. They need to settle down into an actual domain so that they can loot it to pay off the wizards of Daemonia for their secrets. In that hellishly bizarre alternate plane of reality, its prime surface is seemingly all water. And it's loaded with inhuman necromancers that can only be harmed with magic weapons:

> *An ordinary sword would never have penetrated that purple flesh; only a blade filled with magic could do that task.*

The Lich in the first story is also pretty good and fulfills a similar niche:

> *"In the days when this land was known as Yarth, I was a sorcerer renowned from frozen Thuum in the north to tropical Azynyssa at the equator. My spells could level a city or raise up a tempest on the sea. Even now, after five hundred centuries of sleep, I still come to the call of witch and warlock, to teach the ancient mysteries or to help a suppliant in trouble."*

There are just three short stories here, but they're teeming with monsters. Kothar goes up against gigantic white worm-slug, the sea serpent Iormungar, a giant spider, demons, and even the fabled bull-man known here as "the Minokar." These are all pretty straightforward, though, perfectly at home as fodder for tabletop games. But they do not get near they same kind of introduction, development, description as the ones in Robert E. Howard's "Xuthal of the Dusk" or even "Rogues in the House." Next to those, it seems

Fox's monsters are tuned more for action like what you see in four color comics.

Another big difference is Conan ends up in all kinds of situations. He might be on the run from the law and end up on a merchant ship that is attacked by pirates. He might begin a tale on the run after a disastrous battle only to end up exploring a mysterious island with a beautiful princess in tow. He could even be a deposed king, thrown into some horrible dungeon full of the abandoned experiments of a wicked sorcerer. Kothar's more of a one-trick pony. He takes on a job with one sorcerer in order to take out another sorcerer. Again and again, even.

Only a fraction of the old Conan stories deal with sorcerers, but that's pretty much all that's served up here. And to be honest, I don't find myself having a reason to want one or the other to come out on top in the end. The scantily clad women that take up with Conan are absent as well, as are the many cultures and nations that are depicted there. This makes the stories seem rather more capricious; Kothar is a pawn for these far more powerful witches and warlocks, and he goes from one magical challenge to another. Without a grounding in the human aspect of fully realized civilizations, all of the fantastic elements rapidly become rather arbitrary.

The descriptions of Kothar's motivations are emblematic of this problem:

> *He was up and running, bent over, gripping his scabbard with his left hand, regretful that he had not kept on the mail shirt, cursing the streak of romanticism in his nature that made him champion of the weak and helpless, like the Lady Alaine and pretty Mellicent. They were no concern of his; at best, what he did here was only a gamble. He should be galloping for the domains of the robber barons, where money would be easy to win for such a warrior as himself.*

Kothar just sort of bops around from one patron encounter to the next. He's a sucker for a pretty face, and he goes hungry because of it. Somehow I have a hard time *believing* that even if it can be hand-waved due to the curse on his magic sword. In contrast, Howard's Conan is as fully realized as J. R. R. Tolkien's Gandalf. You can imagine what those two characters would say to questions you might put to them. And in Conan stories, every paragraph is crafted so that his likeability is maintained and contrasted with the crookedness and evil of his foes. When he triumphs, it is positively thrilling to see his more "civilized" opponents get their comeuppance.

And the women! Some of Kothar's witchy woman dream sequences here get perilously close to the sort of graphic luridness that was included in the *Conan the Barbarian* movie from the eighties. Howard's Conan stories were racy, but they were never quite that gratuitous about it. Yet what struck me about the women was just how different they were from one another. Belit treats Conan like a glorified cabin boy when he's not knocking heads at her command. Yasmela is in a state of abject terror and clings desperately to him for the security he provides. Olivia ends up tagging along out of happenstance and actually ends up rescuing Conan later on. Natala nags and complains, even after Conan goes to great lengths to keep her alive. And so on. These female characters may not be everyone's cup of tea, but they are *characters*, and they contrast greatly with one another even when they fulfill more or less the same role. You see the same thing with Howard's pantheon of gods: Crom, Bel, Mitra, and Set are not just swear words! They are fully developed fictional deities, and they're an integral part of the cultures of his fantasy setting.

I don't mind Fox's Kothar stories. They're actually much closer to the typical fantasy role-playing game scenario *because* of their simplicity. What bugs me is that the impression that most people have of Conan is that the stories must be every bit as trashy and formulaic as his imitations. That just isn't the case. Yet even though the action and the pacing seem to anticipate the sort of typical fare that would become ubiquitous in later role-playing and computer games, there are enough standard tropes missing here that it's interesting to see how things play out without them. Like an odd reductio ad absurdum, Gardner Fox's small volume of tales demonstrates why *Dungeons & Dragons* had to meld so many disparate and contradictory themes together in order to get a coherent, playable game.

It was perhaps inevitable that *Dungeons & Dragons* would reach beyond the tropes of vanilla swords and sorcery. Unrestrained sorcery is thoroughly chaotic and evil; its incoherence and randomness make it difficult to adapt to gameplay in a satisfying way. The *threat* of it makes for good drama, but it's better if it is partitioned off from the game world even if numerous Lovecraftian cults are at work to aid in unleashing it. It is ironic, but adding medieval Christian-themed clerics and paladins, each specially equipped to counter these forces, actually is the key ingredient that allows for *more* sorcery-themed foes to be added back into the mix. Tolkien's fantasy races provide many useful stereotypes that are perhaps more manageable for novices game masters than fully realized and historically accurate cultures. Finally, Jack Vance's magic system adds playable spell effects and abilities to the game without requiring player-characters to sell their imaginary souls for them. *Dungeons & Dragons* appears at first to be a Frankenstein's monster of pulp literature fragments, but it turns out that each of these components serve to solve problems that are immediately evident in the adventures of less well-known heroes like Kothar.

Changeling Earth
by Fred Saberhagen

This offbeat novel first published in 1973 begins with the dread Emperor of the East enjoying the slow impalement of one of his people. He then meets with his various chiefs and magicians to discuss the threat posed to their empire by Ardneh, some strange being that seems in league with the West. The novel appears at first to be heading down the same path as Roger Zelazny's *Jack of Shadows*, with an evil wizard anti-hero doing his thing in a magic-filled world where science does not work. Instead, the chapter closes with the emperor being struck down in some sort of trick by Ardneh.

The perspective then changes for several chapters, and we get a glimpse of the wider world from the perspective of the West. Their magicians depend on elementals for their magical effects. They dominate the night with their army of owl-like birds. The East depends on demons for their spells, and its armies tend to dominate during the day thanks to their flying lizard minions. Most people are reduced to wielding swords in battles, but most groups of fighting men usually have a mage attached to their unit.

But the entrance of Ardneh into the conflict is starting to turn the tide against the East. This strange spirit comes to all manner of people in the West, prompting them to be at the right place at the right time and giving them clues for how to best take advantage of openings that the East leaves for them. It's hard to tell if this is necessarily a good thing; no one knows who Ardneh is, where he came from, or what his ultimate aims are. If anyone is skeptical of his directives, the still small voice that is Ardneh merely replies, "By their fruits you shall know them." He's given the people of the West sound information time and time again. Isn't that reason enough to trust him?

It turns out that Ardneh is actually a cybernetic think tank that was constructed before the apocalypse. His name is really an acronym: *Automatic*

Restoration Director – National Executive Headquarters. When the doughty
protagonists arrive at his installation with a key component for Ardneh's
scheme, he reveals his true nature to them:

> *"I was built by war-planning men of the Old World, as part of a system of*
> *defense, but not as a destructive device of any kind. My oldest purpose is to*
> *defend mankind, and so I am of the West today, though there was no East*
> *or West when I was built. But my basic nature is one of peace, so it has*
> *taken me long to develop weapons of my own to enter battle. The object you*
> *have brought me will be helpful there, adding to the physical strength I can*
> *exert, if the test I am now conducting has a favorable result. More of that*
> *later. I have spoken of my builders. They meant their defense system to save*
> *the world, and in a sense they did. But they called on powers they did not*
> *fully understand and could not wholly control, and in saving the world they*
> *changed it, so drastically that their civilization could not survive. This was*
> *the great Change of which men still speak, dividing the Old World from the*
> *New. As I will show you soon, the world was changed by another machine,*
> *or rather by a part of me that is a part of me no longer, having done its work*
> *and been dismantled. I, the part of me that still exists, was created to end the*
> *Change when the time was ripe. The builders did not really expect that the*
> *changes in the world wrought by their defenses would be so great that I would*
> *be needed, but they doubted and feared enough to make me and to put the*
> *powers of restoration under my control if and when they should be needed.*
> *They never dreamed, I suppose, that fifty thousand years must pass before the*
> *proper time for restoration came. But only now has it come. The odds for the*
> *survival of mankind, if the restoration is accomplished in this year, in this*
> *month, are better than they have been at any time since the Change, or are*
> *likely to be in the estimable future."*

Continuing his monologue by way of a telepathically delivered animated
short, he divulges the complete origin story of this unusual science-fantasy
setting:

> *Now disaster was only seconds away from most of the major cities of the*
> *land. The part of Ardneh that had been built to change the world was*
> *empowered to act, and functioned as it had been made to do. It laid*
> *hold upon the matter within itself and pulled its energies into a new shape,*

beginning a Change that spread through the substance of the earth like cracks through shattering glass. A round wave-front of Change sprang out with the speed of light from Ardneh's buried site. But the setting in motion of the ultimate defense had taken a few seconds longer than anticipated. One enemy missile fell just before the wave-front reached it and exploded with full force beside a populous city, ending uncountable lives in the blinking of an eye. Other intercontinental weapons, falling like hail a few seconds later failed to explode. Meanwhile, on the other side of the world, surprise; the enemy was employing the same kind of an ultimate defense. Theirs was not, however, controlled by any device as sophisticated as Ardneh, and their simpler mechanisms were never to become alive. This too Rolf understood as in a dream, knowing it was so without knowing how he knew. But the enemy defenses also worked. A wave of Change springing from the other side of the world met that generated by Ardneh, and the fabric of the planet was altered more powerfully than anyone had thought it would be. Those few missiles that fell before the Change exploded, and the vast number that fell afterward were rendered practically harmless. One missile, however, to which Rolf's attention was now silently directed, was caught precisely in mid-explosion by the wavefront emanating from Ardneh. The fireball, the blooming nuclear blast, had just been born and it was not extinguished but neither did it follow the normal course of the explosions that had preceded it. It did not fade, but changed in shape, ran through a spectrum of colors and back again, and writhed up toward the sky as if with agonizing effort. Rolf knew that he was watching a kind of birth, and one of terrible importance.

So this magic-filled post-apocalyptic world is a result of two nuclear damper technologies having unanticipated side effects in the midst of a classic cold war nuclear exchange. The unique thing about this is that unmitigated destruction is the means of injecting powers and principalities into the overarching premise. Ardneh is an artificial intelligence entity empowered to alter the laws of nature in order to protect mankind from total destruction. He functions as a sort of guardian angel for the West. In opposition to him is the demonic force of Orcus, the result of an ill-timed nuclear explosion. The magicians of the East attempt to harness this demon for their own ends but find that he is not entirely under their control.

This is a really weird book. It is far less about action and adventure than it is about the overall setting it depicts. The efforts of its characters are far too often undercut and overshadowed by Ardneh and Orcus. Offhand, the only reason that I can think of that this novel would have been included in *AD&D*'s Appendix N reading list is for its example of being willing to think outside the box when it comes to coming up with a premise for a fantasy setting. Of course, as *D&D* evolved, it became so much more conventional and self-referential[1] that it is now hard to imagine this book having any impact at all on the game's milieux. But when *AD&D* was just about the only game in town, Gary Gygax intentionally designed it with a wide-open multiverse at the Dungeon Master's disposal. Whether as a brief themed sublevel in a funhouse dungeon or as a fully realized parallel world, he intended referees to have the latitude to be as creative as they wished, even going so far as to encourage them to shift temporarily into other game systems![2]

Being a post-apocalyptic tale, it would seem to have far more to do TSR's classic *Gamma World* setting than any sort of swords and sorcery game. It's not a perfect match, of course: *Gamma World* lacks magic and demons and is loaded with tech gadgets of varying degrees of functionality. The most immediate gaming application of the material in this book is therefore somewhat more indirect: it is perhaps best used in reworking the nature of a couple of the game's Cryptic Alliances. Fortunately, the designers of the game explicitly encourage the referee to make these sorts of changes:

> *As if the monsters and creatures of GAMMA WORLD weren't fearsome enough, many of them have banded together into semi-secret organizations called CRYPTIC ALLIANCES. Some are remnants of organizations that existed during the Shadow Years... some are of very recent origin.... The possibilities for cryptic alliances are many and varied, limited only by the referee's imagination. A suggested list of basic groups follows. The referee should feel free to add or change them as he sees fit. Even changing the names and some of the characteristics of some of these groups will keep the players guessing.... (Gamma World first edition, page 27)*

As you can see, the political situation of the default *Gamma World* campaign setting is a big contrast to the thinly veiled cold war era superpowers setup we see in *Changeling Earth*. It's more of a complete zoo, an insane mutated wilderness with enclaves of off-the-wall secret societies occasionally exerting greater influence within relatively small locales marked out on the area map. Outside these relatively limited areas, agents from any of the Cryptic Alliances *can* be found, but it's more likely that random encounters will involve wild mutant creatures, robots, or independent humanoid tribes.

Here is one of the Cryptic Alliances that got only marginal attention during the game's heyday:

THE FOLLOWERS OF THE VOICE These are beings of all types who worship computers, believing that machines created the world and can again restore peace and order. They are always encountered near installations that have computers whose logic circuits agree, at least in part, with their philosophies. In some instances, the large computers, such as the think tank, have taken over their followers, and rule with dictatorial powers. Roving bands of the Followers of the Voice are occasionally encountered as they roam vast areas in search of computers or machinery to use as "shrines" for their strange religious rituals. (Gamma World first edition, page 28)

Looking back, it's not hard to imagine why oddball groups like this would have failed to get much play back in the day. In the first place, the mutations and high-tech weapons are so much fun, few gamers cared about much in the game besides looting the next installation. Secondly, information on Cryptic Alliances was pretty sparse in the third edition rule set. People who came to the setting with that particular iteration would have had so little to go on that they would more than likely drop the parts that weren't immediately playable. But combining this particular nugget with what we see in this Fred Saberhagen novel could lead to some interesting gaming situations.

The Followers of the Voice don't have to be the superstitious simpletons that mindlessly venerate ancient computer devices. There might really be a voice coordinating disparate groups across the post-apocalyptic wasteland. Perhaps the power that is directing them gets more intelligent and threatening as they obtain the necessary parts to bring its primary installation up to a more effective working order? If the voice represented an intellect from before the apocalypse, it would be able to direct adventuring groups to potentially unspoiled caches of materiel. It may even be able to help them find a means of entering ancient military complexes and disabling its defenses once they are inside.

A lot of the other groups are pretty straightforward. The Knights of Genetic Purity want to eradicate all mutated humans. The Iron Society, in turn, wants to kill off the remaining pure strain humans. The Zoopremisists see to the interests of the mutated animals even though they are few, far-flung, and fanatical. But there is one other group that could benefit from a tune-up courtesy of this obscure Appendix N entry:

> *RESTORATIONISTS These are a group of primarily human and humanoid mutants who have recovered large amounts of information from the past and are seeking to rebuild the lost civilization. Restorationists are usually armed with weapons from the past and frequently have robotic units working with them. They shun other moderate alliances and work single-mindedly towards their goal.* (Gamma World *first edition, page 27*)

The way that the overall intent of how these Cryptic Alliances were meant to be used seems to shift over time is most clearly evident with this particular group. With the first edition, they are mainly background for encounters with non-player-characters. By the third edition, there are elaborate rules governing how players could join them and gain status within them. (Oddly enough, it is implied that the players' party could even be comprised of individuals from different groups.) However, the series of adventure modules released for that iteration of the game were designed under the assumption that the Restorationists were basically the "good guy" group and that the players would be working for them by default.

Going back to the original material and giving it a *Changeling Earth*-style twist, I would look at making it possible for the Restorationists to genuinely threaten to turn back the clock. Science and technology still work in the *Gamma World* setting, of course. Yet the sort of fastidious scientific realism that was endemic in eighties games is conspicuously absent. What if there were reasons for that? What if the oddities of the artifact operation charts were the result of changes to the laws of physics that occurred during the apocalypse at the close of the Shadow Years? Similarly, there is no magic in the *Gamma World* setting. But what if the game's mutation system was made possible by a fundamental shift in the nature of reality?

Perhaps the Restorationists are privy to information that would allow them to change things back. If they have their way, the laws of physics would be restored, mutations would cease to function, and technological artifacts would go back to being more consistently comprehensible. But what would the side effects be? Will mutant creatures simply die when the new change occurs? Will artificial intelligences that have transformed into strange spirit-like forces revert to mere computer code that can't even pass a Turing test? Do average Restorationist operatives even know what would happen? Or does an inner circle of elders carefully guard the true nature of their work against discovery?

Most importantly... how will the players respond to all this once they catch wind of what this Cryptic Alliance is really up to? Personally, I can't imagine them wanting *Gamma World* to ever change on such a fundamental level. It's just one of the most unaccountably fun settings ever developed for a role playing game. The prospect of the game actually turning into a really mediocre version of *Twilight 2000* would more than likely end the campaign. Still, "the last *Gamma World* adventure" could make for some truly memorable action. Whether the indefatigable band of mutated misfits fails to prevent the restoration of the old world or whether they allow it to transpire as a sort of least bad alternative to something much worse, it could be something that players end up talking about for a long time.

Notes

1. As *The RPG Corner* recently posted, "It's no big secret that *D&D* long ago stopped referencing literature and mythology and instead became a self-referential genre unto itself."

2. See pages 57-58 and 112 in the *AD&D Dungeon Masters Guide* for details.

The Face in the Frost
by John Bellairs

Ursala K. Le Guin called this book "authentic fantasy." Lin Carter said it was "absolutely first class." Quite simply, though, this book is just downright *fun*. The dialog of the two main magicians featured in the story is loaded with anachronisms. Every scene practically boils over with vivid details. And the action is varied and exciting. This is not ponderous epic fantasy; it's an engaging read that is extremely difficult to put down. It's almost a shame that it's so short—fewer than 180 pages with quite a few illustrations. But it's loaded with charm, it doesn't waste your time, and it provides one of the best close-up looks you'll find of freewheeling wizardry anywhere in the Appendix N reading list.

The opening hook involves a tome of magic fraught with secrets and danger. The two protagonists, Prospero and Roger Bacon, discover what all is afoot through a few odd journal entries:

February 18: *I stayed up all night, and toward morning, when the letters were twisting and squirming before my eyes, I found that the first two lines made sense.* Laudate Dominum! *All that is required, it seems, is concentration. It seems to be the beginning of an incantation of some sort....* March 14: *At first I was horribly disappointed. I chanted the words but nothing happened. However, I soon came to see that one has to want something specific to happen. I decided that the best thing would be to close my eyes and see what image formed. I saw many things, but one picture kept recurring: the snowy field outside my window, and in the middle of it one gray wolf.... I chanted the words again and went to my window. It was ten o'clock at night, a three-quarters-full moon was in the sky, and in the snow I saw a wolf staring up at me. In that instant I realized that I had* made *him.*

This seems to be a rather big to-do for something as familiar as a "Summon Wolf" spell. In Steve Jackson's classic MicroGame *Wizard* this was one of the easier spells, amounting to an inexpensive way to get an additional figure on the tactical map to fight alongside you. But here we have an ordinary monk with no particular training in magic spending weeks upon weeks to decipher the formula, growing every more haggard in the process, taking on new quirks and disadvantages, and possibly even undergoing an alignment change in the process. There's much more to this than a simple conjuring trick!

> March 17: *More success with the control of the wolf. I have translated three whole paragraphs now. The intense study is affecting my nerves. I constantly think that something is plucking at my sleeves. When I turn around, there is no one there....* April 7: *It seems that the next paragraph is not an incantation at all, but a set of directives. Prerequisites for further action. I cannot believe that such demands need to be met, so I will simply continue to the next spell.... [Later....] I spoke the words I have learned, and suddenly the whole room began to waver and drift like smoke. I felt as if I could put my hand through the table and the walls. I saw everything as through murky water. The floor pitched like a deck, but with difficulty I got to the window. The wolf was out there on the grass, closer than before, but beside him was a man in a monk's robe. The cowl was thrown back, but I could not see his features through the shimmering air. Then his face grew impossibly large and came near, and I saw that it was mine—my face as it might be after a year in the grave. A voice, a dry insect voice, harsh and cracked, whispered,* "Give me the book."

This is good stuff. The magic here is mysterious and dangerous. It's creepy, yet this hapless monk can't seem to stop himself. He refuses to take the proper precautions and ends up in sort of a cross between *The Sorcerer's Apprentice* and *The Twilight Zone*. But this is only the beginning.

Our two heroes have to sort all of this out, of course. In contrast to this monk's handiwork, *their* magic is quite a bit more tongue in cheek. They use a nonsense rhyme to shrink themselves down so that they can ride on a miniature replica of the British man-o-war *Actaeon*. They fire off all the guns on the ship at once with a spell consisting of "the Celtic word for Greek fire couched between two old Dutch swear words." One of them destroys a bridge by yelling at it and then creating a whirlwind by throwing a bunch of tarot cards into the air. The other turns first a tomato and then a squash into a carriage by reciting a bit of nonsense. (For the record, the tomato carriage did not turn out so well.) As if recapitulating Cinderella wasn't enough, the author, later on, takes a page from Jack in the Beanstalk by having a monk send them over a wall by enchanting a Creeping Charlie to wrap itself around them and then *growing* them to the other side.

In contrast to these hijinks, removing a curse is serious business. The scene pictured on the cover is of a grave in the midst of a haunted forest. The inscription on the tombstone is this:

Under this stone we have placed the burnt body of Melichus the sorcerer. He did great wrong. May his soul lie here under this stone with his body and trouble us not.

This is quite a terrible thing to Prospero, and he sets about to undo it with an elaborate ritual:

He took out a pair of brown beeswax candles and lit them, placing them a few feet apart on the carved stone. Between these he opened his large book to the place he had marked the night before. Then he went to the bag again and took out a square glass jar full of saffron-colored chalk powder. Going back to the book occasionally to check the words, he sprinkled the chalk in two concentric circles around himself and the stone, all the while whispering verses. Sometimes he would speak a word aloud, and then stop to listen before going on. In the space between the two circles, with the same yellow powder, he made signs: Hebrew letters, zodiac symbols, old complicated figures that every magician knew. One wide empty space was left, and in it he slowly wrote "Melichus." First he traced the letters in the dirt with his finger, then he poured in the chalk. He got up, took a compass from his pocket, and sprinkled water from a metal jar to the north, the south, the east, and the west.

All of this was required in order for this mage to give a command to the dead to come forth. It's all very evocative, of course, and it makes for a good read, but you don't see this sort of thing turn up in tabletop games very often. Oh, there are perennial complaints about the lack of "realism" in Vancian magic. There're numerous demands that magic be made more... well, *magical*. While innovative games like Ars Magica were designed from the ground up in order to address these sorts of issues, very few of the modifications to classic D&D in this vein ever seem to stick.

Consider the addition of material components in AD&D. To cast "Comprehend Languages," a magic-user has to have a few grains of salt. "Enlarge" requires a pinch of powdered iron. "Feather Fall" requires a piece of down. "Friends" requires the mage to apply chalk, lampblack, and vermilion to his face before casting it. And so on. Most of these are lightweight and common enough that they wouldn't require much in the way of bookkeeping to keep track of them. In fact, the magic-users' robes become a bit quirkier as a result of these rules: "material components for spells are assumed to be kept in little pockets, stored in the folds and small pockets of the spell caster's garb."

This, however, does not do much to inject a sense of wonder and exuberance into the game's magic. Indeed, this is almost painfully drab and mundane. A purer Jack Vance-type approach at least implies an alien culture and science that functions according to its own internal logic. These "pinches of this" and "powders of that" do little more than invoke medieval hucksters and charlatans vainly trying to turn lead into gold. And while there might be occasions where the lack of a certain ingredient could create an interesting problem for players to work around or perhaps an amusing situation, I can't imagine the average group of role players wanting to regularly deal with the sort of hassles that would arise from a magic-user somehow losing just about everything except his precious spellbooks.

That said, there are more than a few cases where spell components do add something more significant to the overall gameplay. In the case of the second level cleric spell "Spiritual Hammer," the cleric must have an actual warhammer on hand to cast it. Given that the warhammer disappears after the spell is complete, this is a pretty severe limitation on a cleric's ability to make use of it. For short excursions within a day's journey from town, the expense of the warhammer is a minor annoyance, the weight of the hammer is enough to matter in encumbrance calculations, and the need for hauling around more than one backup weapon becomes something that has to be taken into account. For a journey of several weeks through a wilderness region, however, the use of this spell can rapidly cease to be an option!

The first-level magic-user spell "Identify" is another good example. The spell components are expensive, costing a whopping one hundred gold per casting. The option of increasing the effectiveness of the spell by crushing up a relatively valuable luckstone and adding it to the brew is intriguing even if it is unlikely to ever actually be done. Thus, the addition of spell components in *AD&D* is mostly about opening up new ways to balance the various spells against one another. As far as chrome goes, it does very little to add to the overall atmosphere and the sense of awe that magic should inspire. Indeed, at low levels of play and in typical adventure scenarios, the game often boils down to the players coordinating a team of misfits and rivals so that they can get into a position where they can extract a maximum value from the use of an insanely small number of "Sleep" and "Charm Person" spells. It might be fun, but it's far from the spirit of characters like Prospero and Roger Bacon.

This tendency of players to only use a handful of the most effective spells no doubt played a part in Gary Gygax's revision of the rules in the *Greyhawk* supplement which was incorporated into *Advanced Dungeons & Dragons*. Not only did he introduce additional variation into magic user characters by requiring them to roll for their "chance to know" based on their intelligence, but they also started the game with only "Read Magic," a random offensive spell, a random defensive spell, and a random utility spell. This left the players in a position where they would have to really apply themselves if they were going to have access to anything remotely like the full spell list:

> ...the ramifications of spell scarcity are bound to aid your campaign, and not only with regard to excess treasure and magic items. A scroll of but a single spell becomes highly meaningful to the magic-users in the game, especially when it is of a spell heretofore unknown. The acquisition of a book of spells from someplace in the dungeons or wildernesses of the campaign is a benison beyond price! PC and NPC alike will take great pains to guard scrolls and spell books. Magic-users will haunt dusty libraries and peruse musty tomes in the hopes of gleaning but a single incantation to add to their store of magic. (Dungeon Masters Guide, page 39)

People who came to the game via one of the popular *Basic Sets* released over the years were unlikely to think in such terms. Even hardcore adherents to the *AD&D* system were unlikely to be aware of this facet of the game: their dungeon masters may have been running a *Basic*-style game with only the more immediately understandable new rules appropriated into the mix. These instructions on spell scarcity were tucked away in an odd corner of the

Dungeon Masters Guide, and players would not have been aware of them unless their DM specifically enforced them![1]

Back in the early days of role-playing, it was often considered bad form for the players to ever look in the DM's books.[2] Of course, many groups would often take the opposite tack and consult the *Monster Manual* during the middle of a fight in order to fine tune their tactics. Players naturally want to master the game and make informed decisions; concise, playable magic rules that the players can completely understand is something that's nearly inevitable in a tabletop game. Not that it isn't impossible to run a game where the players never actually see the rules[3], but it's not something that happens very often. This sort of mechanical reliability is often antithetical to "real" magic, but that's the price for having a playable game.

The ideal place then to create more mysterious and frightening forms of magic is not in the rules that govern the players, but in the adventure situations that emerge from the actions of non-player-characters. Bad things can happen to those guys without violating the players' sense of fairness. Critical spell failures that you'd never think to dole out to an acquaintance of yours at the tabletop can be unleashed with impunity upon random simpletons and fools. These guys thus become not only cautionary tales but also clues for the players as to how best to approach whatever malevolent forces there are that have been unwittingly turned loose. Finally, truly despicable sorcerers, corrupted with the knowledge of *Things Man Was Not Meant to Know*, can toy with spells and rituals that could never be fully articulated in a rule set. The only real limitation from a game design standpoint is that the resulting situation must be something to which the talents of a group of bold and greedy adventurers are relevant.

Rules are primarily there to govern the players and their avatars within the game world. Adventure designers, however, should feel free to indulge in exploring the possibilities that lie far outside their scope. Still, even without getting fancy, just keeping magic scarce can go a long way toward bringing a sense of awe back into the mix.

Notes

1. The implications of these rules were not lost on the designers of Infocom's *Enchanter* series, however.

2. In *Paranoia*, even saying something that indicates you know what's in the referee's material is grounds for the execution of a clone.

3. See Rick Stump's "Making Magic Amazing Without Touching Mechanics" for details on *that*.

Dwellers in the Mirage
by Abraham Merritt

A. Merritt is easily my favorite of the early pulp writers. His descent into obscurity since his heyday might be hard for me to fully comprehend sometimes, but it makes me relish his works all the more. It is as if his books are a secret that I practically get to keep all to myself. I am not alone in my admiration of his works, of course. He was highly regarded by H. P. Lovecraft and played a significant role in the development of the much better-known Cthulhu Mythos. Merritt ranks highly among the influences that Gary Gygax cites as being the inspiration for the game *Dungeons & Dragons*. Finally, James Maliszewski even created his megadungeon *Dwimmermount* as a tribute to the man. So while admirers of A. Merritt today are fewer in number, they are at least in good company.

While the overall structure of Merritt's work is (in keeping with its time) more or less derivative of Edgar Rice Burroughs's winning formula, his execution is nevertheless impeccable. All of the standard tropes are here in all their glory with not a hint of irony: the best buddy Indian sidekick, the cosmic terror, warrior women, a "witch woman" femme fatale, and even the eligible princess type that just so happens to be living among doughty goodhearted savages. It's a potent conglomerate, vividly described and masterfully paced; this volume, in particular, is positively transporting.

I actually prefer this over Burroughs and Lovecraft. The former strikes me a being a bit cavalier and rough around the edges no matter how much of a debt Merritt might have owed the man. And though the latter is rightly regarded as a grandmaster of horror, his characters are generally well insulated from the strange phenomena they encounter. They will follow a trail of unsettling hints for pages on end, all the while remaining in full skeptic mode. Sometimes they insist on a rational explanation of all the strange stuff they find right up until the very end. But usually, one good whiff of the horrors that lurk just outside the collective consciousness of mankind sends them scuttling back to Miskatonic University to foist a massive cover up on the rest of us.

Merritt, in contrast, is much more familiar with his readers. Rather than keeping you at arms length with a formal academic account that carefully lays out all the facts, he puts you inside the head of a protagonist that is far more relatable. Devices such as hypnosis, past lives, and ancestral memories are perhaps a little hokey, but in Merritt's hands, they are powerful tools that make for a uniquely intimate encounter with the weird.

This passage is a pretty good illustration of how he accomplishes this:

The high priest touched my arm. I turned my head to him, and followed his eyes. A hundred feet away from me stood a girl. She was naked. She had not long entered womanhood and quite plainly was soon to be a mother. Her eyes were as blue as those of the old priest, her hair was reddish brown, touched with gold, her skin was palest olive. The blood of the old fair race was strong within her. For all she held herself so bravely, there was terror in her eyes, and the rapid rise and fall of her rounded breasts further revealed that terror. She stood in a small hollow. Around her waist was a golden ring, and from that ring dropped three golden chains fastened to the rock floor. I recognized their purpose. She could not run, and if she dropped or fell, she could not writhe away, out of the cup. But run, or writhe away from what? Certainly not from me! I looked at her and smiled. Her eyes searched mine. The terror suddenly fled from them. She smiled back at me, trustingly. God forgive me—I smiled at her and she trusted me! I looked beyond her, from whence had come a glitter of yellow like a flash from a huge topaz. Up from the rock a hundred yards behind the girl jutted an immense fragment of the same yellow translucent stone that formed the jewel in my ring. It was like the fragment of a gigantic shattered pane. Its shape was roughly triangular. Black within it was a tentacle of the Kraken. The tentacle swung down within the yellow stone, broken from the monstrous body when the stone had been broken. It was all of fifty feet long. Its inner side was turned toward me, and plain upon all its length clustered the hideous sucking discs. Well, it was ugly enough—but nothing to be afraid of, I thought. I smiled again at the chained girl, and met once more her look of utter trust. (Chapter 4)

In the *Call of Cthulhu* adventures I've observed, it's pretty much game over when the players succeed in tracking down the evil cultists. Here, we get all of this as part of the prologue. It's the *opening hook*, not the climax! And as you can see, the hero really is a *nice* guy. He's a skeptic, cut from the same cloth as guys like Clarence Darrow or Carl Sagan. In a film adaption he could even be played by somebody like Jeff Goldblum. If anything, he's a bit smug: patronizing the religious practices of a less sophisticated people. His reorientation with reality comes swiftly, though. He's about to find out that life is a lot more complicated than he ever imagined:

> On swept the ritual and on…was the yellow stone dissolving from around the tentacle…was the tentacle swaying? Desperately I tried to halt the words, the gesturing. I could not! Something stronger than myself possessed me, moving my muscles, speaking from my throat. I had a sense of inhuman power. On to the climax of the evil evocation—and how I knew how utterly evil it was—the ritual rushed, while I seemed to stand apart, helpless to check it. It ended. And the tentacle quivered…it writhed…it reached outward to the chained girl… There was a devil's roll of drums, rushing up fast and ever faster to a thunderous crescendo… The girl was still looking at me…but the trust was gone from her eyes…her face reflected the horror stamped upon my own. The black tentacle swung up and out! I had a swift vision of a vast cloudy body from which other cloudy tentacles writhed. A breath that had in it the cold of outer space touched me. The black tentacle coiled round the girl… She screamed—inhumanly…she faded…she dissolved…her screaming faded…her screaming became a small shrill agonized piping…a sigh. I heard the dash of metal from where the girl had stood. The clashing of the golden chains and girdle that had held her, falling empty on the rock. The girl was gone! (Chapter 4)

A protagonist in this situation can't afford to simply fail a sanity check and then swear off weirdness forever. In the first place, he's complicit with it, an active participant. He's partly responsible for the blood on his hands even though he acted in ignorance. Running away isn't even an option because his destiny is bound up somehow with the horrors that have been awakened. And by the time the action has shifted to being set within the lost world on the other side of a tremendous mirage, the average reader ought to be ready for just about anything. I was not, however, ready for *this*:

Behind her rode a half-score other women, young and strong-thewed, pink-skinned and blue-eyed, their hair of copper-red, rust-red, bronzy-red, plaited around their heads or hanging in long braids down their shoulders. They were bare-breasted, kirtled and buskined. They carried long, slender spears and small round targes. And they, too, were like Valkyries, each of them a shield-maiden of the Aesir. As they rode, they sang, softly, muted, a strange chant.

Whoa.

You know, my whole life I kind of suspected fantasy and science fiction could be like this. I know we hear a great deal about how films and comic books and novels are across the line for this reason or that. It's just that I always felt like we were holding back on some level. And it sure seems that our epic movies are missing something these days. Occasionally, you get a hint that things were different once—that there used to be Amazon women in space and stuff like that. But for a long time now it just seems like people can't invoke that sort of thing except as a parody.

There's just something about the old stories that we can't seem to *do* anymore. It shows up not just in what's off limits but in how things from the past get tweaked for present day audiences. Just like Faramir can't be depicted as simply being more noble and discerning than his brother. No, in the film adaption of *The Lord of the Rings* he has to trudge back to Osgiliath and come face to face with a Nazgul on a winged mount before he can make the right (but counter-intuitive) choice. Just like that scene with Fili and Kili dying in battle protecting the body of their kinsman Thorin—it can't be left alone to be what *it* is but has to be reworked to shoehorn in whatever plot elements people can't live without anymore. Just like *Starship Troopers* can't just be more or less faithfully translated into movie format but rather has to be turned into a two-hour pillorying of crazed warmongers that have to be unfrozen from the sixties just for the occasion.

There's something to all this, and it didn't just happen. Back during World War II, C. S. Lewis wrote in *The Abolition of Man*, "We laugh at honour and are shocked to find traitors in our midst." From a cultural standpoint, we've been laughing and sneering for a *long* time. These now utterly predictable mutilations of classic adventure fiction are a direct result of decades of this sort of mentality. And what are the scriptwriters and directors laughing at when they foist these revisions on us? The capacity of a man to make a sound leadership decision in the absence of an immediate crisis that forces his hand. The fierce loyalty that was once routinely summoned up as a part of Anglo-Saxon family bonds. The dedication and determination of a young man as he strives to become officer material in the midst of a war where humanity's existence is at stake. What is it about the modern mind that it looks at these things and says, "Hey… let me *fix* that?" What is this impulse that makes filmmakers unable to leave this sort of thing alone? It's an adventure story, of all things! Are they really *that* threatening?

I may never completely figure this sort of thing out. And I don't know why it is, but somehow chainmail bikinis and everything else is bound up in all this. It's just an armchair observation, mind you… but it sure appears that if you have lots of hot Viking warrior women in a story, then this is a pretty good indicator that you're going to get all that other stuff in there, too. And right or wrong, I just love Merritt's audacity in not just having them all be redheads, but having them all go topless in their opening scene as well. It doesn't come off as some sort of weird fetish like some Heinlein's later stuff, and it's not especially lurid or titillating the way Pierce Anthony would have played it. It's just a fact, and it seems like Merritt could write it that way without giving a second thought to any potential complaints from the peanut gallery.

But these characters aren't just here to provide a little cheesecake. We do get to see them in a proper battle, and we also get to see them endure the harsh discipline of military order. And they aren't just stormtroopers or video game avatars either; they have hopes and opinions of their own. They're tamped down due to the rigors their society puts them through, but it comes out before the end. It's a nice touch as well that these people really do have a severe shortage of men—and not due to some kind of dumb female supremacist ideology either. The male babies just aren't being born as much among their isolated people group. These Viking-like people have no choice but to press their women into military service.

Inevitably, this scenario has other implications once our square-jawed protagonist enters the scene:

For the first time I seemed to be realizing her beauty, seemed for the first time to be seeing her clearly. Her russet hair was braided in a thick coronal; it shone like reddest gold, and within it was twisted a strand of sapphires.

Her eyes outshone them. Her scanty robe of gossamer blue revealed every lovely, sensuous line of her. White shoulders and one of the exquisite breasts were bare. Her full red lips promised—anything, and even the subtle cruelty stamped upon them, lured. (Chapter 15)

Yeah, she's stunning. Sure, she's captivating. And yes, the fact that she is… you know… a witch woman means that she is the *last* person you'd want to be involved with. But she's also at the center of the action. To sort anything out, the hero pretty much *has* to get involved with this character. I just love the boldness of this type of scenario. It's like that time that Kirk ordered the *Enterprise* across into the neutral zone and Spock (yes, Spock!) had to seduce an attractive Romulan commander while his captain donned a disguise and looted the enemy flagship's cloaking device. It's good drama… especially when you get to see Spock (yes, Spock!) confronted about his subterfuge by the very woman he's betrayed.

Not everybody goes in for the dashing rogue routine though. I mean, you naturally look down on a guy that doesn't even have the *option* to be a dastardly cad. But when it comes to a protagonist, likability takes a hit if the guy actually goes and takes advantage of someone. At the same time, you wouldn't be picking up a book with this sort of cover if you didn't want to indulge in an at least a *few* scenes of that sort. How can you walk the line between these conflicting constraints? Well in Merritt's case, the solution is to have the main character be sort of a reincarnation of that sketchier sort of guy that we'd never really accept in a full-on protagonist's role. When his "old self" gains control of the nice guy's mind, we've got no choice but to read chapter after chapter about the exploits of a top-tier scoundrel. It's positively delicious. And we've got enough plausible deniability that we don't have to feel *too* guilty about it.

Yeah, that's a bit of a stretch, sure. But it works, and the whole situation results in some pretty good dialog:

"What have you seen, Dwayanu?" What I had seen might be the end of Sirk—but I did not tell her so. The thought was not yet fully born. It had never been my way to admit others into half-formed plans. It is too dangerous. The bud is more delicate than the flower and should be left to develop free from prying hands or treacherous or even well-meant meddling. Mature your plan and test it; then you can weigh with clear judgment any changes. Nor

was I ever strong for counsel; too many pebbles thrown into the spring muddy it. That was one reason I was—Dwayanu. I said to Lur: "I do not know. I have a thought. But I must weigh it." She said, angrily: "I am not stupid. I know war—as I know love. I could help you."—I said, impatiently: "Not yet. When I have made my plan I will tell it to you." She did not speak again until we were within sight of the waiting women; then she turned to me. Her voice was low, and very sweet: "Will you not tell me? Are we not equal, Dwayanu?" "No," I answered, and left her to decide whether that was answer to the first question or both. (Chapter 18)

Yeah. That's how it's done right there.

Of course, you can play your dangerous games like that. But there's still that part where you come to your senses and get back with the really sweet girl that you should have been with all along. In some ways, that's a lot more difficult than outplaying a player at her own game. There's something about, oh, I don't know… selling out your friends, hanging with a really bad crowd, and… oh yeah, hooking up with an utterly evil but smashingly good-looking Viking warrior witch woman that puts a damper on things; it pours more than a little ice water on the reunion. How do you talk your way out of *that*?

Well, if it's Grant Ward from the *Agents of S.H.I.E.L.D.* television series, his opening line in a fairly similar situation is, "I figure I let you punch me again, repeatedly." That is, of course, brilliant… if you literally want to *make someone actually want to punch you repeatedly.* Talk about cringe-worthy! And I get that it wasn't just that he took up with a Norse goddess there when she mind-controlled him; it was the fact that she revealed the truth about who he actually had feelings for. Even so, I could not understand how the scene could make any sense. In what universe does a man owe anyone any kind of apology once mind-controlling secret-divulging Norse goddesses enter the picture?

Merritt's take on this same sort of scenario is infinitely more satisfying. The thing is, when your girlfriend actually wants to kill you and she actually has every reason to, and you really were possessed by an ancient warlord that could summon Cthulhoidian tentacles from outside of space and time… well, you've got your work cut out for you. Apologies are not enough. Inviting your girl to punch you in the face is not going to fix it either. First, you have to physically restrain her to keep her from **killing** you, and then you have to put her in a position where she can eavesdrop on you while you start resolving all the remaining plot threads. When she can see not just that the real you is back, but also that your sterling character really is above reproach, well… *look out!*

> *"Leif!" I jumped to my feet. Evalie was beside me. She peered at me through the veils of her hair; her clear eyes shone upon me—no longer doubting, hating, fearing. They were as they were of old. "Evalie!" My arms went round her; my lips found hers. "I listened, Leif!" "You believe, Evalie!" She kissed me, held me tight. "But she was right—Leif. You could not go with me again into the land of the Little People. Never, never would they understand. And I would not dwell in Karak." "Will you go with me, Evalie—to my own land? After I have done what I must do… and if I am not destroyed in its doing?" "I will go with you, Leif!" (Chapter 22)*

Okay, maybe it's not entirely realistic, but it sure makes for a solid conclusion. It is, at any rate, a story of which I am unapologetically among the target audience. Sure, this very nearly boils down to being a trashy romance novel for guys. But Merritt's Leif Langdon is of almost exactly in the same mold as Tolkien's Aragorn: he gets the girl in the end, but he does the things that need doing and preserves his honor in the process. Contrast that with Camelot, where Guinevere takes the man she wants regardless of the consequences, openly betraying her husband and destroying the pinnacle of civilization in the process. My old pulp novel collection is positively prosocial in comparison!

More recent iterations of genre fiction really fail to do much for me, though. The *Agents of S.H.I.E.L.D.* episode I just mentioned ends with the female science expert explaining to the male science expert, "I'm not saying *you* were weak. I'm saying *all men are weak.*" Uh… thanks, I guess! The male character I most identify with from that series finishes the first season by having the snot beat out of him by a woman he jilted. It's almost sadistic how long the beating goes on. And when trying to pitch the Disney movie *Frozen* to me, people tell me how awesome it is because *the handsome prince turns out to be a real douchebag in the end!* As if that is some sort of fantastic literary innovation. They don't seem to notice that they are talking to, you know, a bona fide handsome-prince type. That's the kind of character *I* identify with, after all. And when writers use that stock character as a punching bag, then wipe their feet on him, I naturally take it a little personally.

Maybe I've overlooked the more recent stuff that would be right up my alley, but I've got to say that this A. Merritt story really does it for me. When I finished the last chapter and set the book aside, I was positively cheering like the people in all those clips of fans supposedly reacting to the conclusion of the Legend of Korra series. *This* is the sort of story that has nearly been erased from what is even conceivable anymore, yet here it is, undiluted and without the slightest hint of snark or self-consciousness. I love it. Maybe I'm a hopeless romantic or something, but hey, at least I'm not a masochist. Half the time I turn on the television anymore I get the feeling that someone's working overtime trying to erase people like *me* from the collective consciousness. I'm sick of it. Until this sort of weird cultural myopia runs its course, I'll stick with works of guys like A. Merritt.

Lest Darkness Fall
by L. Sprague de Camp

It's a perfectly reasonable impulse to want to have your own favorite volumes of fantasy literature retroactively included in the Appendix N book list. Indeed, it was not surprising to see a few glaring omissions addressed in the latest edition of *Dungeons & Dragons*.[1] That said, I'm generally flabbergasted when the discussion turns toward who should get booted from one of gaming's most notable honor rolls. Roger Zelazny gets brought up in spite of the wide-ranging appeal of his *Amber* series—a series that inspired one of the most innovative role-playing games around! (Amber Diceless, naturally.) Gardner Fox, too, is brought up even though he created the Lich—easily one of the most significant *D&D* monsters that wasn't inspired by those weird plastic toys from Taiwan. John Bellairs gets mentioned here in spite of his hilarious anachronisms and compulsive readability. Most surprising to me, however, is to see L. Sprague de Camp's work singled out for a place on the chopping block. That's really shortsighted though. The guy covered a great many things that are of especial interest to gamers, including some things that they consistently neglect. Cutting de Camp out of the Appendix N library does a great disservice, both to him and to gamers in general.

You see, *Lest Darkness Fall* is a tale of inadvertent time travel that's loaded with stuff that can help you bring the oft-shortchanged domain level of play to life. Not sure what to do once your kingdoms are all set up and ready to go? Why not follow de Camp's lead and have emissaries from the surrounding kingdoms come calling one after another to demand their piece of Danegeld? If the player chooses to pay them all off, he'll bankrupt himself. If he gives them all the brush off, then he better be ready to fight them all... *simultaneously*. (And of course, if the player chooses to ally with one power in order to crush another, his hardscrabble alliance of "free peoples of the West" will just have that much less materiel when the beastman armies crash the big board a few strategic turns later!)

Then there's stuff like gadgeteering, inventions, and spell research. This book highlights exactly why it is that Gary Gygax would write, "YOU CAN NOT HAVE A MEANINGFUL CAMPAIGN IF STRICT TIME RECORDS ARE NOT KEPT" in all caps *precisely* like that in his *Dungeon Masters Guide*. Sure there are plenty of game changers that you can conceivably whip up. But it isn't going to come together overnight. Not every project will come to fruition. Even the ones that can actually be accomplished are often going to be irrelevant by the time they can actually be brought to bear. And you can't expect the world to just leave you alone to sort all this out at your leisure.

If you think that every single engineering project you can conceive will play out exactly the way that it did for Captain Kirk when he had to fight that big reptilian Gorn in single combat, then you've got another think coming. Face it, in most games, your character is not like the android from David Weber's *Off Armageddon Reef*. You don't have all the recipes for everything all safely backed up in your memory banks. There's no telling if you could even get the proportions of sulfur, charcoal, and potassium nitrate correct. And even if you did, it's not a sure thing that you'll be able to manufacture enough to be useful or that you'll be able to create an effective killing machine with it on short notice. And even if you could pull *that* off, do you have enough social savvy to protect yourselves from rivals that can have you brought up on charges of witchcraft for even accidentally insulting them?

And this is the area where *Lest Darkness Fall* really comes alive. Telescopes, brandy, Arabic numerals, double-entry bookkeeping, and Morse code are all well and good. But yellow journalism, blackmail, dirty politics, and down-home barbecues are even better—especially if you're of a mind to take over the ancient world and prevent the onset of the dark ages. The way he writes, it's pretty clear that if L. Sprague de Camp was a Dungeon Master, charisma wouldn't be the dump stat that everyone else seems to think it is! And nowhere is de Camp's grasp of human nature clearer than in his depiction of our "book smart" protagonist's encounter with women of the past. It starts innocently enough with a drunken fling with his housekeeper:

He moved carefully, for Julia was taking up two-thirds of his none-too-wide bed. He heaved himself on one elbow and looked at her. The movement uncovered her breasts. Between them was a bit of iron, tied around her neck. This, she had told him, was a nail from the cross of St. Andrew. And she would not put it off. He smiled. To the list of mechanical innovations he intended to introduce he added a couple of items. But for the present should he… A small gray thing with six legs, not much larger than a pinhead, emerged from the hair under her armpit. Pale against her olive-brown skin, it crept with glacial slowness… Padway shot out of bed. Face writhing with revulsion, he pulled his clothes on without taking time to wash. The room smelled. (p 82-83)

But as our "skeptical inquirer" type hero continues his meteoric rise in business, politics, and war he necessarily moves on to more attractive prospects. He hits the jackpot even: he finds someone who is both ravishingly beautiful *and* also able to afford the kind of personal hygiene that could maintain her appeal to a man with 20th-century grooming standards. She's better connected than Princess Leia. And even better, her home world hasn't been blasted into asteroids. And even better than *that*, she's seems to be developing feelings for the protagonist ever since he rescued her from having to be married to a positively odious guy. It's a classic fairy tale plot point. *It's almost too good to be true!*

Mathaswentha sat up and straightened her hair. She said in a brisk businesslike manner: "There are a lot of questions to settle before we decide anything finally. Wittigis, for instance." "What about him?" Padway's happiness wasn't quite so complete. "He'll have to be killed, naturally." "Oh?" "Don't 'oh' me, my dear. I warned you that I am no halfhearted hater. And Thiudahad, too." "Why him?" She straightened up, frowning. "He murdered my mother, didn't he? What more reason do you want? And eventually you will want to become king yourself—" "No, I won't," said Padway. "Not want to be king? Why, Martinus!" "Not for me, my dear. Anyhow, I'm not an Amaling." "As my husband you will be considered one." "I still don't want—" "Now, darling, you just think you don't. You will change your mind. While we are about it, there is that former serving-wench of yours, Julia I think her name is—" "What about— what do you know about her?" "Enough. We women hear everything sooner or later." The

little cold spot in Padway's stomach spread and spread. "But—but—" "Now,
Martinus, it's a small favor that your betrothed is asking. And don't think
that a person like me would be jealous of a mere house-servant. But it would
be a humiliation to me if she were living after our marriage. It needn't be a
painful death— some quick poison..." Padway's face was as blank as that of
a renting agent at the mention of cockroaches. His mind was whirling. There
seemed to be no end to Mathaswentha's lethal little plans. His underwear
was damp with cold sweat. (p 145-146)

And there you have it. This is not the over-the-top idealized presentation
of women that you get in a rip-roaring Edgar Rice Burroughs novel. Neither
is this the "man with boobs" shtick that you see in everything from *Chronicles
of Riddick* to *Agents of S.H.I.E.L.D.*. This is women as they are, with their own
ambitions, their own unique strengths, their own passions and jealousies, and
their own effortless mastery of intrigue. As enticing as she might otherwise be,
our smart-aleck know-it-all from the future just isn't up to the job of dealing
with her. (And if you think that all women that predate the suffragettes had to
have been passive, wilting violet doormat types, then you clearly haven't read
too many characters cut from the same cloth as de Camp's Mathaswentha!)

The other thing here is that the author is depicting the ancient world as
being one without privacy, without tolerance, without due process, without
habeas corpus, and without anything remotely like a principle of "innocent
until proven guilty." Indeed, anyone that grew up in a small town will readily
recognize just how potent a force the local gossip ring can be. And in contrast
to Robert E. Howard's vivid portrayal of civilization being set up expressly to
pervert justice in favor of foppish nobles over honest thieves, here we see just
about everyone as being free game! It's the "nice" people who especially seem
to bring it on themselves. The guy that quietly lets go of a workman that is
caught embezzling is liable to be brought up on outlandish charges. Jilted
lovers and political rivals are equally liable to make false accusations that have
drastic consequences. Even bribing the right people isn't always enough to get
out of trouble: the various functionaries and bureaucrats are more liable to
fight over who has the authority to torture confessions out of people than see
anything remotely like justice served. It's a mess!

It's no wonder that the nuances of these sorts of social interactions are
rarely dealt with in the average role-playing campaign. Tabletop gaming is

necessarily going to play to its own particular strengths, whether it's looting a dungeon or playing out an epic fantasy battle. And unless they're *Diplomacy* fans, the average player of these types of games is going to be of a mind to escape from the kind of social pressure that goes with navigating society, establishing a dynasty, and dealing with ostracization. People just like to be able to go into a town in *Ultima II* and not have to worry about the guards coming after them unless and until they really have stolen something from one of the shopkeepers. Outwitting the shopkeeps in *Nethack* is a blast, sure, but gamers don't necessarily want to deal with some sort of shotgun wedding scenario when they come back to town and discover that the saucy tart they met last session is suddenly with child. Neither would they want to put up with every single townsperson not only ripping them off but doling out false accusations to the Watch about the players when they get called on it. Indeed, a town where that sort of thing happens routinely is liable to see every single level-zero peasant wiped out when the player-characters finally reach their breaking point. Heck, the entire place would get burned to the ground if the players are anything like the people I've gamed with.

But it doesn't have to be this way. The trick for game masters wanting to invoke culture, society, and local color is to make sure that none of these trimmings is seen as a barrier to the players getting what they want out of the game. If you know for a fact that the players are interested in dipping into domain-level play, then marriage, titles of nobility, and land grants should top the list of things thankful potentates are willing to dole out to adventuring groups that have accomplished deeds of renown. This works equally well in everything from *Dungeons & Dragons* to *Traveller* to even *Car Wars*, yet it's not something that people tend to think of when they design adventures or set up campaigns.

Traveller adventurers are generally assumed to be more concerned with making starship payments than setting down roots.[2] And the default reward for a band of hardened autoduelists is $100,000 in cold hard cash, which will generally be blown immediately for repairs and vehicles that will probably get wrecked in the very next session. Even in *Dungeons & Dragons*, where domain play is an explicit part of the end game, people tend to assume that they have to wait for players to get to the right level before it can start. As if there aren't jobs for which the only people available for them are the ones that aren't ready for them yet! Part of the friction here is that the very concept of adventure is seen as being at odds with civilization… or at least, something that occurs mostly on its frontier. High society just isn't always what players are looking for in their flights of fancy, and it's not what many game masters are used to running either.

Now, I want to explain how to work around all these pitfalls and tendencies, but first let me explain a general method for running a wide-open campaign. What most people do most of the time in a long-running campaign is simply connect one prepackaged module or scenario after another into a loose continuity. The rules are generally silent on precisely how to do this. (Indeed, the rules were generally written before the modules were even published!) But even if there is a well-articulated default campaign system, it generally gets forgotten or deprecated as the system continues to be developed. The tested and tightly scripted modules are what tends to catch on in actual play because they give a "good enough" result that requires less confidence, fluency, and specialized knowledge to implement.

Consequently, campaign development rules often end up getting the least amount of development and coverage in classic role-playing games. Oftentimes, the game master is presumed to just *know* what he needs to do, and he's often expected to ignore entire sections of the rules wholesale. This leads to a weird situation where campaigning is something people do *in spite of* the rules under the assumption that everyone else must already be doing it just fine. So here are (completely spelled out) my pointers on running a campaign. This is stuff I wish someone could have told me back when I was thirteen years old and had all those endless summers to fill with nonstop gaming sessions. After this, I'll break down my pointers on how to actually get to the domain type game that a lot of us never really got around to doing.

- First, realize that the average role-player is looking for a recognizable scenario that he believes he has the capacity to excel at. Put the typical game group in the middle of a wide-open wilderness hex crawl, and you can expect them to just be at a loss as to what to do. Part of the problem is that there's often not enough information there for them to make any meaningful decisions. (Or worse, the appearance of total freedom is nothing more than a mediocre illusion.) That sinking feeling they don't tell you about? It's usually them dreading the hours of stumping around trying to find where an actual adventure is. I know that the early installments in the classic *Ultima* series were pretty well built this way, and they were kind of a big deal. But at the tabletop with real live players, people mostly want you to help them "get to the bangs"[3] instead of playing hide and seek with the fun.

- In the typical fantasy role-playing game, try to open the game with several adventure hooks right out in the open. Traditionally, you would drop hints and rumors about this stuff over the course of several sessions while hoping the players will gradually figure it out after a half dozen role-played encounters in the taverns and so forth. Don't count on it! While they will find impossible uses for pointless oddments that they pick up from throwaway encounters, taking notes on every nuance of your campaign setting just isn't that high on the list of things that players like to do. It's more than likely going to be the game master that will keep up with that stuff via session reports if anybody's going to do it!

- Go ahead and explain the adventure hooks out of character and in "meta" terms. You are not role-playing anything at this stage; you're helping the players make an informed choice that will ensure they get the sort of gaming in that they are looking for. Have some variety, too. You'll more than likely have the usual dungeon within a day's march of the frontier outpost. You'll have indications of potential standalone encounter situations at varying distances from home base. You might even have adventure situations that are a month's travel away or more. With all of these, you'll be able to come up with in-game justifications for whether or not you'll actually play out the journey according to your system's specific game mechanics. Note that if you are insisting on playing through piles of random encounters like that, you're off the hook for prepping in advance very much of the adventure that awaits the end of the journey! And when you rough out a dungeon and the players drop down to a new level faster than you expected, all you really need is a decent random encounter table to let you wing it.[4] Having lots of things for the players to do does not mean you necessarily have tons of upfront planning to do.

- Another thing you'll want to pay attention to: in addition to having a variety of adventure types, you'll also want to have a range of difficulties on the list of available options. Some of them should be so obviously hard that the players all scoff at them. The old text adventures by Scott Adams and Infocom are great examples of this. Those programmers understood that you could really hold someone's attention if you taunt them with something impossible while at the same time giving them several other things scattered around for them to tinker with and solve in preparation for dealing with the real challenge. *Enchanter, Zork,* and *Adventureland* are all masterpieces of the form for just this reason. When the players come across the key to something that has stymied them in the past, it creates this great "eureka!" moment. Confronting the players with an insanely challenging problem early on also reinforces the idea that every single encounter is not designed from scratch to be a self-contained easy win.

- For each of your adventure options, there needs to be something at stake, and there must be consequences for the campaign state that follow from how they are engaged with and/or resolved. Ignoring things can have consequences, too. It might be a good idea for the players to pass on messing with the dragon that lairs a hundred miles away when the party is weak, but dealing with it may become a much more pressing matter when a Witch-king arises in a neighboring domain that knows how to put that monster to strategic use! This one point is the thing I find the least acknowledgment of in all the old gaming books. I don't think I've ever read any adventure designs that actually even acknowledged that campaign state was even a thing. I know that with dungeons where the players are making multiple trips there, I tend to have the various monster tribes adapt to the players tactics over time. (Kobolds killed so many player-characters in one game that they actually became the general store for all the other monsters. They traded all the iron spikes and torches for whatever else they needed.) You need to do something similar with the situations at the villages and castles the players come across. Basically, for each major encounter or scenario, there need to be some sort of consequences that ripple out into the setting and the non-player groups, both civilized and not. When you place any sort of adventuring situation into your campaign world, you'll want to have some kind of notion of reasonable consequences for a range of outcomes, both successful and otherwise.

- If this sounds like a lot to keep up with, don't sweat it. Classic introductory modules like B2 "Keep on the Borderlands" and X1 "The Isle of Dread" are already set up exactly how I describe here. The only thing I'm doing that's different here is explaining how to frame these big jumbles of adventure opportunities so that the players are aware of just how much they can do. Running the game isn't that hard. Convincing jaded players that they actually have real autonomy and that they really are gaming in a "living" world; that's the hard part. You can give that to them and they still won't see it—they'll often make a beeline to the thing that they think they are "supposed" to do, never realizing the full potential of classic role-playing games! That's part of why you give them brief out-of-character rundowns of everything and give them straight answers about the relative stakes and difficulties and formats. It does come off as a bit like the old "Choose Your Own Adventure" books, but it allows them to see what you're offering them instead of what they *assume* you're offering them.

- Another thing to keep in mind is that you'll often see things in the older adventure designs that are regions that are intentionally left vague and undeveloped. *This is for a darn good reason.* Some game masters think they're so smart because they have this idea of dropping the B1's "Caverns of Quasqueton" in as module B2's "Cave of the Unknown." *Fight that impulse!* (Though that is kind of cool, actually, I know.) In the first place, you need to have the sort of confidence that will allow you to portray a random keep without going through the hassle of working out every last floor plan for the place. (You laugh, but *Traveller* referees get caught up with that except that in their case they're detailing dozens of worlds at a time!) Mainly, though, you need to leave the blank spots blank because you're going to need something totally unexpected once the campaign gets started, and these undetailed regions are going to be the perfect place for them to emerge. Think of it as "just in time adventure design" based on *requirements that are discovered in the course of play!*[5]

- You'll notice that I haven't talked much about your sweet setting background and your awesome cast of non-player-characters. There's a reason for this: *everybody hates your stuff*. It's not you. Really, it's not. It's just that players care about your campaign setting only so far at serves up adventures that they want to play. All that continuity stuff that you fret over... nobody cares. The longer you talk about it, the more you sound like a pitiful wannabe novelist. And your Mary Sue characters? The players would kill them in a second if you didn't make them stupidly powerful. Even the barkeeper and stable boy are just seen as knuckleheads that are keeping the players from getting to what they want by sitting on crucial information. Quit that! Oh, sure, the players will tease you when you make up a silly name for a character on the spur of the moment, so have a list of good ones handy to draw from during play. But they need personalities only so far as it facilitates the game. If these characters take on a life their own in the course of play, so be it, but they are not the best place to dedicate your prep time. Good strong archetypes—clichés even—are the way to go because the players will know what to do with them when they come across them. Really subtle characterizations can be just another form of hiding the fun, so don't bother getting too fancy with this stuff.

- Most players that have played a lot know that there are plenty of good reasons to play anti-social orphans that only work with other player-characters. The girlfriend characters and the extended family are viewed as liabilities more than anything else—hostages in the hands of the game master to be used to bully the player into doing whatever stupid thing he has in mind. What they are actually doing is fighting the game master in order to preserve their autonomy in the face of his meddling. They don't like this stuff any more than they like any other kind of railroading.

- Finally, if you have a crack team of players that engage beautifully with everything you throw at them and that want to pitch in with developing the setting and that really have better ideas about how the game should work than what you have... then you definitely want to embrace all this and incorporate their contributions as well as you can. You'll burn out if you try to do it all yourself anyway. Yes, a lot of my advice here assumes that the players are a little more passive, but not every group is like that. If you're running your game and you're feeling like you're having a hard time keeping up with just how awesome your players are, then that is a great place to be. In that situation, your job really amounts to little more than light refereeing, note taking, and general facilitation. Go with it! It's much better than being the guy that is treated like he's solely responsible for everyone else's fun. As your campaign develops in this direction, what you'll see is that aspects of various game-mastering responsibilities are actually being shared with the players. As the game master, you are ultimately responsible for the integrity of the game. But answering most player suggestions with "yes" or "yes, but" isn't going to break anything. Players don't have access to complete information about the overall campaign state. You still need to retain the capacity to say "no" and to make the call as to whether or not to actually say it. Nothing the players declare or suggest impacts the campaign state until it's run through an actual ruling on your part.

Now, as you dig through that deluge of points there, you'll begin to get a notion of why it is that the action in your role-playing campaigns never quite looks much like what you read about in L. Sprague de Camp's *Lest Darkness Fall*. I'm explaining all this so that you understand the panoply of forces that are stacked against your ever getting to something like that. It's just not how people play by default! And all those gamer friends of yours with dreams of running the perfect campaign with lots of real world history and realistic people? You know, those guys that never really got a long-running campaign off the ground? There is a reason why this stuff doesn't just come together all that often.

If you are really serious about going from having players roll 3d6 in order all the way up to running domain-level play incorporating elements ranging from gross injustice to marriage and epic military battles, here's what you need to keep in mind once you've already mastered the basics of running a more conventional campaign:

- Do not make the player-characters the targets of gossip campaigns, pointless swindles, and backstabbing political maneuvers. Make the non-player-characters be the target of that sort of thing and put the players in a position where they can do something about it if they choose. Don't expect the players to do this out of the goodness of their hearts; reward them with money, information, and patronage if they intervene and do the right thing.

- *Do* expect the players to resort to violence if non-player-characters mess with the players. If the players are more interested in other things and leave hapless peasants and petty nobles to their own devices, then consider increasing a sense of general chaos, but don't use this as an excuse to punish the players directly.

- If you want the characters to develop a supporting cast of allies, vassals, liege lords, henchmen, and yeah, family, then make all of this stuff be a resource to enable the players to get the kind of game *they* want. Think of it as sort of a Monty Hall campaign, where all the easy loot is on tap to reward digging into and developing the domain game. Interesting stuff can happen to *other* people's family members. But as far as the players are concerned, all of this stuff is a means to getting free land, free help, get out of jail free cards, and plum assignments.

- Do not expect players to run their kingdoms consistently with medieval or ancient value systems. If they want real truth, justice, and the American way plastered all over an otherwise realistic historical setting, then let them. (Robert E. Howard let a red-handed barbarian pull that off; there's no reason why your players can't as well.) If they do go beyond generic justice and order and actually free the slaves, then not everyone will be happy with that. But if you want some background color for just that eventuality, then you can see how de Camp handled that very thing in *Lest Darkness Fall* if you're interested.

- Do not force the players to babysit, manage the farm, or take anything remotely like a day job. Even if they get married or take on a half dozen titles, let them go adventuring if that's what they really want to do. Take a page from the *Honor Harrington* series and introduce a steward to manage the estate, a helpful mother-in-law (or witch!) to fill in on the home front, and/or some sort of executive officer to hold down the fort in the player-characters' absence. Domain play is meant to add **additional options** for play, not to limit the players or to create chores for them.

- And yes, these are all *options*. Domain battles are just one more type of game session, and if the players would rather loot a bigger dungeon or tromp a wilder wilderness instead, then let them. Even if the players aren't interested in messing with their domains directly in actual play, you can add in adventure hooks that have stakes that tie back into their general state and well being. And, of course, if someone is more interested in miniature battles would like to step in, you can always (with the players' consent) let *them* play out the actual wargames in the party's place.

- Have the pressure on the players be primarily from external forces. Players will find a use for every conceivable spell, number stat, and item of equipment on their character sheets if they're in a tough fight. Put a massive army of beastmen on their borders, and they'll start looking for every possible advantage that they can milk from their domains! (Hint: make the domain status report look as much like a character sheet as you can manage!)

Nothing I'm saying here is all that new, to tell you the truth. I'm just reiterating the standard advice for not railroading the players, not engaging in adversarial play, and not front-loading all of the adventure design. Along with that, I'm also generalizing the basic idea of the "sandbox" to incorporate additional elements that people seem to not get around to playing as much. If this sounds like a lot to take in all at once, **don't panic**. Just start with the standard town and dungeon setup and ease into things from there. It worked for Gary Gygax way back in the seventies, and it can work for you today! But read this book by L. Sprague de Camp. It'll help you wrap your head around the sort of things you can do to make the domain game come alive. It's a good read—and there's a darn good reason for why it made the Appendix N list in the first place.

Notes

1. See Patrick Rothfuss's "Thirty years of D&D" for the lowdown on 5th edition *D&D*'s Appendix E.

2. The online JTAS from Steve Jackson Games has an adventure called "The Last Hand-to-Mouth Adventure" by John G. Wood that demon-

strated how to transition away from the typical *Firefly*-style campaign setup.

3. This is Ron Edwards's terminology, which I first saw in his game *Sorcerer*.

4. See "The Dungeon as Mythis Underworld" by Jason "Philotomy" Cone in Knockspell #2 for more on this.

5. See Lawrence Schick's post "The 'Known World' D&D Setting: A Secret History" over at *Black Gate* for a particularly famous example of this technique: *We dubbed this setting the "Known World," to imply there was more out there yet to be discovered, because we didn't want to paint ourselves into a corner.*

The Blue Star
by Fletcher Pratt

I've long been mystified by the incredible range and diversity of literature that role-playing game designers of the seventies seemed to take for granted as being common knowledge. How is it that they seemed fluent in so many obscure authors, many of which were writing more than half a century before? Compared with my experience growing up in the eighties, I just wouldn't see a lot of the classic authors on the shelf at the local B. Dalton's. Libraries would be loaded with Piers Anthony and Anne McCaffrey, but they would have almost nothing from the Gary Gygax's Appendix N list. Except for a selection of the "big three" of science fiction—Asimov, Heinlein, and Clarke—there would be very little fantasy and science fiction on the shelves from before about 1970 or so. What happened?

Part of the answer to this has to do with the fact that great authors and good books just seemed to stay in print longer back then. A. Merritt is all but forgotten now, for example—and sure, it's no surprise to see his works dominating Avon's paperback lineup in 1951. But Merritt's work stayed in print on into the late sixties. His books would have been on the rack right next to classics like *The Foundation Trilogy* and *Glory Road*.[1]

Coupled with this trend would be the sort of intentional literary archaeology embodied by Ballantine's Adult Fantasy series. In the wake of *The Lord of the Rings'* runaway success there was a noticeable uptick in demand for serious works of fantasy, and Lin Carter scoured the stacks for anything that could meet it.[2] Fletcher Pratt's *The Blue Star* is a prime example of this: it was an obscure work published in 1952 as part of an anthology. And it was hand-picked by Lin Carter to inaugurate the new line of books that targeted an "adult audience" that craved "fantasy novels of adult calibre."[3]

And boy does that ever sum up the nature of this book. It is a far cry from anything I've read from the old pulp magazines. Oh, it's not a ponderous slog like Willam Hope Hodgson's *The Night Land*, but it clearly isn't kids' stuff, and it does take a while to get into what Pratt is serving up. If you wanted a breezy bit of swords and sorcery action, then *this isn't it!* It's like *Downton Abbey* but with witchcraft. The cultures, characters, religions, and intrigues are all fully realized and impact every turn of the plot. And this is not written for children either. Just like the wildly popular television series, rape is something of a recurring theme. And though we don't get a lot of gory details when it becomes a major plot element, it does tend to create a much harsher tone than what you typically get in the average fantasy novel. It's *different*, but it's a great book to read if you want to see what fantasy could be like in the absence of Tolkien's overwhelming influence.

For those wanting to adapt Pratt's approach to witchcraft into their own tabletop adventures, the biggest factor in how it is premised here is the fact that it is a hereditary ability. Powerful interests keep records of this sort of thing and see to it that that ecclesiastical authorities don't catch wind of who needs to be watched. Latent abilities become active only after the witch has lost her virginity[4], and with the titular Blue Star she can bestow the ability to read minds upon her lover. This dangerous alliance is reminiscent of Ron Edwards's game *Sorcerer*. It's both personal and interpersonal and quite unlike the more common portrayal of magic as being little more than re-skinned technology.

> *Rodvard shivered slightly. Lalette said; "Open your jacket," and when he had done so, hung the jewel round his neck on his thin gold chain. "Now I will tell you as I have been taught," she said, "that while you wear this jewel, you are of the witch-families, and can read the thoughts of those in whose eyes you look keenly. But only while you are my man and lover, for that power is yours through me. If you are unfaithful to me, it will become for you only a piece of glass; and if you do not give it up once I ask it back, there will lie upon you and it a deadly witchery, so that you can never rest again." (page 28)*

And that bit about him having to remain true to her in order to keep his new gifts is not a bluff. If you're involved in "the great marriage" with a practitioner of "the art," the witch is going to know if you cheat on her:

...a flash of lightning wrote in letters of fire across the inside of her mind the words Will you go with me now? *and though there was no meaning in what they said, she understood that it told the unfaithfulness of her lover. (page 109)*

This is of course unlike any fictional treatment of witchcraft that I have ever seen. There are a lot of implications to setting it up this way, and everything in the action and the setting is derived from this. But if you *do* like the more traditional approach to witches, that's here, too—right down to the ugly old woman with the feline familiar and sinister cauldron:

She was fat and one eye looked off at the wrong angle, but Rodvard was in a state not to care if she had worn on her brow the mark of evil. He flopped on the straw-bed. There was only one window, at the other end; the couple whispered under it, after which the housewife set a pot on the fire. Rodvard saw a big striped cat that marched back and forth, back and forth, beside the straw-bed, and it gave him a sense of nameless unease. The woman paid no attention, only stirring the pot as she cast in an herb or two, and muttering to herself. Curtains came down his eyes, though not that precisely, neither; he lay in a kind of suspension of life, while the steam of the pot seemed to spread toward filling the room. Time hung; then the potion must be ready, for through half-closed lids Rodvard could see her lurch toward him in a manner somewhat odd. Yet it was not til she reached the very side of the bed and lifted his head in the crook of one arm, while pressing toward his lips the small earthen bowl, that a tired mind realized he should not from his position have been able to see her at all. A mystery; the pendulous face opened on gapped teeth; "Take it now my prettyboy, take it." The liquid was hot and very bitter on the lips, but as the first drops touched Rodvard's tongue, the cat in the background emitted a scream that cut like a rusty saw. The woman jerked violently, spilling the stuff so it scalded him all down the chin and chest as she let go. She swung round squawking something that sounded like "Posekshus!" at the animal. Rodvard struggled desperately as in a nightmare, unable to move a muscle no more than if he had been carved out of stone, realizing horribly that he had been bewitched. He wanted to vomit and could not; the cottage-wife turned back toward him with an expression little beautiful. (page 96)

The book tends to focus primarily on Rodvard and what he does with his ability to read thoughts. It provides him with a significant edge in the political arena, but when you're a penniless clerk, it really doesn't do that much to turn you into a superman. The old hag, for example, is far more concerned with offending Rodvard's witch than anything else. And rightly so, Lalette seems to be able to dole out potent curses when she's pressed sufficiently:

> *"It is the watch to daybreak. No one aboard will ever know." "No, no, I will not," replied Lalette, (feeling all her strength melting), though he did not try to hold her hands or put any compulsion on her but that of the half-sobbing warm close contact, (somehow sweet, so that she could hardly bear it, and anything, anything was better than this silent struggle). No water; she let a little moisture dribble out of her averted lips into the palm of one hand, and with the forefinger of the other traced the pattern above one ear in his hair, she did not know whether well or badly. "Go!" she said, fierce and low (noting, as though it were something in which she had no part how the green fire seemed to run through his hair and to be absorbed into his head). "Go and return no more." The breathing relaxed, the pressure ceased. She heard his feet shamble toward the door and the tiny creak again before realizing; then leaped like a bird to the heaving deck, nightrobed as she was. Too late: even from the door of the cabin, she could see the faint lantern-gleam on Tegval's back as he took the last stumbling steps to the rail and over into a white curl of foam. A whistle blew; someone cried: "A man lost!" and Lalette was instantly and horribly seasick. (page 130)*

Very little of this sort of action appears in the book, however. Even when it does happen, it's only in response to a crisis situation. The consequences of being an outcast on the run from the civil authorities are apparently too great for her to act with impunity. She never achieves anything like the stature of a Morgan Le Fay, and one necessarily wonders what she could have accomplished had she had the opportunity to select a more capable man as a mate. With this particular specimen in tow, it's much more important for Lalette that she gain some sort of refuge and cover than anything else.

The abilities conferred by a Blue Star are a significant and secret trump card for whoever would seize control of the state, however, so she and Rodvard are much more of interest to the sort of people who could actually leverage their talents to good effect at the domain level. But the ability to read minds seems to get reworked over the course of the book to be much more restricted—only about reading *particular* types of emotion:

> *"You bear a Blue Star." (It was not a question, but a statement; Rodvard did not feel an answer called for, therefore made none.) "Be warned," said the second Initiate, "that it is somewhat less potent here than elsewhere, since it is the command of the God of love that all shall deal in truth, and therefore there is little hidden for it to reveal." "But I—" began Rodvard. The Initiate held up his hand for silence: "Doubtless you thought that your charm permitted you to read all that is in the mind. Learn, young man, that the value of this stone being founded on witchery and evil, will teach you only the thoughts that stem from the Evil god; as hatred, licentiousness, cruelty, deception, murder." (page 159)*

And so it is, except for a passage early on where Rodvard reads someone's mind as if he could see a running internal monologue that's in English, every other scene involving the use of the ability consists more of him sensing the nuances of more negative emotions related to lust or a desire for violence or other wrongdoing.

The various political factions and religions depicted in the book really do seem to be thought through, though. They are their own thing and not a thinly veiled attempt to rake a particular real world group over the coals. In fact, none of them stands out as being the "good guys." There is a baseline culture that has a strong aristocracy and a strict ecclesiastical authority. Within it is sort of a "cryptic alliance" or secret society that is intent on overthrowing the upper crust there. This country is at war with a nation that blends aspects of Gnosticism and communism into its own weird society. Its religion is not entirely bunk but clearly grants some real-world abilities, especially in regard to witchcraft. And devotees of this ideology also exist within the base culture through the presence of at least one other significant ethnic group.

Fletcher Pratt's world building is much more the focus of this book than any of the usual tropes of adventure fiction. He, in fact, turns more than a few of those tropes on their head: for instance, when Rodvard manages to somehow rescue Lalette from a life of involuntary prostitution, he does not earn her undying gratitude in the process.[5] And the things Pratt emphasizes are of a far different stripe than what Tolkien tends to focus on: you don't see any elaborate maps, genealogies, myths, histories, or epic poetry here. The investment is almost entirely within the realm of culture, human institutions, ideas, and beliefs.

Before reading this, I didn't even realize that I *would* be interested in something like that. And I had to get about a third of the way through it before I could fully grasp what it was that I was getting into. Having completed the book now, it's hard not to wonder about what we've lost in the transition to a more derivative and formulaic approach to fantasy fiction. But I have to admit that this Ballantine Adult Fantasy Series was an incredibly good idea. I'm glad that it happened, and I'm even gladder that I can get these books today. Even if it's not that big of a surprise that this particular sort of fantasy wasn't overwhelmingly popular and failed to persist too long on the shelf at book stores and libraries.

Notes

1. See the Avon pages in the *Internet Speculative Fiction Database* for detail. In addition, note that in the seventies, Merritt's books would have been coming out right alongside Zelazny's *Amber* series.

2. See "Lin Carter and the Ballantine Adult Fantasy Series" over at *Black Gate* for more on this.

3. This is from Lin Carter's introduction to *The Blue Star*, written in 1969: "Some of the most sophisticated novels of the last two centuries have been fantastic romances of adventure and ideas; books which few, if any, children would be capable of appreciating. The astonishing success of J. R. R. Tolkien's *The Lord of the Rings*, Ballantine Books' editions of Mervyn Peake's *Gormenghast* trilogy, and the extraordinary fantastic novels of E. R. Eddison have proved beyond a doubt that an enthusiastic adult audience exists for fantasy novels of adult calibre. The trouble is that many of these books are long out of print, scarce and rare, known only to a handful of collectors and connoisseurs. Some of them have never been published in the United States and are difficult to find."

4. Lin Carter also points out in his introduction that the mother loses the ability to work witchcraft at the moment that her daughter gets it.

5. Given that the relationship began with rape and later moved on to rank unfaithfulness, this is hardly a surprise. From start to finish, this couple never follows the standard script for a fairy-tale romance. That is to some extent both refreshing and disappointing at the same time.

Kyrik: Warlock Warrior
by Gardner F. Fox

Compared to Gardner Fox's other *Conan* knockoff,[1] this one is actually pretty good. Instead of a collection of episodic stories, this book serves up a complete short novel. Instead of taking place in the far future on a distant world, this tale is set in a mythical past. Instead of a goof bumbling around with a magic sword that ensures victory at the cost of keeping the protagonist in a permanent state of poverty, this book features a guy that can rise as far as he cares to go. And instead of a single feminine foil to tag along on the hero's adventures, this book features *three*: a beguiling sorceress, a saucy gypsy girl, and a lascivious demoness.

Kyrik's got his hands full playing his romantic interests off each other to be sure, but being a good guy, he's mostly about the business of taking back his kingdom and getting even with the people responsible for putting him away for all those thousands of years. The book's like something out of a weird parallel universe where cheap supermarket novels were tailored to regular guys' tastes. It's kind of strange that it even exists.

No, Fox is no Robert E. Howard. He rips through one scene after another without really developing the suspense. He also tends to get pretty talky as well. *It's almost like he's used to writing for a comic book where someone else can come along after him and flesh out what he has in mind.* I will say this though: the man knew how to pay off what he sets up. It's kind of hokey—about like the ending of the original *Star Wars* movie that came out at about the same time—but it's strangely satisfying. If this had been done a decade or so later, it would have ended up being pointlessly blown up into something three times as long. Worse, it could have been written from the start just to sell the next book of a series that would never actually see completion. Or maybe the last

couple of installments would have that "contractually obligated" feel to them
as they peter out.

Given my gaming advice from when I covered *Lest Darkness Fall*, it was
funny to see how Fox made a point have the hero set up a regency at the end
so that he could be free to adventure however he pleased. I've also advised
game masters to allow their players to run their domains as anachronistically
as they wished—and it's funny to see this odd idea taken to almost ludicrous
extremes:

> He went with his guard about him out into the city streets. There were people
> here, staring and worried, and Kyrik went among them to take their hands
> and speak with them, promising a lessening of their taxes, an easing of their
> lives. There would be no more torturers; if a man committed a crime and
> deserved to die so that the rest of society would be safe, then it would be clean,
> swift death. Through the night he went, into the taverns and the alehouses,
> and spoke with the common man and his woman, and left them with tears
> in their eyes. Peace and contentment was come upon all Tantagol, he assured
> them, there would be a celebration at his expense when men could feast and
> become drunk and make love, and there would be no curfew, nor any spies
> to stare upon them and report their words. (page 146-147)

Barbarians… they not only have a preference for consensual sex over rape, they're
also fiscal conservatives that know how to party.

Hard-nosed realists will have a hard time with that, but It's really about
the only way to make this sort of character at all likable. The author is on the
hook to put the spotlight on someone the reader will *want* to see succeed, and
that character needs to still be likable even after he pulls off his caper. It may
not make any sense to have uncivilized swordsman end up being the second
coming of America's Founding Fathers, but people eat it up anyway. It works.

From a pure fantasy gaming standpoint, one of the more interesting parts
of the book is that the sorceress character actually ends up losing her coffer
of spell components.[2] This doesn't entirely strip her of her abilities: she can
still summon up a cloud of "blackness shot with lightnings" if she has enough
time to gather "certain herbs" that are relatively common in the wild.[3] And she
seems to be able to cast a soap bubble-themed *Sleep* spell without any arcane
ingredients.[4] But by the final climatic encounter, the loss of that coffer really
does prevent her playing a part as some sort of *deus ex machina* for the hero.

Given that novice dungeon masters are loath to separate players from their spell books,[5] it's pretty useful to see how all of this plays out in the context of a straight ahead swords and sorcery story. The action here closely mirrors the wild inventiveness of players that are bereft of their tested "I win button" strategies.

While Aryalla's magic is not too far off from what you'd see in a typical *AD&D* session, her debut in the pages of this relatively obscure novel nevertheless involves her summoning three demons at once:

> *A moment she paused, glancing about the room. Then her hand loosened clasps, the garment fell away and she stood proudly nude in the lamp flames. Drawing air into her lungs, she then stepped into the center of the pentagram. From the casket with the silver clasps she drew powders, rare and tinted with the hues of the rainbow, and of these she made piles, here and there, and touched them with the flames from the lamp wick. A blaze of colors lifted like pillars from the pentagram, went upward toward the beamed ceiling hid amid the shadows. A faint perfume came into the room. She raised her bare arms. "Demons of the worlds beyond our ken! You who dwell where no man's eyes may see, where no man's limbs may go except that it be your will—heed me! Open wide your senses, hear my words!" Aryalla paused to draw breath. "Kilthin of the frozen weald of Arathissthia! Rogrod of the red fire-lands of Kule! Abakkan the ancient, bent with the wisdom of ten thousand times ten thousand nether worlds! I appeal, I cry out my needs, I summon you to this plane, this land where I wait your coming." (page 19-20)*

These guys sound like they'd look fantastic in four colors and on a lavish two-page spread. But she doesn't do anything too creepy or horrific with these things. For instance, she offers no sacrifices and doesn't sell her firstborn son to them or anything like that. Other than reversing Kyric's transformation into a bronze statuette, the purpose of this trio of demons is mainly to provide information. The next creature of the occult which we run into is a different matter, however:

> *"You did yourself a good turn when you slew Isthinissis. Devadonides counts on him for much help in those necromancies of Jokaline." Kyrik remembered what Illis had whispered to his mind in the temple. He asked in surprise,*

"How can a big snake—or whatever Isthinissis was—help Jokaline the wizard?" "He wasn't just a snake. That was only his earthly form. He is a demon god, in his own world. Or so I've heard it said. But it was as a reptile that he could work the wonders Jokaline asked of him. His snake body served as some sort of—of gateway through which his demonic powers could pass. Without that body, he isn't as strong as he was. (pages 114-115)

I can't say that I've ever seen anything quite like that in a game: a wizard that gets a set of spell points, spell slots, and/or special abilities that are tied to having a demonic monster holed up in a temple a few hexes away from his domain capital? That's just awesome! You get the idea that he has to feed it a regular diet of virgins in order to keep the mana flowing, too. Without this gateway to demonic power, the wizard Jokaline is nowhere near as big of a problem at the end. Not when Kyrik has so many powerful allies working with him to help him successfully navigate the gauntlet of traps that protect the guy. This all leads to the obligatory epic showdown:

Toward the greater pentagram he hurled himself, toward Jokaline. The old man screeched, shouted indistinguishable words. The great prism set into the floor darkened, grew black, shot through with flames. 'Absothoth comes,' whispered Illis. Kyrik was inside the pentagram, had caught the old man in a mighty hand, whirled him upward off his feet, hurled him. Through the air he flung him, right at the great prism. His old body hit the crystal facets of the living gem, collapsed at its base as he slid down those smooth, hard sides.... Kyrik whirled. The prism was melting, flowing into nothingness. And from its deep a dark being was rising upward, amorphous, evil, its fangs showing in a triumphant grin. What served for its eyes—red stars that glittered with demonic fury—glanced down at the gibbering Jokaline who sought to crawl away from the base of the great prism that was its doorway into this world, away from that which he had summoned. Outside the great pentagram Jokaline was prey to that which had served him and obeyed his commands across the many years. Well he knew that hatred Absothoth held for him and so he tried to flee. "Great Absothoth! Mighty lord of the nether hells! Always I have worshiped you. Always have I given sacrifice in your name. Living men, living women, all have been fed to you—by me!" The black being laughed, booming laughter that rang in the chamber. "Only by sacrifice could you command me, Jokaline. You gave me helpless humans to further your own ends, to keep me in thrall to you. Now—I find you outside the pentagram!" Something like a black hand, a clawed paw, darted. It sank into Jokaline, held him motionless under the paws of a cat. (pages 132-134)

This was all being written right about the same time that the *Dungeons & Dragons* game was gaining the sort of supplements that would grow it into the much larger "Advanced" incarnation of the franchise. Like, everything else in the Appendix N list, it *could* have had a direct impact on that game's rules, but in the case of demonology, the game just seems to go off on a bewildering tangent. Consider the attributes for demons and devils that were laid down in the iconic 1977 *Monster Manual*:

- All devils have a range of spell abilities at their disposal: Charm Person, Suggestion, Illusion, Infravision, Teleportation, Know Alignment, Cause Fear, and Animate Dead. Demons may use Infravision, Darkness, Teleportation, and Gate. Most demons and devils have additional spell abilities beyond this to such an extent that they are essentially high-level spellcasters that don't have to track spells used per day.

- Most demons and devils have the ability to gate in additional demons. The chance of success and a table detailing the summoned types are included with each monster entry. (It is not stated as to whether or not summoned demons can or cannot summon additional creatures when *they* are summoned.)

- All devils can direct their attacks against two or more opponents if the means are at hand.

- All but the weakest demons and devils have a specified level of magic resistance.

- Most powerful demons and devils have psionic abilities, and their attack modes and defense modes are painstakingly broken down.[6]

The game's off-the-wall approach to demons and devils illustrates how even though *D&D* was inspired by a diverse range of fantasy and science fiction, it rapidly diverged from it to become very much its own distinct thing. Most of this stuff is the result of cobbling things together out of pre-existing game elements rather than a serious attempt to translate an explicit set literary antecedents into game form. And *AD&D* strenuously differentiates between demons and devils. This fetish for taxonomy continues in *Monster Manual II*, where **daemons** are added into the mix as yet another class of creature. This kind of hairsplitting seems to be a consequence of a syncretistic cosmology emanating throughout every aspect of the game. Every conceivable pantheon is incorporated into the "official" *AD&D* campaign setting by relegating them to their own individualized plane of existence. Devils, for instance, form a rigid Lawful Evil hierarchy—and in an homage to Dante, hell itself is broken up into a sort of nine-level dungeon. The overall effect here is reminiscent of DC comics buying up its competitors and then cordoning them off in their own separate parallel universes.

A lot of contributors to the game seemed to perfectly able to overlook the peccadillos of the *Monster Manual* format,[7] but the institution has garnered more than its fair share of critics over the years. For instance, Wayne Rossi over at *Semper Initiativus Unam* has pointed out that the release of the first *Monster Manual* not only eliminated the original game's science-fantasy elements, but it also established for demons, dragons, and humanoid monsters a bewildering range of canonical types.[8] He suggests that it would have been better if they'd replaced color-coded dragons and named demon princes with random tables. The funny thing is, Gary Gygax did, in fact, include such tables in an utterly forgettable appendix to his *Dungeon Masters Guide*.[9] Unlike John Pickens's earlier article along these lines,[10] Gygax's tables take great efforts to create not just the combat statistics, but also a very specific look for the creature, with a range of possible results for the eyes, nose, moth, arms, legs, skin, and even body odor.

Far more interesting is an article by Gregory Rihn from about the same time and whose material was specifically passed over when the *Dungeon Masters Guide* was compiled. It suggests using the spell research rules to allow magic-users to discover the names of demonic entities. The names of more powerful creatures are treated as being higher-level spells, though you don't always end up with the exact sort of demon you were aiming for. Once the name is known, a separate ritual for summoning the critter must also be researched. Lesser demons require tributes or sacrifices each time they are called up. The more powerful demons will require a thousand years of service in the afterlife or even permanent forfeiture of the spellcaster's soul. In addition to gaining access to new spells and information on the names of other demons and the all-around fighting ability of the monster in question, deals with these creatures can also involve details that spill over into the domain game:

> *In making a pact with Asmodeus, the archfiend may offer twenty years of service in return for a promise that the operator worship him, build a place of worship consecrated to him, dedicate half of all his treasure to him, raise an army and stamp out good religions in a given area, and perform sundry other little jobs. Plus, of course, the operator must forfeit his soul at the end of the contract.*

While this is certainly in line with works ranging from "The Devil and Daniel Webster" to "The Devil Went Down to Georgia," it's nevertheless hard to imagine individual players caring too much about the actual souls of their various player-characters. That's why it's such a delight to read how Lewis Pulsipher hammered out game effects of just this sort of thing:[11]

> *The demon offers to aid the character on occasion in return for his soul, and the souls of others through sacrifice. The character, when killed, cannot be resurrected by any means other than a Wish. Even if a Wish is used, sooner or later the demon prince will discover that he has been robbed, and will thereupon immediately hunt for and obliterate that character.*

Awesome.

In both of these articles, you get far more concrete rules for how to handle demons and devils in the course of play than anything you'll find in the "official" supplements. But as good as they are, they also omit any mention of the demons' amulets and devils' talismans, two offbeat items that garner a couple of paragraphs in Gygax's original *Monster Manual* entries. Items along these lines actually turn out to be a critical plot element in Gardner Fox's first *Kyrik* novel, being a major aspect of how the demons Illis and Absothoth are depicted. While this may not be the sole source for Gygax's ideas here, it's certainly interesting to see something along these lines worked out into something that could be developed into an actual gaming scenario.

Demons are formidable creatures with a great deal of mythic significance. It's hard to see them slapped into the game as sort of an amalgam of extra tough ogres and high-level magic-users. There really should be more to them than that, but you just don't tend to get much help from the game manuals on that sort of thing. This absence of coherent guidance is something that was carried forward into the second edition of the game: the *Dungeon Masters Guide* for that particular iteration makes no mention of any of this! This was no doubt an *intentional* omission, done to appease the Puritanical mobs that supposedly made it their mission to clean up pop music, role-playing games, and River City.[12] This a topic that has a major impact on the game's depiction of magic, clerics, and the overall cosmology, and it was simply erased from the core books in order to avoid offending people at the exact moment that a more coherent synthesis was what the game needed most!

Which brings us to Ron Edwards, who can fairly be characterized as being part of a wider correction in response to TSR's tendency toward watering down the game over time. His take on demons may seem somewhat unconventional, but it too has a precedent in this battered old Appendix N book. While Kyrik the **Warlock** Warrior can be easily translated into *Sorcerer* terms, it's something of a surprise to see that his demon Illis follows the game rules almost to the letter. Being a self-styled Goddess of Lust, she naturally has a **desire** that is in line with that. She is capable of concealing her human form by transforming herself into a small snake, which wraps around the hilt of Kyrik's sword, but her **telltale** of eerily whispering warnings and suggestions will give away her occult status. Finally, she doesn't dole out favors just for the kicks; she also has a **need** that is straight out of the *Sorcerer* rulebook:

> He hastened back toward Illis in her worshipping chamber. She was moving about the room, graceful, lissome, and once more Kyrik wondered at her shape and form in those demon lands. She laughed at the sight of him and his bloody sword and ran to him on bare feet. Her fingertips touched the bloody blade, wiped it clean. As might a child, she put that finger to her mouth, licked off the blood. Her blonde eyebrows rose questioningly. "Do I shock you, Kyrik darling? Is my thirst for blood so baffling to your human mind?" His wide shoulders lifted, fell. "There are night creatures who need blood for life. To you it's a tasty thing. Who am I to condemn your demon ways?" (page 92-93)

Gardner Fox's short novel, unpretentious though it may be, is loaded with game-inspiring material like that. It's not just that it shows a good half dozen demons in action either. It also shows several different ways that those monstrous cross-planar entities can be leveraged in the context of typical adventuring situations. The fact that its subject matter was subjected to some sort of purge in the eighties only makes it that much more interesting today. Just the idea that this sort of thing is across the line makes it more fun to check back into it today, but the fact that *D&D*'s treatment of other planes never quite set well with me is one more reason why the sequel to this is going on my reading list. "Kyrik Fights the Demon World"? Yeah, that's something I have to see!

Notes

1. That would be Kothar, which we covered back on page 81.

2. See page 105.

3. See page 121.

4. See page 128.

5. See "Dungeon Masters Rulebook (Red Box version)" at Technoskald's *Forge* for an example of this sort of reticence. (Going by James Ward's "Notes From a Semi-Successful D&D Player" in *The Dragon #13*, Dungeon Masters in the bad old days had no such qualms: "a set of extra spell books for the magic user is a must. Those things are too easy to destroy, steal, or lose. I know the cost is extreme, but considering their need for you to simply exist as a magic user, they are a must.")

6. Note that just as Gary Gygax would later regret including the monk class in the core *AD&D* game, he would also acknowledge a need to remove the unusual psionics system in subsequent editions of the game: "Quite frankly, I'd like to remove the concept from a medieval fantasy roleplaying game system and put it into a game where it belongs something modern or futuristic." — (*Dragon Magazine issue #103*, page 8)

7. Going by "Demons, Devils and Spirits" in *Dragon #42*, Tom Moldvay seems perfectly able to operate within the constraints of the *AD&D* game system.

8. See "Nuking the Monster Manual" over at *Semper Initiativus Unam* for more on this.

9. Gary Gygax's "Random Generation of Creatures From the Lower Planes by Gary Gygax" first appeared in *The Dragon #23*.

10. Jon Pickens's "D&D Option: Demon Generation" appeared in *The Dragon #13*.

11. Lewis Pulsipher's "Patron Demons" appeared in *Dragon #42*.

12. While the actual extent of the influence groups like B.A.D.D. merits further investigation, it's clear that role-playing game designers behaved as if there was a real threat. Even as late as 1995, TSR bent over backward to distance themselves from the sort of game depicted in the Tom Hanks TV movie *Mazes and Monsters*. This is documented in the writers guidelines they published on AOL at the time.

The King of Elfland's Daughter
by Lord Dunsany

First published in 1924, Lord Dunsany's *The King of Elfland's Daughter* was rescued from obscurity by Lin Carter's work with the Ballantine Adult Fantasy series. It was an excellent choice for that project, too. Here we find the forgotten themes that set up the cadence of twentieth-century fantasy literature. Here we have a take on elves, trolls, and witches far different from anything on the shelves today. Here we have an undiluted synthesis of the fantasy elements that echoed on into the stories we read growing up. It's breathtaking in its own right, but being exposed to it somehow makes later, better-known literature snap suddenly into focus due to its shared connection to forgotten lore.

Take, for example, the way that time is treated as a recurring theme up to about midway through the twentieth century. It seems to behave in rather a strange fashion in Lothlórien where the Fellowship of the Ring "could not count the days and nights that they had passed there." And children returning to Narnia could never tell for sure just how much time would have passed there while they were away. In the book *Three Hearts and Three Lions*, Holger Carlsen's quest would have ended in disaster if he had gone in to Elf Hill, where "time is strange." Fantasy since then has gradually developed into something that tends to be much more naturalistic— as if "realism" were now somehow integral to the genre. Something like the *Game of Thrones* series lacks these sorts of time-related elements altogether.

But Lord Dunsany's Elfland combines these ideas into even broader, more fantastic strokes. Time simply doesn't exist there. Were a mortal to lose a decade of his life somehow, an elf wouldn't even begin to know how to sympathize. And they, in turn, not having first-hand knowledge of anything having to do with aging, could not easily come to terms with the potential for losing their strength or their beauty to the "harshness of material things and all the turmoil of Time." Indeed, even its most mundane consequences are liable to overwhelm them:

> *Orion slept. But the troll in the mouldering loft sat long on his bundle of hay observing the ways of time. He saw through cracks in old shutters the stars go moving by; he saw them pale: he saw the other light spread; he saw the wonder of sunrise: he felt the gloom of the loft all full of the coo of the pigeons; he watched their restless ways: he heard wild birds stir in near elms, and men abroad in the morning, and horses and carts and cows; and everything changing as the morning grew. A land of change! The decay of the boards in the loft, and the moss outside in the mortar, and old lumber mouldering away, all seemed to tell the same story. Change and nothing abiding. He thought of the age-old calm that held the beauty of Elfland. And then he thought of the tribe of trolls he had left, wondering what they would think of the ways of Earth. And the pigeons were suddenly terrified by wild peals of Lurulu's laughter. (Chapter 22)*

Elfland is not just timeless though; it is also elusive. The "friends of Narnia" in C. S. Lewis's tales never know when or how they will find a way in as the means of traveling there changes with each adventure. In Tolkien's lore, Eärendil's finding of the Undying Lands is a positively mythical accomplishment. But Lord Dunsany's take on this is much closer to what Poul Anderson did in *Three Hearts and Three Lions*. The place of the elves is an actual region that exists on the borders of "the fields we know." Unicorns stray out of Elfland occasionally, just as our foxes skirt the "frontier of twilight" between the two worlds. Strangely, the mundane people who live nearby don't even seem to be aware that anything even exists in that direction:

> *And then Alveric began to ask him of the way, and the old leather-worker spoke of North and South and West and even of north-east, but of East or south-east he spoke never a word. He dwelt near the very edge of the fields we know, yet of any hint of anything lying beyond them he or his wife said nothing. Where Alveric's journey lay upon the morrow they seemed to think the world ended. (Chapter 2)*

Just because you have found it once, it does not mean that you will necessarily be able to do so again:

When Alveric strode away and came to the field he knew, which he remembered to be divided by the nebulous border of twilight. And indeed he had no sooner come to the field than he saw all the toadstools leaning over one way, and that the way he was going; for just as thorn trees all lean away from the sea, so toadstools and every plant that has any touch of mystery, such as foxgloves, mulleins and certain kinds of orchis, when growing anywhere near it, all lean towards Elfland. By this one may know before one has heard a murmur of waves, or before one has guessed an influence of magical things, that one comes, as the case may be, to the sea or the border of Elfland. And in the air above him Alveric saw golden birds, and guessed that there had been a storm in Elfland blowing them over the border from the south-east, though a north-west wind blew over the fields we know. And he went on but the boundary was not there, and he crossed the field as any field we know, and still he had not come to the fells of Elfland. (Chapter 10)

But the border between the worlds is capricious, and the Elf King can actually cause it to recede in order to prevent people from finding a way into his land:

Then the Elf King rose, and put his left arm about his daughter, and raised his right to make a mighty enchantment, standing up before his shining throne which is the very centre of Elfland. And with clear resonance deep down in his throat he chaunted a rhythmic spell, all made of words that Lirazel never had heard before, some age-old incantation, calling Elfland away, drawing it further from Earth.... So swiftly that spell was uttered, so suddenly Elfland obeyed, that many a little song, old memory, garden or may tree of remembered years, was swept but a little way by the drift and heave of Elfland, swaying too slowly eastwards till the elfin lawns were gone, and the barrier of twilight heaved over them and left them among the rocks. And whither Elfland went I cannot say, nor even whether it followed the curve of the Earth or drifted beyond our rocks out into twilight: there had been an enchantment near to our fields and now there was none: wherever it went it was far. (Chapter 14)

This is utterly fantastic—exactly the sort of outright magic that was deliberately set aside as fantasy developed from the Tolkien pastiches of the eighties on to the more "grimdark" style of today. And though people borrow from Tolkien all the time, they rarely borrow *these* particular elements.

Lord Dunsany's work really is something else though. The "desolate flatness that stretched to the rim of the sky" that Alveric finds in the place where he'd hoped to find Elfland is stunning. His half-elven son's ability to hear the horns of Elfland blowing at eventide is positively *fantastic*. But there is one other ingredient here that further heightens the distance between our world and that of Elfland. You see this plainly in Poul Anderson's fantasy where Christendom and Elfland are diametrically opposed to each other—even going so far as defining the opposite ends of what would become the *Dungeons & Dragons* law/chaos alignment spectrum. This is far different from the watered down "good versus evil" approach that most people played it as. It originally had more to do with the inherent conflict between the mundane and the magical—between the human and the alien.

You see this opposition forcefully expressed by the Freer:

"Curst be all wandering things," he said, "whose place is not upon Earth. Curst be all lights that dwell in fens and in marish places. Their homes are in deeps of the marshes. Let them by no means stir from there until the Last Day. Let them abide in their place and there await damnation. Cursed be gnomes, trolls, elves and goblins on land, and all sprites of the water. And fauns be accursed and such as follow Pan. And all that dwell on the heath, being other than beasts or men. Cursed be fairies and all tales told of them, and whatever enchants the meadows before the sun is up, and all fables of doubtful authority, and the legends that men hand down from unhallowed times. Cursed be brooms that leave their place by the hearth. Cursed be witches and all manner of witcheries. Cursed be toadstool rings and whatever dances within them. And all strange lights, strange songs, strange shadows, or rumours that hint of them, and all doubtful things of the dusk, and the things that ill-instructed children fear, and old wives' tales and things done o' midsummer nights; all these be accursed with all that leaneth toward Elfland and all that cometh thence." (Chapter 31)

Tolkien is, of course, at pains to avoid an explicit reference to this sort of enmity. It is nevertheless present in *The Lord of the Rings* when Butterbur scolds Frodo for causing a disruption at the Prancing Pony: "We're a bit suspicious round here of anything out of the way—uncanny if you understand me; and we don't take to it all of a sudden." Bilbo's reputation took a similar hit what with all the "outlandish folk" that were dropping by his hobbit hole. *Bag End's a queer place, and its folk are queerer.*

But there is much more to this than homespun culture or even fear of the unknown. There is a very real divide between elves and men. And there is a theological aspect to it, and it would be a mistake to think that Tolkien was unusual in his tendency to fret about these things in his notes and letters. Tolkien might have had his reasons for wanting to tiptoe around this within the context of his best fiction, but Lord Dunsany had no such compunction:

> *And in those seasons, wasting away as every one went by, she knew that Alveric wandered, knew that Orion lived and grew and changed, and that both, if Earth's legend were true, would soon be lost to her forever and ever, when the gates of Heaven would shut on both with a golden thud. For between Elfland and Heaven is no path, no flight, no way; and neither sends ambassador to the other. (Chapter 32)*

This is almost the exact same estrangement that Elrond faced with the prospect of giving Aragorn his daughter's hand in marriage. It is a bitter thing, and it is no wonder that he would do this for no less a man than one that could reunite and restore the Northern and Southern kingdoms of Gondor. Yet the precise relationship of the elves to heaven is not nearly as explicit there as it could be.

Lord Dunsany is willing to explore this in depth, however. Instead of simply ending the story with the match being made between man and elf after the fashion of the fairy-tale romance, we get to see just how extensive the culture clash between Alveric and the Elf King's daughter really is. The Freer could hardly stand to oversee the espousal in the first place. "I cannot wed Christom man," he says, "with one of the stubborn who dwell beyond salvation." (Chapter 14) But though he did have "rites that are proper for the wedding of a mermaid that hath forsaken the sea," Lirazel could never quite acclimate herself to human ways. She could "never read wise books without laughter," she could "never care for earthly ways," and she could never feel particularly at home. After all, how could the very few years she'd spent among men compare to how "all the centuries of her timeless home" had shaped her?

Their conflicting views of worship would make it all but impossible for them to get along with each other:

And Alveric seeking her in the wide night, wondering what wild fancy had carried her whither, heard her voice in the meadow, crooning such prayers as are offered to holy things. When he saw the four flat stones to which she prayed, bowed down before them in the grass, he said that no worse than this were the darkest ways of the heathen. And she said "I am learning to worship the holy things of the Freer." "It is the art of the heathen," he said. Now of all things that men feared in the valley of Erl they feared most the arts of the heathen, of whom they knew nothing but that their ways were dark. And he spoke with the anger which men always used when they spoke there of the heathen. And his anger went to her heart, for she was but learning to worship his holy things to please him, and yet he had spoken like this.

The presence of these sorts of explicit references to Christianity are shocking today, but for these authors, Christian concepts were integral to the very axioms of fantasy. This strikes us as conservative today, but their works were, in fact, revolutionary. Had Sir Arthur Conan Doyle read tales more like those of Tolkien, Lewis, Anderson, and Lord Dunsany, he would not have fallen for the Cottingley Fairies hoax. The fact that he did indicates that he was very much a product of his times and had a radically different notion of what elvish creatures actually would have been like compared to us. But as influential as Tolkien became over the course of the twentieth century, even so *his* particular take on fantasy would also fade away—much like his Third Age gave way to the far less mythical period that followed it. Lord Dunsany makes it clear just how much we've lost.

Hiero's Journey
by Sterling Lanier

This is pretty much *the* original source for what ended up becoming TSR's *Gamma World* setting. Oh, there are differences, sure. The equivalent of the surviving "pure strain humans" here almost all have some degree of telepathy, precognition, and clairvoyance. There is nothing quite like the mutated plant creatures of the game. And there's a complete lack of any of the truly weird technologies, robots, or cyborgs that are a central feature of *Gamma World* gameplay. But the basic premise of post-apocalyptic mutant mayhem is right here in a fully realized form.

This book is just plain loaded, too. Its main character hails from the north, riding a mutant moose across the wilds with his mutant bear ally. He wields a jury-rigged rocket launcher and lance, engages in psionic battles with some seriously weird creatures, and reverently paints a maple leaf on his forehead when he has time to keep up his appearance. His primary foes are the dreaded Leemutes: mutant humanoids that range from vicious ape-men to cunning rat creatures. (And yes… I did just about fall out of my chair when the Hoppers turned up.)

The best thing about this book is its excellent treatment of many random wilderness encounters. That along with its depiction of a desperate attempt to rebuild civilization in the face of overwhelming odds really captures an essential aspect of the *Gamma World* setting:

The world was full of savage beasts and more savage men, those who lived beyond any law and made pacts with darkness and the Leemutes. And the Leemutes themselves, what of them? Twice he had fought for his life against them, the last time two years back. A pack of fifty hideous ape-like creatures, hitherto unknown, riding bareback on giant, brindled dog-things, had attacked a convoy on the great western highway while he commanded the guard. Despite all his forelooking and alertness, and the fact that he had a hundred trained Abbeymen, as well as the armed traders, all good fighters, the attack had been beaten off only with great difficulty. Twenty dead men and several cartloads of vanished goods were the result. And not one captive, dead or alive. If a Leemute fell, one of the great spotted dog-things had seized him and borne him away. (page 11)

It's the tenuous climb from barbarism, a romantic effort to rebuild society from its own ashes; the glimmer of hope even as a remnant of sanity threatens to succumb to an encircling chaos. But most of all, it's the desperate need that drives these peoples to send their best and brightest out into the wilds, searching for anything that would give them an edge. It's also the things they come across that are so bizarre, that you may never fully understand exactly what they are or where they came from. *This* is what a great *Gamma World* campaign should be like… something like *that*!

As interesting as it is to see the original source of some classic creatures of gaming, it much more intriguing to see what the designers elected to leave behind. For instance, psionic abilities here can only be improved by engaging in deadly psionic battles:

He was amused that his new confidence seemed more than temporary. Beyond, and indeed underlying the amusement, was a hard-won feeling of mental power. Hiero knew without even wondering how he knew, that Abbot Demero or any others of the Council would now be hard-put to stand against him. He hastily put aside such thoughts as vainglorious and impertinent, but they were still there, buried but not dead, in the deep reaches of his mind. He was learning something the Abbey scholars of the mental arts were just beginning to conceive, the fact that mental powers accrete in a geometric, not arithmetical progression, depending on how much and how well they are used. The two battles Hiero had won, even though the bear had helped decide the first, had given the hidden forces of his already strong mind a dimension and power he could not himself have believed possible. And the oddest thing was, he knew it. (page 80-81)

And as if it is not enough that this book provided the lion's share of the inspiration for *Gamma World*, the original source of the *Dungeons & Dragons* game's green slime monster is here as well. (You know it's the *D&D* monster because it's vulnerable to flame.) There's even a significant component of *Traveller*. Anyone familiar with that latter game will immediately recognize the mysterious coyns of the alien Droyne who live on worlds scattered all across the Third Imperium:

> *"Can you really make more sense out of it?" asked the girl. "It seems, well, a bit vague. Most of the stuff could almost be guessed, if you think about where we are, and what we're doing." "First," said the priest as he finished unrobing and packing, "You're absolutely right. It is a bit vague. But I'm not a good talent at this particular form of foreseeing. I know men, friends of mine, who could get a lot more out of it, maybe draw ten symbols or even fifteen at one time, and make an extraordinary and detailed prediction. I've never got more than six myself, and I feel I've done well if I even get a modest clue as to what's coming." They both mounted, Luchare in front as usual, and with Gorm ranging in front, he continued to lecture. "Now, we do have something to go on. The symbols are an odd mixture of forces, you know. Part of it is genuine prediction, part wish-fulfillment and part a subconscious (I'll explain later) attempt to influence events. So— we have the Spear, the Fish, the Clasped Hands, the Lightning and the Boots. A reading of the obvious answers might, I stress might, run as follows: a long journey, or perhaps the next part, will be on, in or over water. Now there are lots of other permutations possible. Oh yes, the journey will start with a bad storm, or in one or something. That's what I get, anyway. And I feel pretty certain that the storm is coming. That's the surest of the signs." (page 134-135)*

Given how much there is to like here—and I hate to have to say this, too—but the story falls apart about half way through. I mean it just flounders. Part of it is that the handling of the romance aspect is just atrocious. And that's not due to the fact that it starts off with a standard princess in distress scenario. It's not even due to the fact that the author is clumsy handling the interracial stuff in a ham-handed manner. (Though the paragraphs dedicated to describing her afro are awesome in the way that only seventies fiction can truly attain.) And I could almost handle the gratuitous sex, but it's just insane that they have to do their thing right in the middle of an epic adventure to save civilization.

The fact that she's a princess never actually becomes pertinent to the story the way that, say, Dejah Thoris was in *Princess of Mars* or even Princess Leia was in *Star Wars*. She's just there to look exotic, to titillate, and to get told to shut up whenever she asks a lame question. After the fifth or sixth time that happens, I really have to wonder why she is in the story at all. And even with all of those cringe-inducing scenes, she still has to be set up so that she can find the "secret MacGuffin" at the end. Sorry, but no. That doesn't make up for her dead weight after all those chapters. It's more like one last insult to the reader for the finale.

A similar thing happens with the group of thirty sailors that end up tagging along with the adventurer at one point. They will follow our square-jawed hero anywhere and look up to him, but I just never quite get sold on that. Sure, he wins a critically important single combat, but he also makes a blunder that costs them their ship. Just as with the romantic arc, there's never this point where he really captures their respect or demonstrates that he can be responsible with it. I mean, I *like* the protagonist. But if everyone around him likes the guy for no reason and constantly fawns all over him, then I might as well watch *Notting Hill* or something instead.

By far the worst error in this vein is in the handling of the venerable, Gandalf-like character Brother Aldo. In the first place, I could not read this character's dialog in anything other than a Morgan Freeman voice. (This type of character is by now a movie staple, but I guess it was a new thing in the seventies.) Secondly, the character is just too powerful. I could have handled him bailing out the protagonist at a critical point, but having him join the party really ruins the suspense. And I get so tired of his constant pontification. While I could respect the guy for being really in tune with nature and for being a Charles Xavier-level telepath, when he imparts his great wisdom about how everything got to be the way that it was, it actually gets downright painful:

> *You look about you, children, came the message from Brother Aldo's mind, and you see in the world, green forest and glade, blue sea and river, yellow prairie and marsh. In them today lurk evil things, yet they also hold uncounted sorts of beauty and wonder. The singing birds, the breathing plants, the shy animals, the savage hunters, all have a place. Alone and unhindered, they change slowly, one kind yielding place to another over the*

centuries and millennia. This is the ordered course of nature, the plan as the Creator designed it.

He almost sounds like Yoda there. And while it's bad form to mix evolution with Intelligent Design, we can cut this guy some slack given that he's living in a weird post-apocalyptic world.

But before The Death, things most rapidly were changing, yes, and for the worst. The entire world as well as simply here in what was once called North-america, was dying. It was being choked, strangled in artificially made filth and its own sickly refuse. He pointed a lean hand at the ring of ruined towers glaring across the lagoon. See there! The whole planet, the good round Earth, was being covered by these things! Giant buildings blotted out the sun. The ground was overlain with stone and other hard substances, so that it could not breathe. Vast man-made structures were built everywhere, to make yet more vast structures, and the smoke and stench of the engines and devices used fouled the world's air in great clouds of poison. He paused for a moment and looked sad. This was not all. The Earth itself trembled. Monstrous vessels, to which that Unclean ship of yesterday would be a skiff, fouled the very seas. Overhead, the air vibrated with the rush of great flying machines, whose speed alone, by its vibration, could shatter stone, carrying ever more goods and people, charged madly along, their poisonous wastes still further fouling the already wearied air.

Now he's starting to sound like Jim Morrison in "When the Music's Over." A little hokey maybe, but still reasonably believable to some extent.

And then, there were the world's people. The warring, breeding, struggling, senseless people! The peoples of the planet could not, or rather would not, be brought to reason. Not only did they refuse to see how they were killing the life of the world, they could not even see how they were killing themselves! For they bred. Despite vast poverty, great ignorance, disease and endless wars, humans were still tough! Every year there were more and more, until the cataclysm was inevitable. Wise men warned them, scientists and humanists pled with them. God and Nature are one, they said, and hence neither is mocked and defied with impunity. A few listened, indeed, more than a few. But not enough. Certain leaders of religion, men ignorant of any science and any learning but their own outdated hagiography refused to heed. Other men, who controlled the world's wealth and soldiery wished more power. They wished yet more men both to make and to consume what they sold and still more men to wage the wars which they fomented in the name of one political creed or another. Races warred against races of other colors, white against yellow, black against white.

Okay, this is really where an editor should have reigned this in. This is just plain nuts. The apocalypse was brought about by a combination of the population explosion, capitalism, racism, and bible-thumping right wing religious fundamentalists. Seriously? As if anyone thousands of years into a bizarre future would still care about the hot cultural issues of the 1970s? I think I liked it better *not* knowing the secret origin of this setting.

The end was quite inevitable. It had to come! Men of science who had studied many species of mammals in laboratories of the ancient world had long predicted it. When over-population and crowding, dirt and noise, reached a peak, madness remorselessly follows. We today call that madness The Death. Across the whole world, by land water, and air, total war raged unchecked. Radiation, hideous chemical weapons and artificially spawned disease slew most of the humans then in existence, and much of the remaining animal life, too.

Fears about overpopulation evidently reached a fever pitch during the early seventies: John B. Calhoun's mice experiments attained a degree of mythical cachet on par with the Book of Revelation. Did this sort of thing make the book more relevant, more accurate, or more scientific when it came out? I couldn't say. It sure looks painfully transparent today.

At any rate, it's clear this material was not considered to be up to snuff for the requirements of the *Gamma World* setting. These passages appear to have impacted the game to some extent, but only after some significant reworking. In James M. Ward and Gary Jaquet's future history, all of the pressing social issues of the late twentieth century were successfully worked through: "the rape of the earth's beauty and resources in the late 20th and early 21st centuries had been halted and reversed, due to man's tools." Thanks to the wonders of engineering and technology, mankind would be living in a golden age by the 24th century.

In the *Gamma World* game, the downfall of civilization can be traced back to a war between two factions, the League of Free Men and the Autonomists. Their disagreement was over whether or not there should be a unified world government. Their acts of terrorism went on for so long and got so far out of hand that a third faction calling itself the Apocalypse declared that they would blow up the entire world if these two groups didn't knock it off. To prove that they meant business, "the capital city of every nation in the world was turned into radioactive slag." That's when all hell broke loose:

> *Again, due to lack of records, it is not known how the location of The Apocalypse base was discovered, or who it was who initiated the attack. Some evidence indicates the action was a joint effort by nearly all the surviving terrorist factions and vigilante groups—united for the first time in the Shadow Years. In the end, though, a massive attack was mounted against The Apocalypse base. In turn, The Apocalypse retaliated with a fury never before witnessed on the face of the earth. Oceans boiled, continents buckled, the skies blazed with the light of unbelievable energies. Suddenly it was all over. The civilization of man had been slashed, burned, crushed, and scattered to the four winds.*

Gamma World is an over-the-top tongue-in-cheek game of real *wahoo!* adventures, but its designers understood the need for a back story that could actually merit being buttressed by pull quotes from the Book of Revelation. Sterling Lanier sacrificed that in order to peddle the hot political narrative of his day and ruined what could otherwise have been a masterpiece of science fantasy.

Star Man's Son
by Andre Norton

Postapocalyptic fiction in the tradition of *Mad Max II* and *Planet of the Apes* was not merely a byproduct of seventies-era dystopianism. Indeed, the genre goes back surprisingly far. Just seven years after the bombings of Hiroshima and Nagasaki, Andre Norton presented everything you'd need to run a pretty fair *Gamma World* campaign in a single volume. It's got disparate tribes of human survivors struggling to regain even a fraction of the know-how of their expired civilizations. It's got modest mutant abilities like night vision, acute hearing, and animal empathy. And it has vicious humanoid rat creatures and small (but cunning!) lizard people. Best of all, it has cities ripe for looting right up against the deadly irradiated deserts of the Blow-up Lands.

But though Norton's novel was ahead of its time in so many ways, it often seems to be more than a little mired in the social issues of its day. While it is interesting that the author managed to produce a credible multi-racial "buddy" story about twelve years before *I Spy* would be a hit television show, she nevertheless lays on the moralizing rather thickly at times. Take, for example, this exchange between Arskane and the leader of his tribe:

"This is he of whom I have told you—he has saved my life in the City of the Beast Things, and I have named him brother—" There was almost a touch of pleading in his voice. "We be the Dark People." The woman's tone was low but there was a lilt in it, almost as if she chanted. "We be the Dark People, my son. He is not of our breed—" Arskane's hands went out in a nervous gesture. "He is my brother," he repeated stubbornly. "Were it not for him I would have long since died the death and my clan would never have known how or where that chanced." (page 178)

This theme of overcoming racism is echoed in the main protagonist's ("Fors") relationship to his own tribe where he is an outcast due to his being a mutant. And though the need to pull together in the face of overwhelming odds makes the increasingly forward-thinking bent of the characters a bit more believable than it would be otherwise, Norton betrays not one hint of irony when she portrays the savage Beast Things as being anything other than subhuman.

Nevertheless, for *Gamma World* game masters this book is a gold mine. The premise of pure-strain humans sending out scouts to explore, to keep tabs on rival groups, and maybe to come back with a little loot is as gameable as anything you're liable to find in the Appendix N list. The chapter where Fors enters a largely intact city on horseback with his giant mutant cat friend can be played practically as is in a game session.[1] For people looking for a way to incorporate larger battles into their game, the final chapters featuring elements of three competing tribes coordinating against a potentially over-whelming incursion of mutants should be inspirational. The rest of the book is practically one good random wilderness encounter after another.

To top it off, the novel even concludes with a premise that could support a whole series of adventures. You see, there's much more to the titular "Star Men" than just a cool name:

> *Our forefathers were brought to this mountain hiding place because they were designed to be truly men of the Stars. Here were they being trained to a life which would be theirs on other worlds. Our records tell us that man was on the eve of conquering space when his madness fell upon him and he reached again for slaying weapons. We who were meant to roam the stars go now on foot upon a ravaged earth. But above us those other worlds still hang, and still they beckon. And so is the promise still given. If we make not the mistakes of the Old Ones then shall we know in time more than the winds of this earth and the trails of this earth. (page 222)*

This is, of course, the premise of the adventure module series for the third edition *Gamma World* that began with "Alpha Factor" and that was meant to conclude with the unreleased "Omega Project" adventure, which would see the intrepid players assembling the components of a spaceship in order to travel to the moon.

The world of Andre Norton's *Star Man's Son* is far more understated than either the *Gamma World* game or Sterling E. Lanier's *Hiero's Journey*. Enough generations have passed since the Blow Up that new tribal cultures have developed that are largely ignorant of the past. But there hasn't been enough time to completely erode the cities of the Old Ones. The most dangerous irradiated regions are becoming less and less deadly as well. If these hardscrabble survivors could just hang on and maybe find a few libraries, they *could* be on their way to conquering space in no time. That is, unless they fail to set aside their racism, their tribalism, and their propensity to wage war amongst themselves, as Norton reiterates time and again. Failing that, of course, the Beast Things will inherit the earth.

Notes

1. I actually played this out when my son insisted that I run first edition *Gamma World* for him.

Ill Met in Lankhmar
by Fritz Leiber

I've resigned myself to the fact that there are only so many writers in the same league as H. P. Lovecraft, Robert E. Howard, and Jack Vance. And it's tough sometimes. I mean, what am I going to do when I finally finish their last books?

Coming across Fritz Leiber as part of this series, though, I am delighted to realize that the stockpile of great reads just got significantly bigger. And he isn't just one of those authors that make me realize just how good the classics of science fiction and fantasy really are. He goes beyond that; I read him, and it just *hurts*. How could I have waited so long to come across this stuff? What was I doing going through life not even knowing this guy's name? And seriously, who is responsible for the fact that "Fritz Leiber" was never on my reading lists? *Why didn't anyone tell me?*

Well, never mind all that; this book is a masterpiece. It's alternately engaging and delightful, humorous and horrific. The stakes change with an entertaining sequence of tempo shifts, and the story keeps the reader wanting more. It's fantastic. I am not at all surprised to see that this piece garnered a Hugo Award for Best Novella back in 1971. Everything about it is pitch perfect.

But the thing I want to convey to you about this book is the fact that it manages to neatly encapsulate the very soul of *Dungeons & Dragons*. Now when I say that, I'm not talking about the fact that the thieves guild depicted here seems to show up in just about everybody's fantasy cities in their role-playing campaigns. And I'm not even talking about how the characters in this story seem to jibe with the depiction of thieves from *Basic D&D* either. Though now that I mention it, the fact that the Grey Mouser is a washed-up wizard's apprentice would tend to explain both the thief's low hit dice as well as the tendency of early RPG designers to give thieves a small amount of magical ability.

No, when I talk about what D&D **really** is, I don't mean to get into all of the usual discussions of differences between the various editions. I'm not talking about the nuances of all the rules or the differences between the classes. I'm not talking about the definition of hit points, the length of a combat round, or the origins of the alignment system. What I'm most concerned with here is the sort of things that invariably emerge in the course of play, many of which are quintessential features of the game, but which nonetheless are not directly addressed in either the rules or the adventure modules.

If you're not sure what I mean by that, then check out this passage from the story:

> *Each discerned something inexplicably familiar in the other. Fafhrd said, "Our motives for being here seem to be identical." "Seem? Surely must be!" the Mouser answered curtly, fiercely eyeing this potential new foe, who was taller by a head than the tall thief. "You said?" "I said, 'Seem? Surely must be!'" "How civilized of you!" Fafhrd commented in pleased tones. "Civilized?" the Mouser demanded suspiciously, gripping his dirk tighter. "To care, in the eye of action, exactly what's said," Fafhrd explained. Without letting the Mouser out of his vision, he glanced down. His gaze traveled from the belt and pouch of one fallen thief to those of the other. Then he looked up at the Mouser with a broad, ingenuous smile. "Sixty-sixty?" he suggested. The Mouser hesitated, sheaved his dirk, and rapped out, "A deal!" (pages 11-12)*

This just perfectly captures the uneasy alliance that exists between party members in a typical D&D session. Sure, occasionally groups work out some sort of rationale for why a random assortment of good-looking adventuring types from all walks of life might come together and strike off into the wilds in search of excitement and loot, but mostly they don't. You might say that these player-characters find each other to be *inexplicably familiar*. And even when they get into trouble due to how they end up working at cross-purposes at times, there's nevertheless something strangely *civilized* about their relationship—often in a way that is completely at odds with whatever rough cultures they supposedly hail from.

This is simply how things work at the tabletop. And no, there's nothing in the rule books that really nail this down as a feature either. People just seem to intuit that this is how things ought to be. Of course, it's also hilarious that two iconic swords and sorcery characters coincidentally meet when both of them are attempting to kill the exact same group of thieves *and then take their stuff*. It only makes Fritz Leiber's anticipation of coming trends in hobby gaming that much more delicious.

But this gets better because check this out:

> *"Now how do we get into the damn place?" Fafhrd demanded in a hoarse whisper. "Scout Murder Alley for a back window that can be forced. You've got pries in that sack, I trow. Or try the roof? You're a roof man, I know already. Teach me the art. I know trees and mountains, snow, ice, and bare rock. See this wall here?" He backed off from it, preparing to go up it in a rush. "Steady on, Fafhrd," the Mouser said, keeping his hand against the big young man's chest. "We'll hold the roof in reserve. Likewise all walls. And I'll take it on trust you're a master climber. As to how we get in, we walk straight through that doorway." He frowned. "Tap and hobble, rather. Come on, while I prepare us." As he drew the skeptically grimacing Fafhrd back down Death Alley until all Cheap Street was again cut off from view, he explained, "We'll pretend to be beggars, members of their guild, which is but a branch of the Thieves' Guild and houses with it, or at any rate reports in to the Beggarmasters at Thieves' House. We'll be new members, who've gone out by day, so it'll not be expected that the Night Beggarmaster and any night watchmen know our looks." "But we don't look like beggars," Fafhrd protested. "Beggars have awful sores and limbs all a-twist or lacking altogether." "That's just what I'm going to take care of now...." (pages 72-73)*

This is really the meat and potatoes of almost every *D&D* session I've ever run. There's always this thing that the players have to do. And the players invariably come up with these insane plans to accomplish it. I don't even have to do anything, really. As soon as they perceive the objective, they're off hashing out elaborate workarounds for every conceivable problem. They sometimes get so into working this sort of thing out that they'll brush me off when I suggest that we should maybe get started on, you know, actually *playing* the game. And the thing about these schemes is that they're almost always about something that the rules hardly even address at all. I mean, how can you know what a monster is really going to say when the players interrogate him? What's going to happen when the players leave a ludicrous commemorative plaque by the dungeon entrance and then overhear a non-player party arguing over what it means? How do you adjudicate combat when the players are on a slippery surface between boiling mud pots with all the players tied together with a single fifty-foot length of rope?

And that's just the random stuff that comes up in the course of the game! The things that the players come up with once this other stuff comes out are even crazier. For example, what is going to happen when the players send in a possessed hill giant and an invisible thief into a banquet hall so that their magic-user can take over the hill giant chieftain's mind in order to distract a company of drunken monsters with a speech while the rest of the party moves into position to unleash fireballs, poisonous snakes, and insect swarms all in perfectly optimized positions on the tabletop battle-map? What are all the monsters in the rest of that dungeon going to do when *that* particular disaster gets started? Heck, how are the monsters that see all this first hand going to behave? Nobody knows! Not the players, not the dungeon master, not the adventure designer… *nobody*.

The only thing that's certain is that the plan will completely fall apart when it comes into contact with game-reality. For instance, when the players decide to camp out in the giant chief's banquet room and find themselves rudely awakened by loud banging on each of three different entrances into their temporary safehold! That sense of jaw-dropping panic that consumes the players when they are overwhelmed by trouble of their own making is eerily similar to what Fritz Leiber describes here:

"Night Beggarmaster!" he called sharply. The limping man stopped, turned, came crippling majestically through the door. Krovas stabbed finger at the Mouser, then Fafhrd. "Do you know these two, Flim?" The Night Beggar-master unhurriedly studied each for a space, then shook his head with its turban of cloth and gold. "Never seen either before. What are they? Fink beggars?" "But Flim wouldn't know us," the Mouser explained desperately, feeling everything collapsing in on him and Fafhrd. "All our contacts were with Bannat alone." Flim said quietly, "Bannat's been abed with the swamp

*ague this past ten-day. Meanwhile I have been the Day Beggarmaster as well
as Night." (pages 117-118)*

This is where the fun begins: when the players' "brilliant" plans land them
in a situation where they are completely out of their depth. The action takes on
an entirely different tenor. It's amazing that it occurs so predictably given how
little you can do to actually prepare for it. And their creativity is astounding.
The dungeon master will be reminded of rules that no one normally bothers
with. New applications for standard character abilities will spontaneously be
developed. Odd things on peoples' character sheets that nobody ever thought
to use suddenly get brought out. And all of these things collide in this zany
cascade of events that takes on a life of its own.

Of course, the only thing better than the players miraculously pulling
themselves out of the ensuing mess with just the right die rolls and tactics
is when they realize just how badly they've been beaten and just what it is that
they've lost in the exchange. There's just something about those times that
the players return from the dungeon with their noses bloodied—and worse,
when they have nothing to show for it. Risking life and limb for a mere fifteen
experience points is just plain insulting, really. It's worse when casualties are
left behind. But that is the point when a goofy collection of oddballs and
miscreants suddenly pulls together to become a well-oiled killing machine.
It's a frightening thing to behold. Even the players can be taken aback by the
horrors they set out to unleash.

I won't spoil the story by revealing just what exactly it was the Fafhrd and
the Grey Mouser lost on their first adventure together, but I will show you this
scene from the aftermath of their epic rampage through the thieves' guild:

*Their madness was gone and all their rage too—vented to the last red atom
and glutted to more than satiety. They had no more urge to kill Krovas or
any other of the thieves than to swat flies. With horrified inner eye Fafhrd
saw the pitiful face of the child-thief he'd skewered in his lunatic anger.*

That child-thief is the literary antecedent of every orc baby that has ever
been killed in Keep on the Borderlands.

And this story captures the zeitgeist of great fantasy role-playing. It's got
it all: the random thugs joining together in an uneasy alliance as they set off

in search of plunder, the over the top plans like something out of *Mission Impossible*, the incredibly frantic action when things fall apart, the laser-focused vengeance that consumes a rebuffed party, and even the reflection and remorse when they start to come to grips with all the carnage in their wake. Like I said, you won't find this sort of thing spelled out in the rules or the adventure designs, but you will see it in actual play. It's the stuff great gaming sessions are made of.

That this story that was published four years before the release of the original edition *Dungeons & Dragons* only makes it that much more impressive. Yet these similarities are not a coincidence: in the introduction to that game, Gary Gygax cites Fafhrd and the Grey Mouser's books as being one of four series that really captured the sort of fantasy that the game was designed to produce. But the success of his design work has been so influential that it has since overshadowed the authors that made it possible. Today there are countless gamers that have experienced adventures almost identical to the spirit of Fritz Leiber's creations, but they often don't have any idea who he was.

Fortunately, all is not lost: there just aren't that many wandering monster checks in store for those that seek these treasures of fantasy literature. This stockpile of great reads is here for the taking for anyone that has a craving for adventure.

The Complete Cthulhu Mythos Tales
by H. P. Lovecraft

SPOILER WARNING: Before we start this one, let me say that if you have not read Lovecraft's Mythos stories, you need to stop reading *me* and start reading *him*. I was irked at first by the fact that this particular volume did not put the tales in the order in which they were published. However, reading to the end it is clear that the compilers set them up the way that they did in order to consciously give the reader a particular kind of payoff. It worked for me, and I enjoyed it immensely. I can't tell you if this is the best introduction to Lovecraft's work or not, but I can say that I got a great deal of pleasure from it. The copy I got hold of was on the shelves at Barnes & Noble for a reasonable price.

———————

Lovecraft's contribution to science fiction and fantasy is positively ubiquitous. It's not just comics and movies like *Hellboy*, either. There are also a wide range of games that showcase his creations: Klaus Westerhoff's brilliant *The Stars Are Right*, the sprawling *Arkham Horror* board game, Steve Jackson's whimsical *Cthulhu Dice*, and, of course, Chaosium's seminal *Call of Cthulhu* role-playing game. Even before I'd read any of Lovecraft's work, I knew quite well from sessions of *Dungeons & Dragons* that if you *ever* came across some kind of unsettling bas relief, you probably needed to leave whatever ruins you had found them in with every bit of haste you could muster.

The basic premise that tends to come across with these homages, derivations, and elaborations is that evil cultists are at work around the globe. If they aren't stopped, bizarre extra-dimensional beings will be summoned to our plane, where they will change the earth into some kind of terrible hell world.

A rag-tag group of private investigators, academics, occultists, socialites, and explorers must collect clues however they can, but also be ready to get hold of Tommy guns and dynamite to finish off whatever monstrous servants of indescribable evil they finally track down.

It is great fun. It is the one genre of tabletop game that can stand toe to toe with the most enduring role-playing properties: *Traveller* and *Gamma World* not being the least among them. Even a generic game like *GURPS* can trace its "fright check" rules directly back to Lovecraft's oeuvre, so it can be difficult to get away from him. It's only a very few guys like Edgar Rice Burroughs and Robert E. Howard that can be said to have had a bigger impact on fantasy, science fiction, and gaming. But if there's a problem with Lovecraft's legacy and influence, it's that on the whole, these popularizations really aren't all that much like Lovecraft's actual work.

Oh, there is a crazy cult leader type in there such as this one from "The Horror in the Museum":

"See here, Jones—if I let you go will you let me go? It must be taken care of by Its high-priest. Orabona will be enough to keep It alive—and when he is finished I will make his fragments immortal in wax for the world to see. It could have been you, but you have rejected the honour. I won't bother you again. Let me go, and I will share with you the power that It will bring me. Iä! Iä! Great Rhan-Tegoth! Let me go! Let me go! It is starving down there beyond that door, and if It dies the Old Ones can never come back. Hei! Hei! Let me go!" (page 460)

It's amusing to see him impersonate a monster just like a bad guy from *Scooby Doo*. Of course, when he says that his costume was made from the hide of a "dimensional shambler," you actually believe him. And he really does have a monster in the basement worthy of triggering this epitome of failed fright checks:

With intense effort Jones is today able to recall a sudden bursting of his fear-paralysis into the liberation of frenzied automatic flight. What he evidently did must have paralleled curiously the wild, plunging flights of maddest nightmares; for he seems to have leaped across the disordered crypt at almost a single bound, yanked open the outside door, which closed and locked itself after him with a clatter, sprung up the worn steps three at a time, and raced frantically and aimlessly out of that dank cobblestoned court through the squalid streets of Southwark. (page 463)

And while there are all kinds of cultists all over the world, in Lovecraft's stories there is a lot more to them than just some scheme to bring about the end times. There are more children going missing right around May Eve and Hallow Mass, to be sure. But these cultist types are up to *all kinds of stuff*. Some of them are a glorified hospitality network for strange visitors from other worlds and other times. Some of them are heirs to knowledge and traditions that predate human civilizations. Some of them are simply privy to what's going on and are acting accordingly even if it raises eyebrows among the academic set.

And yes, the standard movie trope of world-wrecking entities from other dimensions does, in fact, show up here, too:

There is no need of going deep into the primal lore behind this business, but I may as well tell you that according to the old legends this is the so-called 'Year of the Black Goat'—when certain horrors from the fathomless Outside are supposed to visit the earth and do infinite harm. We don't know how they'll be manifest, but there's reason to think that strange mirages and hallucinations will be mixed up in the matter. (page 516)

But the truth is, the bulk of these tales do not anticipate the basic plot of, say, *Ghostbusters*. For instance, Lovecraft's story "Out of the Aeons" summarizes the basic theme of Lovecraft's Mythos like this: *There are things about the world and universe which it is better for the majority not to know....* That is of course immediately recognizable from first edition *GURPS Horror* as being the tagline of an entire class of monsters for that game. They were indescribably horrific and usually unbeatable. (There's a picture of a giant tentacled blob monster overwhelming some seaside town that I always thought was meant to evoke this strain of nemesis.) This left the players battling the vile minions of these things, usually striving to prevent them from being summoned in the first place. No, you couldn't do anything about cross-dimensional horrors, but you *could* beat up on a range of their servants. But again, this style of interpretation is not the key to Lovecraft's horror stories. And that sort of thing is not at all what he meant when he wrote that sentence.

A much clearer summation of the overall thrust of Lovecraft's Mythos stories can be found in "The Thing on the Doorstep": *There are horrors beyond life's edge that we do not suspect, and once in a while man's evil prying calls them just within our range.* Most people attempting to do something in the spirit of Lovecraft's work tend to make the error of allowing the protagonists to be "big damn heroes" by preventing cultists and monsters from upsetting the status quo. But the point Lovecraft was making across his work was that these people were terrified because they managed to uncover the fact that the status quo is *itself* so messed up. And being aware of the truth can only make you crazy. There's not much that can be done about it except not to meddle with this stuff in the first place, but even *that* tends to go wrong for a lot of Lovecraft's protagonists.

I am thinking that there might be some who have read this far without having read the stories yet. And I can imagine them wondering how this can really work. Because what I just wrote sounds like there's not much in the way of *story* here at all. And that's right. "Real" Lovecraft is different. The tales do not follow the standard phases of Joseph Campbell's heroic journey. They do not at all align with the conventions of blockbuster movies. And they are about as far from an Edgar Rice Burroughs-style pulp novel as you can get. (But if you do want a Lovecraft story in *that* style, check out A. Merritt's *Dwellers in the Mirage*. It's awesome!)

No, there are no heroes here. Usually, the protagonist is some kind of professor that starts off with an unnatural desire to know about something that he should leave well enough alone. For the bulk of the work, he is in denial about the incredible things he comes across. Soon, the cognitive dissonance gets positively undeniable, but he keeps talking himself out of what it has to mean. Before long, he's in too deep, and things begin to get exponentially more frightening. But there's always a kicker of some kind—some shoe that drops at the end that not only makes sense of what might have seemed to be extraneous details earlier on but that also increases the horror levels by yet another order of magnitude.

And the thing that makes it so scary is how real it all seems. For this, the unimpressive scholar figure turns out to be just plain perfect in the leading role. He states every detail with unmatched precision because he knows he will be read by a skeptical audience. It's almost like he is delivering evidence for a court case. The level of resolution here is astounding, too. It's almost like an actual scientist is describing his experiences and encounters. It not only takes you to another time and causes your imagination to flesh out every hint, but it also takes you inside the minds of these characters so that you can experience their fear right along with them.

These protagonists are not the first people in history to encounter this stuff though. Not by a long shot. Again, the monsters are already here. *They are the status quo.* This would, of course, be far more well known if those professors at Miskatonic University quit suppressing their findings. But you can cut them some slack because those who know too much die, go insane, or are murdered by cultists. The occult is real. It's been documented for centuries. And there are a great many books besides the famous *Necronomicon* that delve into this topic:

> *It is true that a few scholars, unusually versed in the literature of occultism and magic, found vague resemblances between some of the hieroglyphics and certain primal symbols described or cited in two or three very ancient, obscure, and esoteric texts such as the* Book of Eibon, *reputed to descend from forgotten Hyperborea; the* Pnakotic fragments, *alleged to be pre-human; and the monstrous and forbidden* Necronomicon *of the mad Arab Abdul Alhazred. None of these resemblances, however, was beyond dispute; and because of the prevailing low estimation of occult studies, no effort was made to circulate copies of the hieroglyphs among mystical specialists. Had such circulation occurred at this early date, the later history of the case might have been very different; indeed, a glance at the hieroglyphs by any reader of von Junzt's horrible* Nameless Cults *would have established a linkage of unmistakable significance. At this period, however, the readers of that monstrous blasphemy were exceedingly few; copies having been incredibly scarce in the interval between the suppression of the original Düsseldorf edition (1839) and of the Bridewell translation (1845) and the publication of the expurgated reprint by Golden Goblin Press in 1909. (pages 492-493)*

It's exactly this sort of attention to detail that makes these tales seem so real. I can imagine what each of these books must look like and how they differ from one another. And there's not just one origin story for the beasties. There are all kinds of ways they could have gotten here. But no matter the premise, the implications of each of them are the same: we are a temporary accident in the cosmic scheme of things, we are hopelessly outclassed by a raft of malevolent entities that can chill our blood without a thought, and there is no place to hide and nothing we can do to change this.

> *Primal myth and modern delusion joined in their assumption that mankind is only one—perhaps the least—of the highly evolved and dominant races of this planet's long and largely unknown career. Things of inconceivable shape, they implied, had reared towers to the sky and delved into every secret of Nature before the first amphibian forbear of man had crawled out of the hot sea three hundred million years ago. Some had come down from the stars; a few were as old as the cosmos itself; others had arisen swiftly from terrene germs as far behind the first germs of our life-cycle as those germs are behind ourselves. Spans of millions of years, and linkages with other galaxies and universes, were freely spoken of. Indeed, there was no such thing as time in its humanly accepted sense. (page 533)*

As a result of this, there is trouble to be found pretty much *everywhere*. There are massive alien cities at the South Pole. There are innumerable crypts that are better left undisturbed. If anything is dredged up from the ocean floor, something terrible is sure to happen. Poking around an old Indian mound can lead you to an immense underworld that rivals Pellucidar. There are still places on earth that are peopled by decadent and godlike beings. Yet these terrible creatures are themselves terrified of other more sinister forces and beings. We are not just beset by horrors… *the horrors are as well!*

And did I mention that many of these beings are basically inscrutable space aliens? The idea that science fiction and fantasy were two distinct genres does not at all line up with Lovecraft's impulses:

> *There was a mind from the planet we know as Venus, which would live incalculable epochs to come, and one from an outer moon of Jupiter six million years in the past. Of earthly minds there were some from the winged, star-headed, half-vegetable race of paleogean Antarctica; one from the reptile people of fabled Valusia; three from the furry pre-human Hyperborean worshippers of Tsathoggua; one from the wholly abominable Tcho-Tchos; two from the arachnid denizens of earth's last age; five from the hardy coleopterous species immediately following mankind, to which the Great Race was some day to transfer its keenest minds en masse in the face of horrible peril; and several from different branches of humanity. (pages 540-541)*

Lovecraft's Mythos not only spans across all of the planets and on into other galaxies even and includes creatures that are "Outside" the limits of our notions of space and time, but it also reaches far back into our most cherished myths. One time-traveling character in this book encounters Crom-Ya, a Cimmerian chieftain from the year 15,000 B.C. Yes, the sum of Robert E. Howard's Conan stories are a genuine element of Lovecraft's sprawling history and world building. Yet the reader is not overwhelmed with this incredible amount of information. Indeed, Lovecraft uses this to make everything both more comprehensible and more portentous, as this passage from "The Haunter of the Dark" demonstrates:

> Of the Shining Trapezohedron he speaks often, calling it a window on all time and space, and tracing its history from the days it was fashioned on dark Yuggoth, before ever the Old Ones brought it to earth. It was treasured and placed in its curious box by the crinoid things of Antarctica, salvaged from their ruins by the serpent-men of Valusia, and peered at aeons later in Lemuria by the first human beings. It crossed strange lands and stranger seas, and sank with Atlantis before a Minoan fisher meshed it in his net and sold it to swarthy merchants from nighted Khem. The Pharaoh Nephren-Ka built around it a temple with a windowless crypt, and did that which caused his name to be stricken from all monuments and records. Then it slept in the ruins of that evil fane which the priests and the new Pharaoh destroyed, till the delver's spade once more brought it forth to curse mankind. (pages 584-585)

This brief breakdown might seem overwhelming, but these kinds of details are divulged incrementally over the course of a great many stories. And they are often firmly grounded in people and places of rural New England. In addition, the descriptions of individual monsters are so detailed that they are conveyed as if Lovecraft actually had specimens on hand to work from. That's something that rarely comes across in the more cartoonish depictions of his creations. The depth and breadth of his vision are so convincing that disbelief is not merely suspended, but one actually comes away with the feeling that our reality is one with Lovecraft's. It's too bad that many of the works that are derivative of these stories seem to have missed their point entirely. But that was perhaps inevitable. After all, we really can't handle the truth.

The Broken Sword
by Poul Anderson

This book is superb. It's not just a rip-roaring yarn either. It also explains a great deal about old-school fantasy that you're liable to have not even wondered about. For instance, it reveals that the most important "half-elf" race throughout history was not the product of an epic elf/human romance but was instead the result of a jaw-dropping elf and troll pairing. It shows why it was that it was of utmost importance in the Middle Ages to have your children either christened or dedicated to some pagan god as soon after their birth as was feasible. It reveals that Faerie have long been active all around us, but that even in the heart of the lands of troll and elf-kindred we cannot see them unless we have the gift of Witch's Sight. Going against the grain of more recent trends and impulses, this book demonstrates just how much more *fantastic* fantasy fiction can be when it is grounded in reality and history.

Not that there aren't Elfland-like worlds here that can (with great difficulty) be journeyed to by mortals. Jötunheim, the land of the giants figures strongly in the tale. Not only does this incredible place contain a steading, but it is also a realm that does not "lie on the earth at all, but in strange dimensions near the edge of everything where creation plunged back into the Gap whence it had arisen." While Poul Anderson is often invoked in order to illustrate how fantasy might have evolved without Tolkien's overwhelming influence, the parallels here to Middle Earth's Undying Lands are unmistakable.

Another connection to Dunsany and Tolkien here is that the tale is framed with the idea that the mythic past is actually *our* past. Of course, if our myths are in some sense true, that leads to the question of *whose* myths are true. And the surprising answer that we get here is that *all of them* are true. This is especially surprising given the number of people who have complained about how classic *AD&D* throws together basically every fantastic beast or being that anyone has ever conceived into one sprawling default milieu. The closest thing to this that many people might have come across might be C. S. Lewis's Narnia stories; consequently, they might think that such a world-building choice might be necessarily cute or silly or otherwise geared toward children.

Yet despite being unflinchingly multicultural, the troll army depicted here is both believable and convincingly ferocious:

> *"Most of the goblin tribes we have either overcome or made alliance with,"*
> *said Illrede. "They have old grudges against both trolls and elves, but I have*
> *promised them loot and freedom for such slaves of their race as we have and*
> *a place just below us when we rule throughout Faerie. They are doughty*
> *fighters and not a few. Then we have companies from distant lands, demons*
> *of Baikal, Shen of Cathay, Oni of Cipangu, imps of Moorish deserts, adding*
> *up to a fair number. They have come for the looting and are not wholly to*
> *be relied on, but I will dispose them in battle according to what they can*
> *do. There are also stragglers who came alone or in little bands—werewolves,*
> *vampires, ghouls, that sort. And we have plenty of dwarf thralls, some of*
> *whom will fight in exchange for freedom; and they can handle iron." (page*
> *82)*

Similarly, each part of England fields a different type of elf. Forest elves were brought and then later abandoned by the Romans. From Cornwall and Wales are the most ancient of the elves, "green-haired, white-skinned sea folk." And in Pictland there are shorter, bearded elves with dark skin and (naturally) tattooed faces. But the greatest allies of the elven people are the Sidhe, which constitute an entire pantheon in their own right. Among these, the Tuatha De Danaan were chief, "for they had been gods in Ireland ere Patrick" had come. But in Anderson's telling, these creatures did not simply sail across to sea to some sort of Elfland retirement home. As a faun recounts, it is the coming of the "White Christ" that ultimately puts an end to these mythic beings:

> *"I came from the south, after great Pan was dead and the new god whose*
> *name I cannot speak was in Hellas. No place remained for the old gods*
> *and the old beings of our land. The priests cut down the sacred groves and*
> *built churches—Oh, I remember how the dryads screamed, unheard by them,*
> *screams that quivered on the hot still air as if to hang there forever. They ring*
> *yet in my ears, they always will." The faun shook his curly head. "I fled*

north; but I wonder if those of my comrades who stayed and fought and were slain with exorcisms were not wiser. Long and long has it been, elf-boy, and lonelier than it was long." Tears glimmered in his eyes. "The nymphs and the fauns and the very gods are less than dust. The temples stand empty, white under sky, and bit by bit they crumble to ruin. And I—I wander alone in a foreign land, scorned by its gods and shunned by its people." (page 14)

I'm not sure why passages like this surprise me so much. Christian authors like Tolkien and Lewis were widely considered to be among the best fantasy authors of all time when I was growing up in the eighties. Yet Christian elements such as what Poul Anderson presents here were being steadily retired from fantasy even then. Instead of using real myths and reconciling them with the real world, fantasy authors and game designers more and more took to creating standalone settings with a more generic tone. Nowhere is this more evident than in the way that fantasy settings tended to come packaged with a cheap knockoff of the Greek gods and goddesses. Not everyone went along with this, of course. But it was a trend. It was so unsatisfactory that Steve Jackson's *Yrth* setting intentionally incorporated actual religions like Christianity and Islam in reaction to it.[1]

Just as one data point to illustrate this shift, I want to take a look at the fourth volume in the original run of *AD&D* hardbacks. This is not one that I remember getting a lot of attention, but Gary Gygax's foreword made it clear that this work was *serious business*:

> **DEITIES AND DEMIGODS** *is an indispensable part of the whole of* **AD&D**. *Do not fall into the error of regarding it as a supplement. It is integral to Dungeon Mastering a true* **AD&D** *campaign. Experienced players will immediately concur with this evaluation, for they already know how important alignment is, how necessary the deity is to the cleric, and how interaction of the various alignments depends upon the entities which lead them. Those readers not well-grounded in ongoing campaigns must take my word for all of this, although they will soon discover for themselves how crucial the deities of the campaign milieu are.*

That is insanely audacious, even for a passage written entirely in High Gygaxian. But this was, after all, a new book for what was to become the apotheosis of fantasy role-playing games: the first real installment after the initial core books were out. A few appropriate words were in order because it was put together by a couple of guys that *weren't* Gary Gygax. They basically had to be ordained—anointed for the task, as it were. So from that standpoint, it's completely understandable that the Old Man had to put in a good word for them.

Still, I have to say that the style of argument he takes there to buttress his remarks is quite out of bounds. They are not the words of a sales pitch. They are not merely an endorsement of someone else's contribution to the game. We are in told in effect that the initiated and the enlightened will *immediately* see the value of the book. Those who don't? They just haven't played the game enough to understand. There's nothing you can do with this if you don't "get it" except pretend that you're in on it. No wonder the early days of tabletop role-playing have the reputation for being some kind of cargo cult!

The preface by James M. Ward could not offer a greater contrast:

> *The book should be used as a beginning framework for the DM. Sample it, take what is wanted, and start the gods as well as the players in a universe. While* **DEITIES & DEMIGODS** *reveals a great many divine powers and a great many powerful devices, it is the duty of the DM to add to, change, and otherwise modify the information on these pages for use in a campaign. (James M. Ward, page 4)*

Something like that last bit belongs in just about every role-playing game supplement ever made. A lot of people lately seem to get hung up on whether or not the game master has the *authority* to make sweeping editorial changes for his campaign. But the invocation of "duty" here not only suggests the inevitability of this sort of thing but also implies that there's more than a little *noblesse oblige* that should go along with it. I may be reading too much into a very brief passage here, but it seems to me that James M. Ward really "gets" gaming. That being the case, it particularly irks me that this book has taken a lot of heat over the years for things that were cleared up in the opening pages:

> **DDG** *(for short) may resemble* **MONSTER MANUAL***, and in fact does include some monsters. However, the purpose of this book is not to provide adversaries for players' characters. The information listed herein is primarily for the Dungeon Master's use in creating, intensifying or expanding his or her campaign.... The most important thing to remember about this book*

*is that, unlike the other **AD&D** volumes, everything contained within this book is* guidelines, *not rules.* **DDG** *is an* aid *for the DM, not instructions. We would not presume to tell a Dungeon Master how to set up his or her campaign's religious system. (Deities & Demigods, page 5)*

Ah, the number of people who have called out this tome for statting up god-like beings as if they were just another variety of monster! And most people do see this work as being a glorified *Monster Manual*. Of course, many vocal connoisseurs of gaming seem to object to the monster books on *principle*—an attitude I was sympathetic to right up until the moment that I observed nine-and eleven-year-old children encountering the old *AD&D* hardbacks for the first time. They understood nothing of the rules. They didn't even roll up characters like I would have done as a teenager. But they spent literally days on end reading about monsters and marking the ones that most inspired them. These books are not just a repository for the game's implied setting. They are something more.

I think what it comes down to is that the monster books really captured and conveyed the zeitgeist of *AD&D* like nothing else. I mean, few people actually understood the rules in the early days. I'm not even sure that you could even run the game with the rules as written. But even a neophyte Dungeon Master could grasp the contents of the monster books. For players, 80% of what you need to successfully play the game would have been in the character generation and combat sections. For the game masters? I think 80% of the what they needed to *run* a campaign was in the *Monster Manual*. It really was the heart of the game.

But the notes on using *Deities & Demigods* in actual play are quite good and go quite beyond the premise of things that your players can murder for treasure. If you are trying to run these beings just from their individual entries, you'll miss out on this, and I think that's exactly what happened with more than a few gamers. In fact, quite a bit of the material here is right in line with *The Broken Sword* and other literary inspirations:

- "The source of a deity's godhead is in some way connected to his or her earthly worshipers, however it is true that a god's power often increases or decreases as the number of his worshipers varies. Thus deities, and clerics as their agents, constantly try to increase the quality and quantity of their worshipers."

- "The statistics given in this book can be of great aid, but they do not tell *how* a deity should be played. The gods are not lists of armor classes, hit points, and attack forms; treating them as such reduces them to the role of mere monsters. They are, rather, beings whose very presence profoundly effects the course of events."

- "If engaged in combat, deities will almost always call upon whatever aid they can. Some gods have specific aids or attendants listed in the text. Those who do not have creatures listed can still usually summon a retinue of appropriate beings from the Prime Material or the god's plane of origin. After summoning aid, many gods will depart from the field, leaving the retinue to do the fighting for them."

- "The gods are not unwilling to aid their worshipers. The fact is, gods have so many worshipers that they prefer to give aid of a less specific and more general nature– subtle aid that will help their worshipers as a whole. This type of aid usually goes unnoticed in the short run (except by high level clerics, who know what to expect.) Specific aid to individuals is extremely rare, despite the fact that this is the kind of aid deities are most frequently expected to supply."

This last one is reminiscent of the passage from *The Broken Sword* where Odin impersonates the Devil:

"I stand ready to give my soul unto you if you will deliver my enemies into my hands." "That I may not do," said her guest, "but I may give you the means to entrap them if your cunning be greater than theirs." (pages 25-26)

And incredibly, the Devil himself actually turns up later on:

The witch had no time for rites or offerings, but she howled the call which had been taught her, and a blackness deeper than night arose beyond the fire. She groveled. Faint and cold, the little blue flames raced across him. "Help," she whimpered. "Help, the elves come." The eyes watched her without anger or pity. The sound of the hunt grew louder. "Help!" she wailed. He spoke, in a voice that blent with the wind but seemed to come from immeasurably far removed. "Why do you call on me?" "They... they seek... my life." "What of that? I heard you say once that you did not care for life." "My vengeance is not complete," she sobbed. "I cannot die now, without knowing whether my work and the price I paid are for naught. Master, help your servant!" Nearer came the hunters. She felt the ground shiver beneath the galloping hoofs. "You are not my servant, you are my slave," the voice rustled. "What is it to me whether your purpose is fulfilled? I am the lord of evil, which is futility. Did you think you ever summoned me and struck a bargain? No, you were led astray; that was another. Mortals never sell me their souls. They give them away." And the Dark Lord was gone. (pages 80-81)

Taking another look at this iconic game supplement as an adult, I can't help but come to the conclusion that *Deities & Demigods* is underrated. While it was not James M. Ward's and Robert J. Kuntz's intent that Dungeon Masters would import the entire range of pantheons into their campaign wholesale, Poul Anderson's *The Broken Sword* offers a fascinating glimpse into just how you would go about doing just that. Maybe the main problem with the syncretic approach of *AD&D* was that we never took it far enough!

Of course, *Deities & Demigods* is noticeably out of step with, say, *The Forgotten Realms* and the many Tolkien pastiches that followed it. And again, when Steve Jackson produced his own fantasy game in 1986, he went out of his way to provide an alternative to the "superficial mumbo jumbo" that passed for typical fantasy religions of the day. He gave players a way to be "paladins of a 'real' faith [rather] than of the Temple of Gooble the Mostly Omnipotent." But by providing a range of real-world pantheons, the designers of *Deities & Demigods* were equipping dungeon masters to embrace that same sort of world building decision six years before that. It might have struck people as being more and more unusual as the eighties wore on, but Ward and Kuntz didn't really stray too far from the sort of thing that writers like Lord Dunsany, J. R. R. Tolkien, and Poul Anderson had done previously.

Deities & Demigods might not be the sort of "fourth core book" that it was originally pitched as being. Nevertheless, there is a lot of potential to be found within its covers. Anyone looking to make his fantasy campaign's gods and goddesses do more than just provide clerical spells to their followers would do well to take a look at it.

Notes

1. GURPS Fantasy first edition, page 70.

The Maker of Universes
by Philip José Farmer

This is another of those stories that starts off with the protagonist suffering from amnesia. Now, that might seem like a tiresome cliché by now, but really, the freakier your setting is, the more that sort of thing starts to look like a great trick for gradually easing the reader into just how everything works. And this setting gets weird fast. In the opening pages, the protagonist is an old man with an overweight harridan for a wife. By the end of the first chapter, he uses some sort of magic trumpet to open a portal into a fantastic world peopled by mermaids, zebrillas, nymphs, satyrs, and dryads.

And this place isn't *just* some sort of crazy Eden where everyone stays perpetually young. (Even our hero ends up regaining his youth.) It's not only some kind of Zardoz-style nudist colony with people who have had the concept of killing stricken from their imaginations. It's *also* some kind of Big Rock Candy Mountain where alcoholic beverages grow on trees. If you think it can't get any weirder, then hold on. These people were kidnapped from Earth by some sort of insanely powerful godlike being that transplanted their brains into the bodies of these mythological creatures.

But Farmer is still not done. It gets even weirder than *that*. These people aren't just folks that were whisked away from Greece at about the time that Homer was writing. Some of them are actually people about whom Homer wrote:

> *Wolff questioned him further for he was interested in what Ipsewas could tell him about Agamemnon and Achilles and Odysseus and the other heroes of Homer's epic. He told the zebrilla that Agamemnon was supposed to be a historical character. But what about Achilles and Odysseus? Had they really existed? "Of course they did," Ipsewas said. He grunted, then continued, "I suppose you're curious about those days. But there is little I can tell you. It's*

been too long ago. Too many idle days. Days?—centuries, millenia!—the
Lord alone knows. Too much alcohol, too. (page 68)

But wait. There's more! (I'm telling you that Farmer simply does not quit!)
It soon becomes clear that this is not some sort of flat-earth setting. You see,
when it says "World of Tiers series" on the cover, it means exactly that: a
world of *tiers*! The bottom level is some kind of weird paradise. The next
level up is loaded with centaurs and Indian tribes. The one after that has
Teutonic knights that act like they just got up from the iconic round table.
The penultimate level is an Atlantis, where its people are in the process of
undertaking the ill-advised project of recapitulating the story of the Tower
of Babel. And finally, at the very top is the Boss Level—the domain of "The
Lord," who has access to the control panels that allow him to rain down divine
wrath on anyone that dares to defy him.

Honestly, any one of these levels could have supported an entire book-
length adventure on their own. I kept thinking that Farmer would come
back around and explain how all of these figures from Greek myth could have
been actual historical people. He doesn't though. He keeps making his setting
wilder and wilder, repeatedly increasing the scope until it's almost impossible
to keep up with it anymore. Or care. You see, the man that created this
insane "World of Tiers" and that abducted all manner of people from all eras
to populate it in weird bio-engineered bodies is not alone. There are others of
his kind that have created similar worlds and that come and go from earth as
well. And just like Roger Zelazny's *Nine Princes in Amber*, they've all ended
up in a nonstop war among themselves.

"The Lords are heir to a science and power far surpassing Earth's. But the
scientists and technicians of their people are dead. The ones now living
know how to operate their devices, but they are incapable of explaining the
principles behind them or repairing them. The millenia-long power struggle
killed off all but a few. These few, despite their vast powers, are ignoramuses.
They're sybarites, megalomaniacs, paranoiacs, you name it. Anything but
scientists." (page 104)

Now that's a familiar trope right there. I mean, everyone wants their fancy
toys, but no one wants a situation that completely destroys "game balance" or
its literary equivalent. You see this in everything from *D&D*'s magic items to

Gamma World's ancient artifacts to *Traveller's* relics. You see it echoing in *The Lord of the Rings*, with the Númenóreans being nothing but a shadow and a remnant of their former selves but still able to take charge of the Palantiri that are rightfully theirs. You see it the charlatanry of the wizards in Jack Vance's *Dying Earth*. This sort of thing is the backbone of adventure fiction.

Because unrestrained technology ends up turning settings into gray goo, world builders invariably develop some kind of Ordnung to keep everything in the Goldilocks zone. One place to look if you want to see how shameless authors can get about this is at the way they nerf firearms. Farmer does not cover up what he's doing here with even the hint of a fig leaf:

> *"By the way, why don't the gworl—or the Indians, from what you've told me—use firearms?" "It's strictly forbidden by the Lord. You see, the Lord doesn't like some things. He wants to keep his people at a certain population level, at a certain technological level; and within certain social structures. The Lord runs a tight planet." (page 106)*

You mean everything's set up just so in order to optimize everything for the kind of adventure story we love to read? That's actually kind of brilliant. I mean why *wouldn't* you do that? *Dune's* critics could never accept that stuff like shield/lasgun interactions, the spice, and the spacing guild could actually *explain* the setting of that science-fiction classic. So why fight it? If you want to write some sort of thinly disguised homage to *A Princess of Mars*, why ruin it with a bunch of hard science and painstaking world design that no one's going to believe anyway?

This is not to say that that Philip José Farmer never thinks anything through. His take on centaurs addresses things I never even imagined could be problems:

> *They were indeed centaurs, although not quite as the painters of Earth had depicted. This was not surprising. The Lord, when forming them in his biolabs, had had to make certain concessions to reality. The main adjustment had been regulated by the need for oxygen. The large animal part of a centaur had to breathe, a fact ignored by the conventional Terrestrial representations. Air had to be supplied not only to the upper and human torso but to the lower and theriomorphic body. The relatively small lungs of the upper part could not handle the air requirements. Moreover, the belly of the human trunk*

would have stopped all supply of nourishment to the large body beneath it. Or, if the small belly was attached to the greater equine digestive organs to transmit food, diet was still a problem. Human teeth would quickly wear out under the abrasion of grass. Thus the hybrid beings coming so swiftly and threateningly toward the men did not quite match the mythical creatures that had served as their models. Their mouths and necks were proportionally large to allow the intake of enough oxygen. In place of the human lungs was a bellowslike organ which drove the air through a throatlike opening and thence into the great lungs of the hippoid body. These lungs were larger than a horse's, for the vertical part increased the oxygen demands. Space for the bigger lungs was made by removal of the larger herbivore digestive organs and substitution of a smaller carnivore stomach. The centaur ate meat, including the flesh of his Amerind victims. (pages 118-119)

And the chapter-long running battle between the centaurs and the Indians is fantastic. It's some of the best action I've read in any Appendix N book. But Farmer also grasps what the real payoff of this sort of thing should be:

They rode on for two weeks and then were at the edge of the Trees of Many Shadows. Here Kickaha took a long farewell of the Hrowakas. These also each came to Wolff and, laying their hands upon his shoulders, made a farewell speech. He was one of them now. When he returned, he should take a house and wife among them and ride out on hunts and war with them. He was KwashingDa, *the Strong One; he had made his kill side by side with them; he had outwrestled a Half-Horse; he would be given a bear cub to raise as his own; he would be blessed by the Lord and have sons and daughters, and so forth and so on. Gravely, Wolff replied that he could think of no greater honor than to be accepted by the Bear People. He meant it. (page 133)*

This is the sort of moment I really wanted Andre Norton's Fors to have in her seminal work, *Star Man's Son*. This is the sort of respect I wanted Sterling Lanier's Hiero to earn before he charged off into the wilderness with a bunch of sailors that reflexively treated him like he was some kind of chief. And again, I would have gladly read an entire novel about just the Indians and the centaurs, but Farmer has the equivalent of *three* game settings to trek through here before he gets to the climatic battle at the end with its cascade of multiple big reveals. We go from each moment being delivered with lavish detail, to days passing in a single paragraph, and on into months of travel being summarized in a single sentence. And so it is that a transition that would normally be a major plot element gets a quick gloss just before the finale:

> *By now through some subtle process, Wolff had become the nominal leader. Before, Kickaha had had the reins in his hand with the approval of all. Something had happened to give Wolff the power of decision-making. He did not know what, for Kickaha was as boisterous and vigorous as before. And the passing of captainship had not been caused by a deliberate effort on Wolff's part. It was as if Kickaha had been waiting until Wolff had learned all he could from him. Then Kickaha had handed over the baton. (page 221)*

Eh, I just don't buy it. I mean, sure, there's plenty of plot to justify this. But this sort of transition is exactly the sort of thing I want to experience vicariously when I kick back with this sort of novel. A quick note explaining that this just sort of happened somehow really doesn't cut it.

I enjoyed this book a lot. Yes, this is essentially an entire world that boils down to being a gigantic upside down dungeon. And many of the settings it contains are a brilliant fit for gaming. In fact, the kind of world building on display here is almost identical to that used by Steve Jackson in his *Yrth* setting: real cultures placed in fantastic circumstances and then left to adapt over time. Even better, they're equipped with all the ancient artifacts and trimmings a gamer could want.

But as a novel, at some point, it all gets to be so much that I lose my capacity to care about how things turn out. I've had similar reactions to Isaac Asimov's post-trilogy *Foundation* stories, John Varley's *Titan* novels, and David Brin's second *Uplift* series. Sometimes authors get so intent on making something so epic, so mind bending, and so over the top that they forget the sort of things that actually make it meaningful in the first place.

But if this book was a letdown, I sure wouldn't mind having a few dozen more like it. It's a masterfully executed page-turner that's just plain loaded. If you're struggling with coming up with a game setting, it should inspire you to take whatever measures are needed in order to really make it work. Farmer does as much as anyone to show us just how big of a palette we have to work with. I think we've gotten a little more conservative, a bit more derivative, and just a tad more predictable with our fantasy settings since Farmer's time. Reading him will inspire you to think outside the confines of habit and received conventions.

The Sword of Rhiannon

by Leigh Brackett

This book is just plain *good*. As far as I'm concerned, Leigh Brackett's work can sit on my shelf in a place of honor right beside the work of A. Merritt and Edgar Rice Burroughs. And I'm not the only one who has had that reaction. Ace actually thought this novel was good enough to run opposite Robert E. Howard's *Conan the Conqueror* as part of its classic Doubles line. That's a tough act to have to follow, but Brackett really pulls it off.

Reading this book, it becomes clear just how much the top blockbuster movie franchises owe to the pulp era. Protagonist Matthew Carse, ex-fellow of the Interplanetary Society of Archeologists, makes for a very credible Indiana Jones figure. In fact, the basic outline of the story here is a wild search for the Martian equivalent of the Ark of the Covenant. And given that Brackett had a hand in developing the plot of the first *Star Wars* sequel, it's no surprise that themes of redemption play a prominent role here as well.[1] It's shocking to think how influential she must have been. If you passed over the pulps because you thought they would read like a bad episode of *Lost in Space*, then you'll be in for a pleasant surprise. If you're short on cash, don't look though. Once you read one Leigh Brackett work, you'll want *more*. And you're liable to watch all the movies that she had a hand in as well—classics like *The Big Sleep* and *Rio Bravo*.

Leigh Brackett's writing is lean and savvy. She knows how to hook a reader and to hold his attention. The action never lets up. Everything that's introduced ends up getting leveraged later. Everything that ends up being important is well established by the time it takes center stage. She has a knack for understanding and conveying the key emotional beats of the narrative. More than any other writer from the Appendix N list, her work reads as if it were a fast paced movie script in novel form.

It's the characters that really get me, though. The rascally Boghaz plays a similar role as Sallah from *Raiders of the Lost Ark*. If you recall, he was the good-natured "best buddy" character that provided a sense of camaraderie along with his comic relief. Boghaz is almost precisely of that archetype:

> *Presently Boghaz found an opportunity to whisper to Carse. "They think now we are a pair of condemned thieves. Best let them think so, my friend." "What are you but that?" Carse retorted brutally. Boghaz studied him with shrewd little eyes. "What are you, friend?" "You heard me—I come from far beyond Shun." From beyond Shun and from beyond this whole world, Carse thought grimly. But he couldn't tell these people the incredible truth about himself. The fat Valkisian shrugged. "If you wish to stick to that it's all right with me. I trust you implicitly. Are we not partners?" Carse smiled sourly at that ingenuous question. There was something abut the impudence of this fat thief which he found amusing. Boghaz detected his smile. "Ah, you are thinking of my unfortunate violence toward you last night. It was mere impulsiveness. We shall forget it. I, Boghaz, have already forgotten it," he added magnanimously. (page 53)*

What a guy!

A casual reader might think that this is just Brackett's take off on *A Princess of Mars*. And there's no doubt it owes a great deal to that book. But as far as the storytelling is concerned, the tale we get here is much more in line with A. Merritt's oeuvre. The main thrust of the plot here concerns a high-stakes gamble in which a possessed hero has to enter into a romance with an evil space princess in order to accomplish his objectives. While this trope has long since been retired from everyday use, it can nevertheless produce an unparalleled amount of sultry, pulpy drama. And while fans today might have difficulty accepting this sort of premise, I believe that Brackett succeeds in making it work as well or better than anybody:

> *"Sit down," said Carse, "and drink." Ywain pulled up a low stool and sat with her long legs thrust out before her, slender as a boy in her black mail. She drank and said nothing. Carse said abruptly, "You doubt me still." She started, "No, Lord!" Carse laughed. "Don't think to lie to me. A still-necked, haughty wench you are, Ywain, and clever. An excellent prince for Sark despite your sex." Her mouth twisted rather bitterly. "My father Garach*

fashioned me as I am. A weakling with no son—someone had to carry the sword while he toyed with the scepter." "I think," said Carse, "that you have not altogether hated it." She smiled. "No. I was never bred for silken cushions." She continued suddenly, "But let us have no more talk of my doubting, Lord Rhiannon. I have known you before—once in this cabin when you faced S'San and again in the place of the Wise Ones. I know you now." "It does not greatly matter whether you doubt or not, Ywain. The barbarian alone overcame you and I think Rhiannon would have no trouble." She flushed an angry red. Her lingering suspicion of him was plain now— her anger with him betrayed it. "The barbarian did not overcome me! He kissed me and I let him enjoy that kiss so that I could leave the mark of it on his face forever!" Carse nodded, goading her. "And for a moment you enjoyed it also. You're a woman, Ywain, for all your short tunic and your mail. And a woman always knows the one man who can master her." "You think so?" she whispered. She had come close to him now, her red lips parted as they had been before—tempting, deliberately provocative. "I know it," he said. "If you were merely the barbarian and nothing else," she murmured, "I might know it also." The trap was almost undisguised. Carse waited until the tense silence had gone flat. Then he said coldly, "Very likely you would. However I am not the barbarian now, but Rhiannon. And it is time you slept." He watched her with grim amusement as she drew away, disconcerted and perhaps for the first time in her life completely at a loss. He knew that he had dispelled her lingering doubt about him for the time being at least. (pages 132-133)

There's a reason why the genre is referred to as "planetary romance." And yes, if you were going to make a trashy romance novel targeting an audience that's made up largely of adolescent boys, then *this is how you do it.*

Of course, the best days of this type of story are long gone by now. It was practically ubiquitous up through the sixties, but today it's shocking to see it delivered with not even a hint of snark or irony. Mentioning the very idea of this sort of thing in mixed company is liable to produce a whole raft of negative responses. We live for the most part in a culture where people are primed to turn up their noses at this sort of thing.

Now, I eat this stuff up. It is by far among my favorite things about the Appendix N list. I have been vaguely dissatisfied with movies and novels for decades now, but I could never explain to you *why*. And maybe I missed something, but I'm telling you that we are now as a culture so vigilant about suppressing this sort of story that before I started reading these old books like this, I couldn't even *imagine* that they existed. Which leads to the question of just how exactly did we get from Leigh Brackett to... I dunno... *Mad Max: Fury Road*.

Well, it's been a long and winding road; that's for sure. It all started, I guess, about the time fans of comic books began self-consciously denouncing a good chunk of their favorite medium as thinly veiled "male power fantasies". People acted as if they needed some kind of excuse to indulge in such guilty pleasures. This transitioned to a point where, say, *Galaxy Quest* (1999) could relentlessly lampoon Captain James T. Kirk's propensity to turn the tables on space-faring femme fatales.

There was a dim echo of this sort of shtick cropping up in the 1996 film *Star Trek: First Contact*, but you really don't see it much anymore. I mean, I give them credit for trying, but I have to say it loses something seeing this sort of thing play out between a nervous android and a mass-murdering cyborg sociopath. Even something as aggressively pulpy as 2004's *Chronicles of Riddick* carefully sidesteps the issue. Indeed, the "strong female character" presented in that property seems to conflate both the "best buddy" figure and the "love interest" in one stroke. Consequently, the film simultaneously loses both a sense of romance and camaraderie as well. As entertaining as it might have been, I can't help but feel that it's missing something.

Meanwhile, there's no shortage of hand-wringing over the fact that boys just tend not to read as much anymore.[2] There's all sorts of speculation in the press about what might account for that and what might be done about it. But somehow no one ever seems to mention the fact that we've spent decades collectively ridiculing the sort of books that boys have traditionally enjoyed. The fact that they have largely just quit reading altogether doesn't surprise me in the slightest.

Notes

1. Note that there is no hint of Darth Vader's ultimate redemption in Leigh Brackett's script for *The Empire Strikes Back*. Indeed, Anakin Skywalker and Darth Vader are two separate people! The half cadence

that is set up there is more centered on Luke's succumbing to tempta-
tion. Had the story been developed more from that Brackett put forth,
it would probably have been Luke's sister serving to redeem *Luke* and
not Vader.

2. Robert Lipsyte's "Boys and Reading: Is There Any Hope?" from *The
New York Times Sunday Book Review* would be just one example of this
sort of thing.

A Martian Odyssey and The Complete Planetary Series
by Stanley G. Weinbaum

Stanley G. Weinbaum is another of those names whose cachet depends a great deal on the age of the person you're talking to. In one generation, he would have immediately been recognizable as a major literary figure on par with someone like Edgar Rice Burroughs in terms of his raw influence. In the next, the trio of Heinlein, Clarke, and Asimov would take the lion's share of the credit for pioneering "real" science fiction while Weinbaum quietly lapsed into A. Merritt levels of obscurity.

But if you're the kind of person who rolled your eyes every time the *Star Trek* franchise introduced yet another alien race that was differentiated only by a personality quirk and a new style of prosthetic forehead, then you want to know about this guy. If you fell out of your chair every time it was revealed that these alien creatures could interbreed with humans, then you want to know about this guy. If you felt like throwing popcorn at the movie screen every time George Lucas introduced yet another world whose entire concept was bound up into a single earth climate, then you want to know about this guy. And if you are the sort of person who always felt really strongly that "strange new worlds" should have a little bit more to them than just a slightly different matte painting serving as the backdrop... again, you want to know about this guy.

If that's you in a nutshell, then Stanley G. Weinbaum is your hero because in the mid-nineteen thirties, he just about single-handedly pioneered your kind of science fiction. H. P. Lovecraft said of him, "I saw with pleasure that someone had at last escaped the sickening hackneyedness in which 99.99% of all pulp interplanetary stuff is engulfed. Here, I rejoiced, was someone who could think of another planet in terms of something besides anthropomorphic kings and beautiful princesses…."

Weinbaum was a very big deal. Revolutionary, even. Oh sure, there *is* a stunning red-haired space pirate femme fatale with a secret base on Pluto in these stories. And most of us are going to have a hard time grappling with the idea of a fog-shrouded Uranus with a vast, unexplorable surface that you can actually walk on. Nevertheless, when you read his work, you see exactly the sort of world building that is taken for granted in almost any *Traveller* campaign today.

Consider the extreme conditions of this tide-locked incarnation of Venus:

One breath of unfiltered air anywhere near the warm edge of the twilight zone was quick and very painful death; Ham would have drawn in un- counted millions of the spores of those fierce Venusian molds, and they'd have sprouted in furry and nauseating masses in his nostrils, his mouth, his lungs, and eventually in his ears and eyes. Breathing them wasn't even a necessary requirement; once he'd come upon a trader's body with the mold springing from his flesh. The poor fellow had somehow torn a rip in his transkin suit, and that was enough. The situation made eating and drinking in the open a problem on Venus; one had to wait until a rain had precipitated the spores, when it was safe for an hour or so. Even then the water must have been recently boiled and the food just removed from its can; otherwise, as had happened to Ham more than once, the food was apt to turn abruptly into a fuzzy mass of molds that grew about as fast as the minute hand moved on a clock. A disgusting sight! A disgusting planet! That last reflection was induced by Ham's view of the quagmire that had engulfed his shack. The heavier vegetation had gone with it, but already avid and greedy life was emerging, wriggling mud grass and the bulbous fungi called "walking balls." And all around a million little slimy creatures slithered across the mud, eating each other rapaciously, being torn to bits, and each fragment re-forming to a complete creature. A thousand different species, but all the same in one respect; each of them was all appetite. In common with most Venusian beings, they had a multiplicity of both legs and mouths; in fact some of them were little more than blobs of skin split into dozens of hungry mouths, and crawling on a hundred spidery legs.

And contrast it with this region of the world's night side:

Outwardly the plateau presented the same bleak wilderness of ice and stone that they had found on the plain below. There were wind-eroded pinnacles of the utmost fantasy of form, and the wild landscape that glittered in the beams from their helmet lamps was the same bizarre terrain that they had first encountered. But the cold was less bitter here; strangely, increasing altitude on this curious planet brought warmth instead of cold, as on the Earth, because it raised one closer to the region of the Upper Winds, and here in the Mountains of Eternity the Underwind howled less persistently, broken into gusts by the mighty peaks. And the vegetation was less sparse. Everywhere were the veined and bulbous masses, and Ham had to tread carefully lest he repeat the unpleasant experience of stepping on one and hearing its moaning whimper of pain. Pat had no such scruples, insisting that the whimper was but a tropism; that the specimens she pulled up and dissected felt no more pain than an apple that was eaten; and that, anyway, it was a biologist's business to be a biologist. Somewhere off among the peaks shrilled the mocking laughter of a triops, and in the shifting shadows at the extremities of their beams, Ham imagined more than once that he saw the forms of these demons of the dark. If they were, however, the light kept them at a safe distance, for no stones hummed past. Yet it was a queer sensation to walk thus in the center of a moving circle of light; he felt continually as if just beyond the boundary of visibility lurked Heaven only knew what weird and incredible creatures, though reason argued that such monsters couldn't have remained undetected.

For each of his worlds, Weinbaum pays careful consideration to their seasonal variations. Even where the science is now dated, there's usually enough here that updating these planets wouldn't require *that* much work. In fact, the only substantial change in principle between Weinbaum's science fiction and what we have today is that his worlds would have to be sprinkled throughout the galaxy now. It's mainly the concentration of worlds with a breathable atmosphere all being present in a single solar system that most strains suspension of disbelief.

Perhaps more than any other author on the Appendix N list, Stanley G. Weinbaum's entry is the most difficult to explain. It's the sort of thing people might point to and say, "Look… that list of books is just a random list of stuff Gygax liked. It doesn't necessarily have anything to do with *AD&D* or gaming or anything else!" And people do say that sort of thing. And I kind of get why it is that they would.

In the first place, that list of books really does look almost completely random to many readers who grew up in the eighties. I mean, a lot of people would not even have heard of a great many of the names on that list. It used to astonish me that the stories referenced in it were drawn from well over half a century. But even the more obscure authors on that list would have been in bookstores throughout the sixties—and not just in things like Ballantine's Best Of line or its Adult Fantasy Series. Many publishers would have had new cover art put together so that many readers might not even have realized right away that they were getting hold of something "old" or out of date.

Gygax's tastes were *not* weird, though. There are Hugo award winners like Fritz Leiber on that list… big-name authors of the time like Fred Saberhagen. There are foundational classics like the works of Lovecraft and Howard. And there is a whole bunch of stuff that could have been on the rack at just about any drugstore. It's stuff that just about any dedicated reader could have been into at the time. When Gary Gygax writes that the books "certainly helped to shape the form" of *AD&D*, there really isn't any reason to doubt him.

But maybe it's not so much that Gary Gygax was weird but that science fiction and fantasy from before 1980 or so were weird. And I mean literally weird—as in the "Weird Tales" kind of weird. H. P. Lovecraft's stories do not follow the accepted conventions of today's horror genre. Heck, even Robert E. Howard's Conan stories are surprisingly different from the "swords and sorcery" tales that followed in their wake. In fact, the bulk of the Appendix N list is made up of works that are from a genre that barely even exists anymore.[1] "Science fantasy" runs through everything from Vance's *Dying Earth* to Zelazny's *Amber* series, from Farmer's *World of Tiers* to Saberhagen's *Changeling Earth*, and from Moorcock's *Hawkmoon* to Lanier's *Hiero*. And yet that vein of fantasy fiction seems to have all but dried up right around the time that the Death Star's towers stopped firing at the X-wing fighters that were cruising down its trench.

But before then, it was practically ubiquitous. There was nothing extraordinary about it other than the fact that it was awesomely entertaining. But then something happened. Somewhere, somehow, *somebody* decided that fantasy, horror, and science fiction were all separate genres that should have very little overlap. Now I'm not saying that there was some sort of smoke-filled room where a group of nefarious publishers and psychohistorians came up with a plan to do this. It is enough for me that we can agree that in the space of one generation, people could look back at entire swaths of fiction that were popular before they were born and not even know how to classify it.

It is in that older and (for some) nearly unimaginable context that Gary Gygax put together a recommending reading list of "Fantasy/Swords & Sorcery" authors in the December 1976 issue of *The Dragon*. Stanley G. Weinbaum is the guy that did Campbellian science fiction before John W. Campbell even had the idea to do it... *and Weinbaum is on this list!*

Why is that? I think the reason is that the boundary between fantasy and science fiction wasn't as hard in his day.[2] Because Weinbaum's work was on the shelf right next to other popular authors of the time. And finally... because if you're going to create imaginary worlds and then turn gamers loose in them, then you're invariably going to engage in the sort of world building that Stanley G. Weinbaum pioneered. Indeed, Gygaxian Naturalism[3] isn't just some weird quirk that came out of nowhere. Gary Gygax picked it up from the science fiction and fantasy he was reading. And the incredible diversity that infused the literature he enjoyed is a big part of why his game has such enduring appeal. We'll be playing it and be arguing about it for decades to come.

Notes

1. See "D&D's Appendix N Roots are Science Fantasy" on *Roles, Rules, and Rolls* for more on this.

2. Remember also that in the early days of the magazine, *The Dragon* billed itself as "The Magazine of Fantasy, Swords & Sorcery, and Science-Fiction Game Playing".

3. This is a term that was coined by James Maliszewski on his blog *Grognardia*. See his post "Gygaxian 'Naturalism' " for details.

The Jewel in the Skull

by Michael Moorcock

Fantasy did, in fact, exist before the advent of the watered-down Tolkien pastiche. To someone who didn't grow up with older books, they're almost impossible to imagine. So it was for me when I first heard that Michael Moorcock was, in effect, the Anti-Tolkien[1]. I mean... how could such a thing even *be* when for all intents and purposes, Tolkien fairly well *defines* modern fantasy?

Well, if you want to know... if you *have* to know what it was that publishing, libraries, and movies have mostly turned their backs on, then read this book. It's not even a hundred and eighty pages long, and it is a very fast read. It's not some sort of monstrous series where every book segues into the next, where each book ends on a cliffhanger, and where about four novels in, everything suddenly takes on that soul-numbing "contractually obligated" feel. No, this book is a good reading value. When you finish, you'll still *want* eighteen hundred more pages in this vein!

But what is the "Anti-Tolkien" like in a nutshell? Well... take everything that's awesome about every heavy metal band in the history of rock and roll and boil it down until you have an elixir of pure *metal*. Now, transmute that into short novel form. That's as concise a way as I can put it. There are no themes of mercy for those that don't deserve it. There are no scenes depicting undying loyalty from servant to master as the weak things of the world head off into the heart of darkness to confound the things which are mighty. There is no unlikely *deus ex machina* for the free peoples of the world to stoically put their faith in as they fight their long defeat. No, what you have here in this book is more of some sort of literary antecedent to the ethos of Black Sabbath's "Paranoid."

Behold:

It was a slithering sound, a slobbering sound; the sound of a baragoon—
the marsh gibberer. Few of the monsters were left now. They had been the
creations of the former Guardian, who had used them to terrorize the people
of the Kamarg before Count Brass came. Count Brass and his men had all but
destroyed the race, but those which remained had learned to hunt by night
and avoid large numbers of men at all costs. The baragoon had once been
men themselves, before they had been taken as slaves to the former Guardian's
sorcerous laboratories and there transformed. Now they were monsters eight
feet high and some five feet broad, bile-colored and slithering on their bellies
through the marshlands, rising only to leap upon and rend their prey with
their steel-hard talons. When they did, on occasion, have the good fortune
to find a man alone they would take slow vengeance, delighting in eating a
man's limbs before his own eyes. (page 11)

That thing won't turn to stone if a friendly wizard can only stall it until
sunrise. Tom Bombadil is not right around the corner ready to bail the
protagonist out the moment he sings a silly song. This thing isn't hoping
to prick you with some kind of magic blade that will slowly overcome you if
you can't make it to the happy refuge of the sparkly elf creatures. No, it just
wants to eat you. And there are stranger and deadlier things out in the wilds
as well.

The world of Moorcock's Hawkmoon series is not a happy place. Instead
of a mythical past where a group of Anglo-Saxon warriors rides to the rescue
in just the nick of time, Moorcock gives us a future where anything remotely
British is synonymous with greed, torture, conquest, and insanity. The people
of that freakish nation all wear horrific animal-faced masks, each different
according to their caste. Their armies march over a silver bridge into Europe
and completely devastate everyone that stands in their way. Country after
country falls to them, and they crucify their enemies' girl children, castrate
their boys, and force the adults to utterly humiliate themselves in the streets
if they want to live. Amarehk isn't coming to bail people out this time like
in all those other world wars. No, Amarehk avoided the worst consequences
of the Tragic Millenium; its godlike rulers are thoroughly isolationist. But
Granbretan will come for them soon enough. It's all too happy to destroy its
enemies piecemeal, and the world is idly standing by and watching it happen.

If you are the sort of person who was irritated by the fact that you never got to actually *see* Sauron in *The Lord of the Rings*, Moorcock throws you another bone here:

> *Eventually Hawkmoon could see the throne globe, and he was astonished. It contained a milky-white fluid that surged about sluggishly, almost hypnotically. At times the fluid seemed to contain iridescent radiance that would gradually fade and then return. In the center of this fluid, reminding Hawkmoon of a fetus, drifted an ancient, ancient man, his skin wrinkled, his limbs apparently useless, his head overlarge. From this head stared sharp, malicious eyes. (page 67)*

And if you felt shortchanged by the fact that you never got more than a hint of what things were like in Sauron's torture chambers, then Moorcock again delivers:

> *This lead into a small, blindingly lighted chamber of white metal that contained a machine of intense beauty. It consisted almost entirely of delicate red, gold, and silver webs, strands of which brushed Hawkmoon's face and had the warmth and vitality of human skin. Faint music came from the webs, which moved as if in a breeze. "It seems alive," said Hawkmoon. "It is alive," Baron Kalan whispered proudly. "It is alive." "Is it a beast?" "No. It is the creation of sorcery. I am not even sure what it is. I built it according to the instructions of a grimoire I bought from an Easterner many years ago." (page 64)*

And instead of building up a menace like the Nazgul that is little more than a source of suspense and a means of constricting the trajectory of the plot, Moorcock just up and gives you the sort of epic action sequences you've always wanted. Yes, Tolkien *did* succeed in giving us the march through Birnam Wood that Shakespeare really ought to have given us in the first place, but his use of the eagles really leaves a lot of people cold. One reason for that is that Tolkien never gave us the epic aerial battle we always wanted. He left that to Michael Moorcock:

> *Count Brass raised his sword in a signal, and there was a great flapping and snapping sound. Looking behind him, Hawkmoon saw the scarlet*

flamingoes sweeping upward, their graceful flight exceedingly beautiful in comparison with the clumsy motions of the metal ornithopters that parodied them. Soaring into the sky, the scarlet flamingoes, with their riders in their high saddles, each man armed with a flame lance, wheeled toward the brazen ornithopters. Gaining height, the flamingoes were in the better position, but it was hard to believe that they would be a match for the machines of metal, however clumsy. Red streamers of flame, hardly visible in the distance, struck the sides of the ornithopters, and one pilot was hit, killed almost instantly and falling from his machine. The pilotless ornithopter flapped on; then its wings folded behind it and it and it plunged downward, to land, birdlike, prow first, in the swamp below the hill. Hawkmoon saw an ornithopter fire its twin flame-cannon at a flamingo and its rider, and the scarlet bird leaped in the air, somersaulted, and crashed to earth in a great shower of feathers. (pages 120-121)

There's some grit and grime mixed in with Moorcock's fight sequences as well. They're not like those in many of the other Appendix N titles. Weapons break. Shields splinter. People get stunned and fall unconscious. Raw strength is a huge factor, but psychology probably matters even more. And people get just plain tired, too. In the end, a lot of fights come down to who has the ability just to get up and deal one last blow when both combatants are already completely exhausted.

Strategy, tactics, and morale all come into play as well. The battles presented here read like they were drawn from real-world actions by guys like Stonewall Jackson or Nathan Bedford Forrest. The combat that results is a consequence not just of the technology and magic but also of the character and attitude of the leaders involved. Moorcock does not take a lot of time to pontificate on these matters, but it's clear he's given thought to this and conveys his vision with one piece of all out action after another.

J. R. R. Tolkien created a sort of an English analog to *The Kalevala*; in a sense, he created a national myth for Great Britain. And to the extent that Tolkien creates a positive picture English and Western people standing against dark forces from out of the east and the south, Moorcock does the exact opposite: His Granbretan is the source of ultimate evil. As shocking as that contrast is, perhaps more surprising is the fact that the antithesis of

Tolkien-style high fantasy is not Robert E. Howard's approach to swords and sorcery. No, the thing that is antithetical to high fantasy is the often brutally dystopian science-fantasy genre.

That sort of wild far future fantasy has all but disappeared today. Concurrently, a lot of people who have been frustrated over the years in their attempts to get the *Dungeons & Dragons* game to better emulate high-fantasy tropes they've come to associate with the fantasy genre. When this doesn't work the way that they want, they usually impose "railroad" style adventures upon it or else just throw up their hands and declare that the system is "broken." Oh sure, there are elves, hobbits, and orcs that look as if they were pulled straight out of Tolkien's oeuvre. But the implied setting of *D&D* and the sort of adventures that people tend to have in it are nothing much like his stories. This leads to no small amount of friction and cognitive dissonance.

The science-fantasy elements of the game were far more pronounced in the early days, of course. A very significant chunk of the books that inspired the game were of that genre, and many people who played the game early on had no problem thinking in terms of it.[2] When the big publishers pushed to crystallize fantasy series around generic high-fantasy themes, *D&D* largely followed suit in order to keep up with the times. And just like Gygax would push to have the monk class removed from *AD&D* once *Oriental Adventures* was on the market, so too would *AD&D* have its science-fantasy elements gradually bled out of it once *Gamma World* could become the repository for everything in that vein.

They could hire Larry Elmore to paint a new set of covers, and they could fine tune the rules in order to adapt to new audiences. But even after taking all those changes and accommodations into account, there's a certain attitude that remains in the mix. Consequently, I would argue that you're probably going to get more gaming inspiration reading Michael Moorcock than you would by reading Tolkien. He can give you a far better understanding of the sort of world that is implied by the rules. Because yes, it's not just Moorcock's work that sprang from an "Anti-Tolkien" approach to fantasy. *D&D* did, too.

Notes

1. See Peter Berbegal's "The Anti-Tolkien" from *The New Yorker* back in December of 2014.

2. Again, see "D&D's Appendix N Roots are Science Fantasy" at *Roles, Rules, and Rolls* for more on that.

The Trail of Cthulhu
by August Derleth

This is unmitigated fan fiction. It is brazen and utterly shameless about it, too. As I read this, I kept looking back to the front to confirm that these stories really did appear within the pages of *Weird Tales* magazine. They really did! Evidently, the editor liked them well enough for it to be worth their time to keep having August Derleth back again and again. But it's shocking to see that this sort of thing not only predates the Internet but that it also was worth publishing in both magazine and paperback format.

I admit, Derleth really does understand the basic structure of a Lovecraft story. He has the protagonist that spends most of the tale in denial about the freaky stuff he's coming across. He has the suspense gradually building as otherwise innocuous events add to the guy's cognitive dissonance. He knows how to implement those Lovecraft style "kickers" where you suddenly find out that this thing you were fretting about is actually much more horrific than you thought could be possible.

It's not bad. But it's not Lovecraft. And it's because of derivative works like this that when we say "Lovecraftian" today, we aren't really referring to Lovecraft's writing half the time. No, we usually mean something much closer to *this*. Heck, the moment we start talking about the "Cthulhu Mythos" we've fairly well departed from Lovecraft already. He wrote most of the stories that now fall under that heading more or less independently. Even when he did have aspects of several horrors colliding within a single story, he didn't tend to throw too many at the reader at once. He usually only gave a brief glimpse of just one aspect of his setting. In contrast, Derleth serves up a circus featuring a rundown of the entire menagerie with each installment. And there are always multiple monster types getting into each other's business.

Lovecraft's oeuvre is so compelling this pretty much works anyway. And if you're a fan, you can't help but get into it. For instance, this scene from early on had me all at once slapping my knee, pointing, face-palming, and shouting in an odd combination of glee and horror all at once:

Never have I felt such extreme and immediate revulsion as I did at the sight of the man on the stoop. There was, admittedly, no streetlight for some distance, and the light which flowed from the hall was so dim as to be more confusing than helpful, but I am prepared to swear that not only was there a grossly batrachian aspect about the fellow's face—irrationally and yet perhaps not inappropriately, there flashed into mind at once the oddly fascinating depiction by Tenniel of the frog footman of the Duchess in Alice in Wonderland—*but that his fingers, where one hand rested upon the iron rail of the stoop, were webbed. Moreover, he exuded an almost overpowering odor of the sea—not that smell so commonly associated with coastal areas, but of watery depths. One might have thought that from his oddly wide mouth there would issue sounds as repulsive as his aspect, but on the contrary, he spoke in flawless English, and inquired with almost exaggerated politeness whether a friend of his, one Señor Timoto Fernandez, had called here. "I have no acquaintance with Señor Fernandez," I answered. He stood for a moment, giving me a contemplative stare which, had I been prey to imaginative fear, would most certainly have chilled me; then he nodded, thanked me, bade me good night, and turned to walk away into the foggy darkness. (pages 11-12)*

Okay, I really do jump at the chance to return to Innsmouth to see what's going on there a few years after what Lovecraft showed us in one of his most famous stories. I want to know more about Devil's Reef. I want to see what goes on in those Esoteric Order of Dagon meetings. I want to know more about what these horrific beings are really up to. Even if it's put together by a guy that can't hold a candle to Lovecraft, I really *would* read something like that.

But I have my limits. The pastiche thing can go too far, as this passage indicates:

"Certain parallels present themselves with damning and inescapable deductions to be drawn. For instance, Dr. Shrewsbury vanished within a year of the publication of his book on myth-patterns. The British scholar, Sir

Landon Etrick, was killed in a strange accident six weeks after he permitted publication in the Occult Review *his paper inquiring into the 'Fish Men' of Ponape. The American writer, H. P. Lovecraft, died within a year of publication of his curious 'fiction',* The Shadow Over Innsmouth. *Of these and others, only Lovecraft's death seems devoid of odd accident. NB: Some inquiry into H. P. L.'s allergy to cold is indicated. Also note a pronounced aversion to the sea and all things pertaining to it, carried so far as to inspire physical illness at sight of sea food. The conclusion is unavoidable that Shrewsbury and Lovecraft, too—and perhaps Etrick and others, as well— were close upon the track of some momentous discoveries concerning C." (page 109-110)*

You know, I read that, and I don't know if I want to cry or pull my hair out. On the one hand, it's a fitting tribute to a brilliant man that died too soon. On the other hand, it's kind of tacky.

That is not, however, the thing about this book that makes me want to throw it against the wall. Really, the most irritating thing about this is the patron-like character that knows more about the occult than just about every Lovecraft protagonist put together. His solution to everything is to find the portals through which Cthulhu is threatening to break and then to blow them up with nitroglycerin or dynamite. He has an unlimited supply of magic items that protect him and his minions from most Mythos-type antagonists. If the really scary stuff is ever threatening to show up, he has a potion he can drink and a whistle he can blow that will together summon a giant bat creature that he can fly to a magic safe house in space.

In other words, these are precisely the sort of innovations you need to apply to Lovecraft's work in order to make it compatible with the typical movie plot or role-playing game scenario. In fact, if you were running a convention game and incorporated elements of what is presented here to players who are familiar with Lovecraft's themes but that have not read the stories in this volume, you could probably make a few people very, very happy. One section in particular that I would recommend incorporating into your game would be the chance for the players to find the Nameless City and actually summon the Mad Arab Abdul Alhazred, the author of the infamous Necronomicon:

I watched Professor Shrewsbury encircle the sarcophagus and both of us with a large band of blue powder, which he immediately set afire. This burned eerily but brightly, so that the entire room was illumined, and the sarcophagus stood out in high relief. My employer then constructed a series of cabalistic designs on the floor and the sarcophagus, again completely encircling it. Thereafter he took from his person certain documents which resembled those transcriptions from the Necronomicon he had given me to read, and from one of them he recited in a clear voice. "Him who knows the place of R'lyeh; him who holds the secret of far Kadath; him who keeps the key to Cthulhu; by the five-pointed star, by the sign of Kish, by the assent of the Elder Gods, let him come forth." This he recited three times, at each adjuration completing a drawing on the floor. At the conclusion of his recitation, he waited. Now there occurred a most unusual and slightly disturbing phenomenon. I felt myself surrendering something of myself, as were I drained of my very life-force, and at the same time there was a movement above the sarcophagus, at first little more than a stirring of air, then a gradual misting, and then before my eyes the remnants and tatters of clothing in the sarcophagus began to lift up into the air and take ragged shape about the misting which was growing steadily denser, losing its opacity for darkness, so that presently there hung above the sarcophagus a spectral image, a blasphemous caricature of a man which had neither body nor face, but only a semblance of each, with black, glowing pits where eyes should have been beneath a torn burnous and a dark shapeless body, very thin, upon which the tatters of garments which long ago were flowing robes hung loosely. This terrifying apparition hung in the air motionless. (page 162-163)

If you play it right, that is sure to be a crowd-pleaser—although I would recommend role-playing a sufficiently creepy voice rather than follow Derleth's lead by having the players play out a tedious game of twenty questions with this thoroughly iconic figure.

There's not much else here that I'm inclined to adapt to my games. I personally think Derleth's framing of the Cthulhu Mythos pretty well neutralizes the whole point of Lovecraft's stories. Mostly, though, I just can't understand it. Each installment has a few passages where he sums up the relationship between a good dozen monstrosities, but these brain dumps read more like name dropping than any serious attempt at conveying something significant about the setting. And unlike similar passages by Lovecraft, they are all more or less interchangeable.

Of course, with Lovecraft being gone, I can see why fans would be happy to take just about anything that kept this informal franchise going. On the other hand, there are developments here that I just flat out detest. I cannot stand the particular spin given to cultists here:

> *Their references to the Ancient Ones intimated too of feuds among these beings, between Hastur and Cthugha on the one hand, and Cthulhu and Ithaqua on the other; evidently these beings were united only against the Elder Gods, but vied with one another for the worship of their minions and the destruction or seduction of such inhabitants of their regions as came within their orbits. (page 198)*

This is not at all what I took from my own reading Lovecraft. The codification of all these bizarre creatures into a formalized Mythos has undercut the verve and the fantastic diversity that made them so compelling in the first place. And the cultists that were all so different from one another in Lovecraft's work, the way they all seemed to be up to something different—that's gone. This makes for a fairly good premise for a fantastic tabletop game like Klaus Westerhoff's *The Stars Are Right*. But really, this sort of thing just doesn't *feel* like a Lovecraft story.

It's the climax that really takes the cake though. I mean, I could see it coming, but I kept reading anyway because I just couldn't believe that August Derleth would really do it.

> *Overhead roared an aeroplane, making for the island. "There it goes," cried General Holberg. "Please look away. Even at this distance the light will be blinding." We turned obediently. In a few moments the sound came, shockingly. In another few seconds the force of the explosion struck us like a physical blow. It seemed a long time before the General spoke again. "Look now, if you like." We turned. Over the place where the Black Island had been loomed now a gigantic cloud, mushrooming and billowing skyward a cloud greater than the size of the island itself, of white and grey and tan colors, beautiful in itself to see. (page 210)*

Yeah. He did it. He nuked Cthulhu from orbit. I don't actually think that would work. I'm inclined to declare that the plot here was derived from completely sophomoric late-night gaming sessions, but tabletop role-playing games were a long way off when Derleth was writing these.

While watching Paul MacClean reviewing the latest edition of *Call of Cthulhu* the other day I was perplexed when he made a tongue-in-cheek reference to some sort of Derlethian Heresy. I had no idea what it could mean at the time, but now I see that it makes quite a bit a sense to pin such a thing on the guy. Derleth had more than a little bit to do with the fact that just about everything you see today with Lovecraft's name on it has next to nothing to do with the man's actual work. And that's just galling. While purists in any genre tend to annoy just about everyone, in this case, I'm inclined to cut them some slack. A shared universe where all kinds of creators could riff off of each other was a great idea in theory. But I'm not too impressed with how it played out in this particular instance.

Swords Against Darkness III
edited by Andrew J. Offutt

While this book was published too late to have any impact on the design of the initial iteration of *Dungeons & Dragons*, it nevertheless merited being singled out in Gary Gygax's list of inspirational reading that appeared in his 1979 *AD&D Dungeon Masters Guide*. Given the wide range of authors presented here, this collection preserves a snapshot of what a significant subgenre of fantasy was like just as role-playing was on the verge of becoming a minor craze. And it's not really that big of a surprise that the influential game designer could get behind a volume like this either. The sorts of situations detailed in the stories here are very much in line with the sort of things people deal with in the course of typical game sessions.

And that's the thing that really sets this volume apart from the other entries on the Appendix N list. When people sit down at a table to throw some dice and have an adventure, you don't tend to see the sorts of worlds and ideas that turn up in so many of the other Appendix N books. You *don't* see the weirdness of Jack Vance's far-future *Dying Earth* setting. You don't see "salt of the earth" barbarians cut from the same cloth as Robert E. Howard's *Conan*. You don't experience the cosmic horror of H. P. Lovecraft. You don't see any Edgar Rice Burroughs-type characters that punch commies and walk off with a beautiful princess either.

Sure, there are games that focus entirely on those properties. But the claim that those works could somehow end up inspiring the original fantasy role-playing game is actually hard to comprehend today. They're just so *different*. Really, the stuff of most *D&D* sessions is going to be more in line with the sort of derivative swords and sorcery that you can easily find in collections like this. A lot of people have never even heard of the heroic fantasy genre that this collection promises, but many of them will immediately recognize it when they read this book. It survives to this day at countless tabletops!

And if I did have to single out one work from this collection that is the most relevant to gamers, it would be Poul Anderson's piece "On Thud and Blunder." It includes a critique of the most common errors in heroic fantasy writing and explains how getting the facts and the history correct not only makes things more realistic but also opens the door to all manner of interesting plot hooks. He addresses everything from economics to religion, warrior women and disease—not to mention armor penetration, two-handed swords, and poisoned weapons. Gamers have, of course, been arguing about these topics for decades, but hearing the author of *The Broken Sword* weigh in on them is just plain fantastic.

This piece has "Gygax" written all over it, too. Yes, Gygax wrote in the *Dungeon Masters Guide* that "the location of a hit or wound, the sort of damage done, sprains, breaks, and dislocations are not the stuff of heroic fantasy." But he is also responsible for including elaborate tables for random ailments, and he made sure to mention that flag lily was a component in medieval cures for venereal disease. As controversial as some of his game design choices were, I think Anderson's piece was something that he nevertheless took seriously. After all, he devoted *six pages* to pole arm nomenclature in *Unearthed Arcana*.

Especially sobering, however, is Anderson's warning to his fellow writers:

> *A small minority of heroic fantasy stories is set in real historical milieus, where the facts provide a degree of control—though howling errors remain all too easy to make. Most members of the genre, however, take place in an imaginary world. It may be a pre-glacial civilization like Howard's, an altered time-line like Kurtz's, another planet like Eddison's, a remote future like Vance's, a completely invented universe like Dunsany's, or what have you; the point is, nobody pretends this is aught but a Never-never land, wherein the author is free to arrange geography, history, and the laws of nature to suit himself. Given that freedom, far too many writers nowadays have supposed that anything whatsoever goes, that practical day-to-day details are of no importance and hence they, the writers, have no homework to do before they start spinning their yarns…. If our field becomes swamped with this kind of*

garbage, readers are going to go elsewhere for entertainment and there will be no more heroic fantasy. (pages 272-273)

Heroic fantasy fiction *did* pretty well disappear in the following decade. But Poul Anderson's craving for verisimilitude found a home among tabletop game design. Indeed, the eighties were a battleground in which every new role-playing product had to be bigger and more comprehensive than the last. Realism was the watchword of gamers in general, and everything from the rules about falling in *AD&D* to the physics of ejection seats in *Car Wars* was hotly debated.

Of course, by the nineties the typical gamer's experience both with role-playing games and the books that inspired them could be summed up in the idea of an action hero racing down a hallway to pick up a first-aid kit that instantaneously replenished his hit points. And by now, arguments about realism are pretty well relegated to how fine the 3D graphics are.

Yet I haven't noticed any excessive outrage among tabletop gamers in response to this trend. Far from being consumed with nostalgia, board gamers are quite happy with the shorter playing times and wider audiences that Euro games bring to the table. While classic hex and chit war games still get played quite a bit, wargamers as a group have taken to the possibilities that block games, card-driven strategy games, and Euro game design elements have opened up for them. If the essence of a conflict can be more readily experienced with half the play time and a learning curve that's not nearly as steep, most gamers are willing to give it a shot.

Is realism passé in gaming? It depends on the genre. Where it counts, though, the realism has to bring something to overall experience. And it cannot anymore come at the expense of either gameplay or accessibility. With computer gaming being ubiquitous and with so many demands on our attention, designers simply cannot afford extraneous detail or complexity like they could back in the eighties. And while I still want to get those old classics played like they deserve, I have to admit that at the moment, we seem to be entering a game design renaissance. We have a lot of great gaming to look forward to.

In order to assess just how relevant these stories were to tabletop fantasy role-playing games, I reviewed them to see how well they fit with the requirements of the typical campaign. Game masters constructing their own settings may find these notes helpful when stocking their wilderness maps.

"The Pit of Wings" by Ramsey Campbell

This story opens with a brief wilderness sequence, but contact with civilization here means encountering injustice that cannot be ignored by heroic barbarian types. In the inevitable clash, combat doesn't have to be initiated by the stock standard reaction roll and initiative sequence. Role-playing the exchange of escalating insults can provide for far more entertaining gameplay. Similarly, "boss" monsters can be more than just a few attack abilities attached to a pile of hit points. It's possible for them to break the scope of the usual combat systems. The end game here demonstrates how the monster itself can be described with a set of three distinct combat situations.

"The Sword of Spartacus" by Richard L. Tierney

This one is just plain awesome. It is exactly the sort of story that Poul Anderson was advocating in his essay. While the plot would be difficult to adapt to a tabletop game session, it could nevertheless serve as a backstory for someone who wants to play an ex-gladiator that's destined for greatness. It's loaded with gaming tropes, though: druids, Etruscan sorcery, relics of heroes from a previous age, undead wizards, and Cthulhu-style demons summoned through gates. The thing that takes the cake here is the idea that ordinary sporting events might have been inherited from people who had very specific religious rituals in mind when they developed them. If you're looking for a game setting that weaves real history with the supernatural, this is an excellent resource.

"Servitude" by Wayne Hooks

This short piece is all about a cursed armband that forces its wearer to kill. The more powerful and influential the victims, the more feelings of love it pumps into the wearer. This produces a state of near invincibility, but the longer it's been since it was satisfied, the harder it is to resist.

SWORDS AGAINST DARKNESS III   219

"Descales' Skull" by David C. Smith

Wishes are a perennial element of classic fantasy role-playing and this story
presents an intriguing way to gain one: by acquiring and reassembling the
skull bones of a dead sorcerer. Seeing as having the consequences of the
wish blow up in their faces and lead the player-character(s) straight to hell
runs against the general gaming requirements of player autonomy, I would
recommend having some other taint factor or mental disadvantage be the
consequence of trafficking with these sorts of evil beings.

"In the Balance" by Tanith Lee

This short but striking piece presents a world where the discipline of magic
is controlled by a monastic order and restricted by a range of moral precepts.
While tests ranging from the Gom Jabbar to the Kobayashi Maru are a staple
of genre fiction, having one that depends upon the content of your character
from the standpoint of traditional morality is rather unusual.

"Tower of Darkness" by David Madison

Small towns and cities with some kind of local trouble are a classic gaming
trope, and every campaign map could stand to have a few of those sprinkled
around. In this story, we get one such town where the people are known to
be sun worshipers. When the adventurers arrive at nightfall, they find all the
inns locked up, and no one will talk to them until they come upon a member
of a group of moon worshipers that offers them hospitality. You can probably
see where this one is going, but this whole situation will certainly give your
players something to argue about. Not to mention a great chance to improve
their status with the locals.

"The Mantichore" by David Drake

The idea that a Manticore could be worth as much in a scenario as we see in this
story is almost hard to imagine. It's not just that fantasy role-playing games
are generally set in worlds where fantastic creatures are merely a fact of life,
either. Most hardcore dungeon crawlers can immediately identify a creature
you're describing based only on the fact that they have the exact same *Monster*

Manual pictures in their head as you do. Big-finale monsters from classic modules are well known even to those who haven't played them because those same critters have been recycled into later products and magazine articles. To get something to happen in your game that's even remotely like this story, the players will have to be facing something that is genuinely unknown, they will have to have heard conflicting rumors on it, and they will have to see evidence of its activities before they encounter it.

"Revenant" by Kathleen Resch

The depiction of vampires as the quintessential bad boyfriend is something that goes back further than you might think.

"Rite of Kings" by John DeCles

The story here makes for a thought-provoking read, but its core element would normally be a disaster at the tabletop. The protagonist has to make a series of three choices based on almost no information. They don't even qualify as genuine riddles, but are more of an opportunity to put the protagonist's flaws on display so that his final comeuppance can have a sufficient punch. In a tabletop role-playing scenario, giving the players a chance to find enough clues to have a chance at making an informed choice at these junctures would help address some of the issues with this. Having each choice impact the scenario in such a way as to not make it unwinnable or impossible to walk away from would be another thing players would tend to expect. Nevertheless, this is so arbitrary, and the number of permutations here is so great that I'm not sure salvaging this sort of thing would even be worth the effort.

"The Mating Web" by Robert E. Vardeman

In spite of their prominence in Tolkien's lore, spiders are often treated as mere vermin in tabletop fantasy role-playing games. And while cutesy attempts to rework classic monsters into misunderstood lonely hearts tends to rub me the wrong way, the treatment we get here is not only a good read, but it is also eminently gameable. This story makes for excellent inspiration on making something a little more out of an otherwise forgettable random wilderness encounter with a giant spider.

"The Guest of Dzinganji" by Manly Wade Wellman

Robot-like creations don't have to be absent from your fantasy world. Gods don't have to be invincible either. This tale features the sole survivor of Atlantis who has killed three different gods with his sword of starmetal... and it rocks! Our games are not like this... and that's too bad!

"The Hag" by Darrell Schweitzer

If there's one thing players should know by now it's that they should never kiss anyone they meet in a dungeon, no matter how beautiful they appear to be. Of course, if there's something stupid to be done, there's almost always one person crazy enough to give it a go, so players will naturally get involved with things best left alone. This particular situation could be thrown at any group that is making nice with a local noble, but the fact that everything culminates into a single individual facing a more or less unfair situation means that it's not the best fit for typical play styles. Nevertheless, game masters looking for inspiration both for giving a backstory for cursed beings and for incorporating the Devil or other demonic entities into play will find this tale worth a look.

"A Kingdom Won" by Geo W. Proctor

When an island people lose the artifact that protected them from the wrath of the gods, everything they have is set to sink into the sea in a matter of days. Without a hero to challenge an evil sorcerer, they will all die before their magic can give them the gills that they need in order to survive in a radically different environment. This could be a perfect opportunity for a bold adventurer to save a princess, win the day, and earn the undying gratitude of an entire people. But what if there is more to this opportunity than first appears? And what if the hero is about to participate in the origin story of a familiar fantasy creature?

"Swordslinger" by M. A. Washil

The more renown the players gain, the more punks are liable to show up looking to pick a fight with them. Again, if you're going to hassle players with this sort of thing, don't forget to play out the dialog leading up to the challenge.

The Carnelian Cube
L. Sprague de Camp and Fletcher Pratt

This book is just plain strange. It's more in line with older works like *Alice in Wonderland* and *The Wizard of Oz* than anything even remotely like *Dungeons & Dragons*. And as much as anything, it reinforces the impression that the fantasy genre as we know it today simply did not exist in the nineteen-forties. It says on the cover there that it's science fantasy, but this is neither a post-apocalyptic mutant-filled wilderness adventure nor a tale of far-future magic where science is forgotten and plate mail is back in style. Perhaps that genre was simply a catchall for titles that don't really fit into *any* conceivable category.

The premise of the story is that archaeologist Arthur Cleveland Finch has acquired the titular cube from an Armenian digger that had declared that it was his "dream-stone." He told Finch that if he slept on it, it would take him to Heaven, which he describes as being "a place where everything is like you want." A colleague then points out that it fits the medieval description of the Philosopher's Stone:

> *"The alchemists were always talking about making gold with it, but when you pinned them down, they always had a metaphysical explanation, something about meaning spiritual perfection by 'gold.' You might say it transmutes the base metal of the actual world into—" "Another nightmare." Finch grinned. "Maybe I will try it."*

Needless to say, it works. And Arthur Finch finds himself in all kinds of trouble in one weird world after another. And I do mean weird. If *Lest Darkness Fall* is any indication, then L. Sprague de Camp supplies both the know-it-all protagonist and a range of historical details. And going by *The Blue Star*, Fletcher Pratt seems to have contributed his penchant for extraordinarily deft world building. Together, these two are a potent combination, effortlessly conveying the sense of entire cultures while making them seem unbelievably real.

But these are not stock standard fantasy or science-fiction settings. These are alternate earths. And while normally people whipping these up tend to be making some sort of thinly veiled political point, if that goes on at all in this novel, then it is too subtle for me to detect. This is not at all like having communists turn up on Venus in an Edgar Rice Burroughs novel. This is not like Kurt Vonnegut's "Harrison Bergeron," an obvious jab at real-world policies and factions. In contrast, de Camp and Pratt just seem to start with their premises, extrapolate from them faithfully, and then let ensuing zaniness go wherever it leads.

In one world, high-ranking politicians form some sort of caste system and are liable to get incoherently violent if something triggers them. They're fairly ineffectual overall, but it's against the law to defend yourself even though the police are never in time to really help. The next world shows an extreme in the opposite direction where Southern notions of chivalry and honor run amok, with rival gangs dominating everything from restaurants to small press publishing. This actually wouldn't be so bad except for the fact that the protagonist's patron is prone to jealousy when it comes to his wife. The kicker is that the guy can actually read minds.

If both of these worlds are shown to be equally barbaric, the final scientifically oriented version of reality manages to go even further. There, nearly everyone is liable to be conscripted into playing parts in massive recreations of everything from the Battle of Waterloo to the reign of Shalmanesar IV. Conditioning ensures that participants won't even know that they're playing a part. And if they come to a bad end, well, that's a small price to pay for great "scientific" results.

These dream worlds are far from being anything like Heaven. Quite the opposite in fact. But if there is one common theme in each of them, it's that bogus intellectual make-work is a foundational element of any good Hell. In the first dream world, Finch takes a job as Genealogist:

"I've had a good deal of experience in history and archaeology." "Youse have? That's much better. The history will give youse your basic research methods, and the archaeology will help youse with the job of faking tombstones when it's necessary." "Faking tombstones?" said Finch, wonderingly. "Sure.

Youse'll see. Rational thing to do; harms no one and satisfies the people that commission youse. Reckon youse had best get a couple of textbooks, and then call me in if youse strike a hard case. De William's Methodology of Geneology—I can loan youse a copy of that—and Morgan's Historic Families of Kentucky are about what youse need to start with. Don't take De Williams' hyperaletheism too seriously, though." "His what?" "Hyperaletheism. Higher-truth theory. His school holds that when one goes back a sufficient number of generations, everybody is bound to be descended from everybody by the laws of probability, so that a faked pedigree showing a descent from Charlemagne is virtually as good as a real one, since the person at issue is bound to be descended from him. He fails to distinguish between genealogies carefully prepared for the district archives and those prepared on commission for patrons." (page 49)

In the world of the ultra-violent Pegasus Literary Society, everything is a sham backed by force. Stopping off for a bit to eat means you're liable to be served whatever the proprietor feels is good for you. If you don't like it, then he'll see to it that you're coerced into enjoying it!

"Come on, boys," said Colonel Lee. "Suh, the honor of the Pegasus will not permit our tastes in food and drink to be dictated to us." "No ye don't!" roared MacPherson. "Ye ha' come to me for nourishment, and nourished ye shall be." The inner doorway was suddenly filled with five more leopard-skinned giants. As Impy fumbled for a gun one of the new-comers pounced on him. Finch had a brief and apprehensive glimpse of the two locked in a struggle for the zenith-pointed firearm which went off with a roar. Then in a moment the whole party of visitors was disarmed and on their stools, with a blonde Hercules behind each. "Eat!" said MacPherson. With sour looks and downcast faces, they pecked at the salads. "Ow!" yelled Basil Stewart suddenly. "What's the matter, Wullie?" rumbled the proprietor. The monster behind Stewart explained: "Pop, this dissipator was trying to stuff his watercress into that fancy coat of his, so you'd think he'd et it." "Beat his harnies out against the wall if he tried it again," said MacPherson, amiably. (page 84)

Finally, the science-themed world combines the first reality's nonsense with the second world's thuggery and then slathers a mathematical veneer over the top. And even though bartenders are called Methymiscologists and everyone glibly chats about the implications of vector analysis over mixed drinks, *repeating* experiments is actually forbidden. The scientific method is replaced with science-themed snake-oil, and the entire planet is eaten up with a "cult of the new" mentality:

> *"Sir, you are anti-familiar with the basis of astrological science. In the procedure of approximatively, we calculate from the sign in the ascendant at the exact moment of birth. But whereas many individuals are unable to recollect this necessary moment, there was introduced some time ago the determination procedure of assumptivizing as in the ascendant the sign occupied by the sun at horizontary ascension." "I see. I should think that would give quite different results. If I were born at sunset the sign in the ascendant might be the Dipper, but by the previous sunrise it might have been the Bridge-Table or something." Beauregard smiled. "Sir, I suspect you are ridiculizing. Ursa Major is not within the zodiacal limitations and there ain't no constellation of the Bridge-Table. The horoscopular reading depends largely upon the relative positions of the planets, and while that is very little changed, sir, in the course of twenty-four hours, very little, you undebatively have a talking point. I feel that way about it myself." "Why in the world do you call the new method the 'accurate' one, then?" Washington Beauregard looked astonished. "Dr. Finch, are you humorizing me again? The entire system of scientific seniority rests on the fact that a new method is better than an old one, since it outroots the errors of earlier practitioners in response to new evidentiary matter." (pages 179-180)*

Reading this book, it becomes clear just how much of our fantasy maps are filled with thinly veiled historical appropriations and outright clichés. There's a reason for that, of course. Whether you're running a game or telling a story, pausing to explain the counter-intuitive aspects of an alien civilization at every turn tends to cause an unworkable amount of drag. It's a completely fair move to admit up front that you're not going to expend any effort with that sort of thing. But if you have a yen to take the opposite tack and really focus on the implications and consequences of cultures that are set up on radically differing premises, then this book will provide you with invaluable inspiration.

The Warrior of World's End
by Lin Carter

Lin Carter is better known for editing the Ballantine Adult Fantasy Series, but this volume from 1974 is anything but a backward glance at the forgotten classics of fantasy. Rather than a mythic past, this tale is set in a far future where the twentieth century isn't even a dim memory. And though this volume came too late to have an impact on the development on the earliest iteration of *Dungeons & Dragons*, the strange group of quirky protagonists presented here is nevertheless immediately recognizable as a group of player-characters from a role-playing game.[1] This is basically gaming fiction from a time when gaming as we now know it really didn't exist yet!

The title character is a Construct, a super-strong "hero" type prematurely set loose from a Time Vault. (And note that we never find out about the peril which was foreseen by the Time Gods and which he was created to forestall.) His Illusionist mentor might well have been the reason why *AD&D* included that specialized variant of the magic-user class. And the knightrix is right in line with seventies-era depictions of both *Red Sonja*, who first appeared in 1973, and *Power Girl*, who debuted in 1976 although she *is* occasionally consumed with an overwhelming desire to go shopping. But more than any other Appendix N book, this *feels* exactly like the implied setting of *AD&D*. Not only are there vast stretches of wilderness with all manner of unruly humanoid races warring amongst themselves, but there is also all manner of domain-like entities competing with one another as well. It's such a perfect fit for tabletop gaming it's almost uncanny.

As wild and chaotic as the setting might be, there is nevertheless a single language that these diverse cultures and monster groups can converse through:

> The naked creature, who certainly appeared manlike, did not seem to under-
> stand the language spoken by the periaptist. This in itself was odd, for the

same universal tongue is spoken across the length and breadth of Gondwane.
And, since the land surface of Old-Earth's last continent in this age totaled
sixty-million square miles—shared between one hundred and thirty-seven
thousand kingdoms, empires, city-states, federations, theocracies, tyrannies,
conglomerates, unions, principates, and various degenerate, savage, barbar-
ian or Nonhuman, hordes, all holding the same language in common—you
could spend a lifetime of journeys without encountering a sentient creature
speaking an unfamiliar language. (pages 14-15)

Game groups that would prefer to hand-wave the languages of the monster
tribes in their campaign in favor of a universal "common" tongue have in this
book a literary antecedent to justify their decision. And for those that chafe
against the sort of human-dominated world that Gary Gygax had in mind
when he added severe level limits to demi-human classes in *AD&D*, this book
provides a look at the kind of setting he might have been trying to avoid:

In these, commonly believed to be the Last Days, trueborn humanity was
a dwindling, perhaps a dying species. Evolution had continued its subtle,
invisible surgery amid the gene pool of Terrene life-forms, and many new
races of beasts as well as sentient humanoids had arisen to challenge Man's
dominance of the Last Continent in the Twilight of Time. The Pseudowomen
of Chuu were but the most harmless of these curious and often inimical
creatures; the Halfmen of Thaad, the Death Dwarfs, the mobile and perhaps
sentient Green Wraiths, the Strange Little Men of the Hills, the Tigermen of
Karjixia, the Talking Beasts, the Stone Heads of Soorm, and many another
breed shared the supercontinent with True Men, and often on an even footing.
(pages 18-19)

Despite the superficial similarities, this doesn't really feel like TSR's *Gamma*
World. There are irreplaceable flying bubble cars that are de facto relics even
though they were in production a mere generation ago. One kingdom has
the resources to outfit its warriors with crystal armor and electric swords. But
there is a uniqueness to most of the artifacts depicted here; it is as if they
were generated by magical engineering rules rather than pulled from canned
equipment lists. For instance, the brass Bazonga bird on the cover would
count as a golem in most *D&D* campaigns even though it's the ultra-rare
gravity reversing element yxium which makes it possible for her to fly.

This really *is* a great premise for a game, though:

You see, there was once a time when all of human civilization had been reduced to one small country, the Thirteenth Empire it is called. It was almost the Last Empire, because except for Grand Velademar all the rest of Gondwane was a savage wilderness where dangerous beasts and wild, uncivilized Nonhumans fought each other for supremacy. When the Thinker was released from his Time Vault, at a place called Aopharz, the end of the world was only a thousand years away. A barbarian horde was arising in Farj and Quonseca; in time it would sweep across Gondwane, trampling the Thirteenth Empire into the dust, slaying or enslaving the last True Men. This could have been the extinction of mankind; at the very least, it would have meant the end of our civilization. (pages 58-59)

With human civilization being reduced to the remnants of a single shattered polity, there is no shortage of trouble to be found. Even better, the fact that there are so few superpowers in this setting means that the foes are at a scale where even a small group of individualistic adventurers could really make waves on the campaign map. Change out several of those Nonhuman domains for thinly veiled Vikings, Teutons, and Anglo-Saxons, and you pretty much have something fairly close to a good chunk of the active *D&D* campaigns from the past four decades![2]

For people looking for inspiration for making a fantasy setting that *feels* different from that of medieval Europe, Lin Carter shows a world where the *Godmakers* cannot keep up with the demand for the new and the different:

A barbarian chieftain from the Largroolian plains desired a new godling with thirteen heads, each more hideous than the last, and the whole carved from a single block of ongga wood twenty feet high; for that order, Phle-sco billed the tribe for five hundred ounces of glelium. A shaman from the community of hermits who inhabited fumaroles in the peak of Mount Ziphphiz in Garongaland commissioned him to create a god of the winds and the airy spaces which should be as light as air itself, but durable as steel. Phlesco executed the commission by shaping an immense bubble of blown glass filled with helium, the glass impregnated with strands of boron twelve molecules thick and ninety million long, and thus unbreakable. For that, his fee was princely.... Each Godmaker had his own specialty, and

none had cause to resent the success of another; Old Galzolb, for instance,
tended to execute colossuses, his principal achievement having been to carve
an entire mountain into the form of the Sleeping God of Xoom in his youth;
sprightly, affable Izzilp, on the other hand, sculpted gods in miniature, and
once reproduced the entire pantheon of the Zul-and-Rashemba mythos on
one side of a single pearl....(page 21-22)

This is a truly pluralistic setting as far as religion is concerned; each tribe has
wildly different mythologies, cosmologies, and beliefs. It's downright raucous
compared to most fantasy treatments of the topic, many of which seem to
assume that religion is largely benevolent, private, and distinct from government. Other fantasy religions are little more than watered-down versions
of the Greek pantheon, which tends to be so unsatisfactory that people will
react against it by either using real-world religions or else eliminating religion
entirely.

In contrast to this, Lin Carter could have a little fun with the topic. (The
moral panic that held sway over gaming in the eighties was nowhere in sight
when he was writing, after all.) When the protagonists show up to a strange
city, they are all forced to wear huge pink on asparagus-green signs that say
this:

BEWARE, O YE FAITHFUL! THE WEARER BE AN ATROCIOUS
IDOLATOR OF FALSE GODS AND INTERDICTED CULTS AP-
PROACH HIM/HER/IT AT YOUR SOUL'S PERIL!

When things get out of hand, there are the inevitable trumped-up charges:

"The male creature is guilty of Tabard Discarding, Interruption of Priestly
Duties, Disturbance of the Civic Tranquility, Ecclesiastical Assault, Defiance
of the Peace Monitors, Unwarranted Flight, Theft of Hierophantic Property,
and Exceeding the Speed Limit," droned a bored Justiciar. "The female,
already adjudged guilty of Lapsed Conversion, is newly guilty of Resisting
Chastisement, Ecclesiastical Assault, Defiance of the Peace Monitors, Un-
warranted Flight, Maintaining a Dangerous Confederate, and in aiding
and abetting each of the nine points of Unlawfulness whereof her accomplice
has just been adjudged guilty. The case is closed; the culprits are to be sold
into slavery for the Public Good." (page 96)

At the other extreme, Lin Carter presents a man who has made himself into a god. Admittedly, this is an old story going back at least as far as Alexander the Great. But there's something different about it when it's combined with drug addiction and an array of fantastic futuristic artifacts:

> *The Elphod was there in all his wrath, moonsilver glittering on his golden armor. An aerial chariot drawn by a dozen Phlygûl had borne him to the scene of battle. He stood erect, thundering imprecations in a mighty voice…. In his right gauntlet the Elphod clutched a curious weapon. A rod of shimmering crystal, it was, terminating into a coppery cup. And that cup held a blazing sphere of naked energy. (page 146)*

The guy's no slouch either. He's like a James Bond villain that has actually been able to get away with his world domination schemes for decades. From his city in the sky, he extorts money from the nearby Tigermen. If they don't pay… *he'll steal their air!*

This is not exactly a lost masterpiece of classic fantasy, but the fact that it's eminently suited to tabletop role-playing makes this volume stand out from the pack. And between the map and the glossary, it's already half way to being a playable RPG supplement just as it is. If you are looking for something to help you break out of the rut of habit and tradition, then this volume makes for an inspiring contrast to the more derivative works that flooded the market in the decades after its release. If you're looking for a fresh way to frame up the implied setting of classic *D&D*, however, then this book will be a goldmine. It doesn't surprise me at all that Gary Gygax included it on his list of inspirations.

Notes

1. They really could pass for a set of iconic characters for *GURPS Fourth Edition*.

2. In "REVIEW: Points of Light," James Maliszewski says that this style of play has "been a setting assumption of D&D from the start."

The Shadow People
by Margaret St. Clair

The cover on this one is outrageously mismatched to its actual content. There simply isn't a Conan clone to be found within the pages of this book. There's not even anything *remotely* like a swords and sorcery tale here. It's as if in 1969, Robert E. Howard had defined fantasy in the minds of typical fans to such an extent that this was the only way to really market a work like this. Either that or the publisher just had this artwork sitting around and elected to save money by not getting something more appropriate. Either way, if you ever needed a canonical example of why you can't judge a book by its cover, this is it!

The novel is *actually* about a couple of hipsters in Berkeley:

We did not consider ourselves members of the hip community, though I sup-pose an outsider would have—I worked on the staff of the local hip newspaper and had a luxuriant mustache, and Carol was ambitious in noncommercial film making. We rarely turned on with anything. (pages 5-6)

And this isn't quite the "real" world either. America in this setting is becom-ing more and more of a police state, primarily due to hysteria over drug use. The rednecks from *Easy Rider* are pretty much in charge of everything. There are riots, food shortages, and oppressive bureaucracies powered by building-sized computers. Much of this would be well in line with extrapolations of late-sixties social upheaval, but Margaret St. Clair takes it further by introducing robot enforcers:

I had taken a zigzag course through the night, hiding in shadows, listening for the patrol, and trying to avoid the sensors of the robofuzz. The machine caught up with me on Durant. In quite a pleasant mechanical voice, it told me to halt. Then it sprayed me with a paralyzing nerve gas and felt around my neck with its prostheses for the Id disk that ought to have been hanging there. For some reason, perhaps that I had eaten so much atter-corn, the paralysant had no effect on me. I shoved Merlin's sword through the grid that covered the thing's viewer and shorted it out in a shower of sparks. (page 92)

Admittedly, the robofuzz are not a major component of the plot. St. Clair blithely introduces them and then hardly even revisits the theme again. Nevertheless, they provide quite a shock to anyone expecting a straight-ahead fantasy story. And they're not the sole science-fiction element incorporated here either. Merlin is just short of being some kind of space alien:

"Who was Merlin, though? You surely don't mean the enchanter in the Arthurian romance?" "No-o-o." Fay seemed to arrange her thoughts. "I think Merlin was a great—magician—who visited our Earth between two and three thousand years ago. I suppose the character of the Arthurian Merlin was ultimately derived from him." "You said 'visited our earth.' Where did the Merlin of the sword come from? Outer space?" Fay wrinkled up her nose. "No, upper space. Do you remember how, in the basement, it seemed that a greater world than ours was impinging on us? I think that greater world is what Merlin came from. The Macrocosmos." (page 145)

But again, as with the robofuzz, this doesn't really come into the story all that much either. The focus is squarely on a psychedelic iteration of Elfland called Underearth. Entrances to this place are scattered around the world, and the passages through cellars and caves seem to violate conventional notions of space and geometry. Elves routinely journey to our world to do anything from pilfering food to making rat-like noises in the walls of peoples' houses to kidnapping women and forcing them to serve as wetnurses for their young.

As with many fairy tales, there is an arbitrary prohibition governing interactions with this mythical place:

"The most important thing is not to eat or drink while you are gone. Remember that…. You must take food and water with you. Don't be tempted to eat what you find or what they offer you." (page 22)

A reddish meal is found in tins scattered throughout the underworld, and they are regularly replenished by elves. A person who eats this food will probably never leave Underearth again. Its effect on people is to first get them high, then to cause them to have vivid hallucinations that they're one animal after another, and finally to induce a period of prolonged misery. In the aftermath of its primary effects, the user will be overcome with fatigue and will usually find a cleft in the caves to crawl into while entering a period of hibernation.

The attercorn is not sustaining in and of itself, however. Elves and men whose diet consists entirely of that meal will eventually become so ravenously hungry for meat that they will be driven to cannibalism. Meanwhile, people who do manage to escape Underearth after consuming attercorn will end up suffering debilitating withdrawal symptoms that range from weakness to severe muscle cramps and on to seizures and worse. This, of course, has even more dangerous complications out in the "Bright World":

"Two or three months ago," he said, "an interesting sample came into my hand. It was an ounce or so of some reddish cereal, coarsely ground, and it had a bitter taste. It was said to be a powerful intoxicant. I turned it over to our—to some chemists I know—and they were interested." I felt a thrill of alarm. "You say 'a sample came into my hands,'" I said, enunciating carefully. "Who gave it to you? What was the source?" "Oh, a man who worked for one of my employers. His name was Hood. I don't know where he got it originally. Anyhow, the chemists got working on it. They were interested, very interested. They ran a lot of tests on it." Sweat was running down my back. That Howie had narcotics-bureau connections was news, and bad news.... "What's this got to do with us?" Carol asked. I doubt Howard noticed the tremor in her voice. "I want more of that meal," he said. "An ounce doesn't go very far when there are a lot of tests to run on it. Also, I want information on the conditions under which the meal was produced. The chemists say the reddish color probably comes from some fungus growing on the grain. What were the conditions under which it grew? You see what I mean." (pages 164-165)

Strange magic is not the domain of Underearth alone, however. The dystopian America of this story is a place where moderately "hip" people can scry with a tumbler of Spanish sherry in order to get a solid lead for whatever adventure hook they're stumped on. Ordinary guys can get surprisingly accurate readings just by laying down Tarot cards and giving them a fumbling "textbook engineer" read.

But the elves of this story are especially strange. They are not the pointy-eared Vulcan supermen of typical fantasy fare of today. Neither are they the dainty, elegant sprites of the Cottingley Fairy hoax. They are weird, frightening creatures that live in an underworld where they are on an almost perpetual bad trip. The only reason they come out into our world at all is because they have the munchies. The weirdest thing about them—and I almost have trouble even imagining this—is that they don't have any bones. They almost couldn't get any weirder except that they also follow some kind of fairy story logic:

> Carol said, "Didn't Fay say something once about a way of compelling elves to an exchange of gifts?" "I think so," I said. "It was when she was having dinner with us once, and she said— umh— yes, I remember." I took an even firmer grip on the elf and bent down so my face was only a few inches from its own. "As I to thee, thou to me," I said as impressively as I could. The elf blinked three or four times and then looked away from me. But it had blinked; I found the pine cone I had been chipping at, and held it out to the creature. Reluctantly and slowly, it took the cone and stowed it away somewhere in its clothing. "Give me what you brought," I told it. The elf didn't move. Well, I hadn't thought this was going to be so easy as Fay had made it sound. "Give me what Fay sent us," I said. And when it still didn't show any sign of obeying, I added, "I command you by the hilt and power of Merlin's sword." That did it. (pages 186-187)

Whether your idea of fantasy is something more in line with seventies-era heroic fantasy or eighties style Tolkien pastiche, this book is likely to be a shock. It's just so different. In a lot of ways, it's very much in line with how C. S. Lewis set up his Narnia stories. There are elements here that are straight out of older works like *The King of Elfland's Daughter* and *The Broken Sword*... but it's jolting to see them applied in a more contemporary context. It's also surprising to see this sort of thing done in something other than a young adult format. But just as fairy-tale lore was once relegated to the nursery, we have largely reserved this type of storytelling as a vehicle for the adventures of school-aged children.

Saying that will, of course, invite people to produce counterexamples from more recent authors—Neil Gaiman and Terry Pratchett not least among them. And it may be the case that readers of fantasy are just not going to be that impressed by some of these older works. In gaming, however, I believe the culture shock is liable to be much more pronounced. And even though *D&D* was itself inspired by a wildly diverse range of fantasy and science fiction, it nevertheless is the culprit here.

The thing that I would pinpoint as the real kicker here would be the page on designing a wilderness from the old Cook/Marsh *Expert* rulebook. Consider these headings from page 54:

A. Decide on a Setting B. Draw a Map of the Area C. Place the Dungeon and the Base Town D. Locate Areas Under Human Control E. Place Areas Under Non-Human Control F. Outline the Base Town G. Fill in Important Details and Points of Interest H. Create Special Encounter Tables and General Lairs

Now, I hasten to say that there's nothing especially wrong with this. In fact, to have a great summer of gaming, all you really need is Part C. Throw in even a moderately detailed wilderness environment as described here, and you can run a campaign for *years* in this sort of framework. Judged solely on the amount of time that people have dedicated to playing this style of game, this is easily the most significant idea to hit tabletop gaming in the past fifty years.

The thing that concerns me most here is Part A:

The DM should decide what the area will be like overall. It may be mountains or steppes, woods or desert. It may be based on a fantasy novel or created entirely by the DM.

It's pretty clear that this passage is concerned almost entirely with the purely naturalistic aspects of terrain. All of the many things that could play into what we mean by "setting" are omitted from the discussion here. The implication is that the DM will simply lean on the classes, races, and monsters of the core rules and pretty well take the overall implied setting of the game more or less at face value. And this makes sense given that this is a follow up to the introductory product that was designed to ease new players into gaming without the benefit of being initiated by someone who had sat in at least once with veterans of the Geneva, Wisconsin sessions.

Still, it's often the things that people take on uncritically in this manner that most impacts the way that they view things. And it's a fact that even though the game emerged from such wildly diverse inspirations, *there's nothing really here to put the gamer in touch with the kind of creativity that inspired the game in the first place.* It's gone, really. And what's worse, there's nothing here that really indicates that it's gone either.

But maybe I'm expecting too much from an intentionally simplified product. That's fair to say. But you can see this overriding philosophy carry over into later, more "deluxe" supplements as well. Consider this passage on setting design from *The Dungeoneer's Survival Guide*:

> *A few fundamental decisions must be made before the world design can properly begin. The scope of the campaign must be determined so that the DM knows what to define. An underground campaign, for example, requires little detailing of continents, seas, and nations on the surface world. A city, town, or village location is probably still necessary if the PC's are themselves surface dwellers—this provides them with a base of operations. (page 100)*

That exact same sequence from the *Expert* book is still the main driving force here. And note that when the question of fundamentals is addressed, little more than geography is what's being referred to. Granted, this is still a very focused supplement for a very focused game system. Yet, I don't see the kind of breakdown I'm looking for in a much more comprehensive book like *GURPS Fantasy Fourth Edition*, either.

Now the first edition of that tome consisted of a magic system and a single setting that was a pretty good fit for the earliest incarnation of the game. This latest iteration attempts to take on the whole of fantasy—the whole spectrum of genres. However, as is often the case with *GURPS*, you pretty much have to know what you want beforehand in order to make the toolkit produce the sort of thing you're looking for. The sections on the different types of fantasy are so concise that there's time for little else than to name drop a few signature authors, for instance. And though the information that's contained here is solid and hits most all of the major themes, the impression that the material leaves is that all of these different approaches amount to little more "skins" to overlay on the *GURPS* engine.

What's really needed here is for more of the dials and options involved with setting design to be exposed. And that's why I think Margaret St. Clair's offbeat novel is so useful as gaming inspiration. It's so far out of the range of what most people even tend to think of as fantasy that it can make people think about things that they don't even realize that they are taking for granted. Following her lead, here are a few things I would pay particular attention to when creating a setting for fantasy gaming:

- **How the Milieu Is Connected to the Real World** – Establishing the setting's relationship to the real world was once de rigueur, but this is increasingly seen as optional. Just as one example, this was the first thing that was done to *AD&D* when it was adapted to Saturday morning cartoons, but it doesn't have to be kids' stuff. On ABC's *Lost*, it was the mundane details of everyone's backstories that gave meaning to the action on the island. Ongoing traffic between Elfland and the real world is not something you tend to see due to its inherently elusive nature, but that's one thing that we get to see in *The Shadow People*.

- **Science-Fiction Elements** – Margaret St. Clair could drop *Robocop* into the middle of her fantasy novel like it was no big deal. And even Tolkien had his share of anachronisms. Truth be told, Lobelia's umbrella, Bilbo's waistcoat, Sam Gamgee's potatoes, and Denethor's heathen kings didn't belong in his mythic past setting, so science fiction does *not* have to be off limits! And there can be much more to it than just the presence of laser pistols and powered armor.

- **The Nature of Elves** – It's interesting how dropping hobbits and their ilk from a setting has a significant impact on the overall tone of a fantasy game. But if you start messing around with elves, there's no telling what will happen. They're that elemental—that fundamental to peoples' views of how fantasy should be. And if you're the sort of reader who is irritated with how vampires and werewolves have lost their edge over the years, it's good to remember that elves got the "sparkle" treatment far earlier.[1]

- **What is at stake?** – If the worlds of elves and men collide, there is bound to be conflict. Too often, elves simply remain in their forests and provide an endless supply of player-characters for adventuring groups to throw into the maw of the nearest dungeon. While Lord Dunsany and Poul Anderson both showed how interactions with Elfland could spill over into significant changes on the campaign map, Margaret St. Clair keeps things focused here on an individual kidnapping victim. This wasn't actually sufficient for the publisher though. The back cover blurb implies that the drug addict elves are planning to subjugate all mankind and reduce them to being mere cattle!

- **Cosmology** – This one has suffered the most over the past few decades. Part of this was that there was a period in the eighties where more realism was the answer to practically every gaming problem. And what's more, eliminating the spiritual dimension was often justified as a means to avoiding offending people, and some of the stranger aspects of fantasy got toned down by people who thought they had better avoid trouble. While I can see the pull of that sort of thinking, if there should be a default for fantasy setting design, it is that creators should at least take a stab at coming up with some kind of cosmology. Certainly, the creatures that populate the fantasy world will have their own views on how reality is organized. Margaret St. Clair's breakdown between Middle Earth, the Underearth, and the Overworld is a venerable and very workable approach that can serve as a great starting point if you don't know where to begin.

A lot of game masters today have radically different assumptions about fantasy than what Margaret St. Clair had. But the thing is that Gary Gygax had more in common with her than with most of us! Questions of cosmology—from the player's choice of alignment to the various planes that corresponded to them in the game's multiverse—were front and center for him. The iconic cover of the *AD&D Dungeon Masters Guide* depicts "three adventurers and an efreet on the Elemental Plane of Fire." If that's not epic enough, the back cover depicts "the fabled City of Brass… floating over a flame-swept sea of oil." I know for myself that over the years, I would have hesitated to take a group of players to such places; my own imagination just wasn't up to the job. But after sitting down and reading the books that inspired the game's contributors in the first place, I have to say that that sort of thing really does seem to be in line with how the game was meant to be played.

Notes

1. A naturalistic approach such as was done in *Underworld: Evolution* reduces vampires and werewolves to goth-themed superheroes whose battles reflect the action of a first-person shooter more than anything else. The movie version of Legolas is little different.

The Fallible Fiend
by L. Sprague de Camp

What if demons weren't monstrous spiritual forces out to corrupt the souls of humans that have dealings with them? What if instead they were rather strong and fairly unattractive but other than that were just plain, ordinary, upstanding folks? Salt of the earth types, as it were.... And what if there was *a reason* they had to make pacts with the human beings of the Prime Plane— an entirely mundane thing, too? What if they would allow themselves to be summoned by magicians and accept a year of indentured servitude in return for ingots of iron, an element which happens to be extremely rare on their home in the Twelfth Plane?

L. Sprague de Camp brings answers to all these questions and more in this short novel marketed by Signet as *science fiction* no less. Not that I ever had questions like those on my mind before. I mean, the stuff in this book is the last thing that I expected to read about in all those other books that have covers featuring some wicked-looking demonic monster trapped inside a wizard's pentagram. For a book featuring a demon as a protagonist, precious few of the usual tropes put in an appearance. Nobody goes to a pit of everlasting torment. Nobody gets possessed. Nobody throws up on well-meaning clergymen.

But check out this profound wisdom of demon civilization:

- *"As we say in my world, perfection waits upon practice." (page 40)*

- *"As we demons put it, well begun is half done." (page 71)*

- *"As we say in demon land, it is an ill tide that washes nobody's feet clean."* (page 89)

- *"As we say at home, self-conceit oft precedes a downfall." (page 104)*

That's Poor Richard's Almanac meets Gaffer Gamgee meets King Solomon right there. And that pretty well sums up demon culture in a nutshell. Oh, they're scaly, they have emotion-sensing catfish whiskers, they have chameleon-like abilities, they're stronger than they look, and their digestive stupors can last well over a day. But they're also monogamous, law abiding, industrious, and honest to a fault. They are Benjamin Franklin's autobiography *in the flesh.*

And next to these guys, humanity necessarily comes off as looking pretty shabby. A magician knows through clairvoyance what peril faces a nearby town, but in order to hold out for as much extortion money as possible, he ends up telling them the details only *after* it is too late for them to do anything about it. A circus owner gives his workers a raise but then wins back their earnings by cheating them at cards. A brigand that takes from the rich and gives to the poor shows promise as being the first truly idealistic person on the Prime Plane, but it turns out that he and his crew are the poorest people they know, so they keep all of their loot to themselves.

This sort of thing could have been thought-provoking or perhaps provided some sort of comment on the human condition. As it stands, de Camp is merely playing this up for laughs. And as the story goes on, the society of demons turns out to be a little too perfect to be believable. They do not practice war and really don't even have a concept of rape. Meanwhile, what about the cannibals that are harvesting entire nations for people they can salt down for the winter? To them, they have the moral high ground because their victims are guilty of waging war on *one another.* In their view, "The only legitimate reason to slay another human being is to eat him." (page 119)

Unless you really want something over the top, you won't find these cultures to be particularly inspiring for your games. Although there is something to the contrast between the nomads, the cave men, the cannibals, and the more urban peoples detailed here. What's really useful is how they behave immediately following the big battle. This really is de Camp's main point with this novel, as the demon character explains:

I have read many of those imaginary narratives that Prime Planers compose for one another's amusement, which are called "fiction." We have nothing like this on the Twelfth Plane, being too logical and literal-minded a species to enjoy it. I confess, however, that I have acquired a taste for the stuff, even though my fellow demons look at me askance as if I had become addicted to a dangerous narcotic. In these imaginary narratives, called "stories", the human authors assume that the climax of the story solves all the problems posed and brings the action to a neat, tidy end. In a story, the battle of Ir would have been the climax. Then the hero would have mated with the heroine, the villains would have been destroyed, and the leading survivors, it is implied, would have lived happily ever after. In real life it is different. (page 125-126)

This is, of course, an indictment against all fantasy and science fiction that followed the Edgar Rice Burroughs-style of storytelling. And it's funny, but *The Lord of the Rings* falls in line with this through the marriages of Aragorn to Arwen and Faramir to Éowyn. *The Hobbit* is actually less clichéd on this point because the death of Smaug does not lead to the standard happy ending, but to Bilbo sneaking off with the Arkenstone in an attempt to forge peace between men, dwarves, and elves.

Gamers are especially prone to make the sort of simplifications that de Camp pokes fun at here. Our rule sets are very strong when it comes to resolving conflicts, whether they be small-scale skirmishes or titanic battles. They are significantly less detailed about how the resolution of one engagement might lead to the next. Even with something simple like what would happen in a dungeon in the weeks following the elimination of a particular faction, you're not liable to get a lot of help from the guides and modules. A good game master pretty much has to arbitrarily take all the variables and incidental bits and frame up a follow-up scenario based on little more than sound judgment, common sense, and a solid hunch on what would be most fun for everyone in involved.

Players, of course, are often looking for something that *feels* like a victory condition to them, even when there isn't one explicitly engineered into the situation. In fact, players of all kinds of role-playing games will create narratives from completely random things that have transpired in a game and then set off to place themselves within the happy ending that they are sure is to be found by following it up. Half the time, it's just as well for the game master to accept the player version of game reality, too. It might be better than what he had in mind in the first place, after all! Or it might just be easier to build on their assumptions than it would be to explain what they were "supposed" to see in the first place.

It's the question of how a series of victories impact a campaign's overall state that's particularly thorny though. Again, there is almost no way for a game designer to anticipate what a game master would really need to make a fair decision on this. The proverbial "want of a nail" phenomenon stands ready to rear its head in even the most carefully constructed scenarios.

My advice for dealing with this is first to take de Camp's advice to heart. Don't be afraid to ask the players what *they* think might happen as a result of their actions. For one thing, they are liable to be far more devious than you are. But really, simulating an entire world is too big of a job for one guy anyway. Take everything that's suggested, take into account the things that the players don't even know about, and then assign the outcomes an arbitrary chance of happening. Roll the dice and follow the results wherever they lead, *especially* if it ruins whatever script you might originally have had in mind.

This is the point where campaigns take on a life of their own: a place where whatever narrative expectations you might have had cease to be relevant and everyone is forced to go off the rails. And even though tabletop role-playing games were inspired by a diverse range of fantasy and science-fiction novels, it doesn't mean that they have to follow the same conventions as genre fiction. In fact, it's the *lack* of an artificial happily-ever-after moment that's part of what keeps people coming back for session after session. Out of the box, the classic role-playing games were designed with the assumption that their campaigns would continue after months of weekly game sessions that could each last well over six hours apiece. And even in this day of innumerable entertainment options and distracting gadgets, they are still capable of maintaining that surprising degree of investment and attention.[1] Even the most subtle aspects of a player's choices can have unexpected ramifications, and not even the game master knows how things will ultimately play out.

Notes

1. See Zak S.'s article "Why I Still Love 'Dungeons & Dragons' in the Age of Video Games" for a great piece on this point.

The Stealer of Souls
by Michael Moorcock

Michael Moorcock's Elric has a tremendous following. And it's true, there's a lot here to like. Elric is the quintessential fighting man that can wield both swords *and* spells. The magic system that's in force in his setting is based on hereditary pacts with demons and is clearly powered by fatigue points. And the sword Stormbringer is at least as popular as the guy that wields it. After all, it not only gives this frail albino uncanny strength and reasonably clear eyesight, but it also consumes the souls of its victims. What's not to like?

Well, plenty if you ask me.

In the first place, Elric is a big crybaby. Sure, everyone cries, sooner or later. Your dog dies. You watch *Old Yeller*. You read *The Lord of the Rings* out loud to your kids and get choked up in the middle of scenes that aren't even really that sad. And sure, we live in a sensitive, New Age future where real men aren't afraid to weep. But somehow, it's a bit much for an epic hero who acts as if he just strode off the bass clef of a Black Sabbath song to blubber away all the way through the climax of his signature adventure.

But hey, maybe I'm out of line here. Human beings have feelings. Who's to say that I wouldn't do the same, right? You just can't know how well you'd hold up when *your* navy is attacked by dragons. But it's not just the fact of his crying that gets to me here. It's not the timing of it in the context of the plot that's cringe inducing here. It's not even his doing it while leading other men in a crisis situation that's so obnoxious. It's the *reason* behind the crying that's the real problem here.

Quite simply, Elric hates himself. And I can't really say that I blame him given the circumstances. But this is absolutely a tremendous flaw to put on a protagonist. I mean, we're supposed to *like* this character. We're supposed to *want* him to succeed. We're supposed to want to invest in him. But it's hard to like a character that doesn't even like himself. And it's pointless to invest in someone who demonstrates he's just not worth it right out of the gate.

Here's how he phrases it when he's trying to give one of his groupies the brush off:

> *He paused for an instant and then said slowly: "I should admit that I scream in my sleep sometimes and am often tortured by incommunicable self-loathing. Go while you can, lady, and forget Elric for he can bring only grief to your soul." (page 41)*

And just as you'd expect, the womenfolk of his world completely buy it. They're drawn in like moths to a flame! I'm really aggravated by this, though– and not just because I'm jealous of Elric's rock star-levels of cachet. After my last Moorcock book, I was all set for something the literary equivalent of "War Pigs". Instead I get The Cure.

Why is he so miserable? Well, let's put this in terms of *The Lord of the Rings* just to make it clear. Imagine if Aragorn was a Black Númenórean and imagine he shows up at Gondor with an army of corsairs. In the process of sacking the place, he kills not only Denethor but Arwen as well. Then, in order to escape the chaos alive, he betrays the great mass of his allies in order to flee with the crew of a single ship. That's the Elric origin story in a nutshell. I left out some of the brooding and moping, but that is pretty much it.

Granted, the killing of Elric's lady friend was due to his magic sword getting out of hand. And yes, it's possible to craft a likable antihero that does something like this. All it takes is showing that each group involved is sufficiently despicable that you don't mind that any of them get their comeuppance. That's how Jack Vance managed to make Cugel the Clever work; the people he hoodwinked mostly had it coming. Cugel was just a bit more devious in playing their own games. Of course, Vance took it further and made sure Cugel got *his* due as well. But Moorcock doesn't do that. It's as if he wants to believe that he's evolved beyond such petty notions such as right and wrong.

Elric betrays people who trust him on little more than a whim. And that's it. It's senseless. Yes, he *feels* bad about the horrible things he's done. But he doesn't want to change himself or try to fix anything. In fact, he's pretty flippant about the whole thing. At one point he's in another adventure and needs help from his own people—the very ones whose kingdom he'd just helped bring down. They'd gone from living like kings to living hand to mouth because of him. A friend of Elric's states the obvious about why his former associates might not work for him:

> *Moonglum smiled wryly. 'I would not count on it, Elric,' he said. 'Such an act as yours can hardly be forgiven, if you'll forgive my frankness. Your countrymen are now unwilling wanderers, citizens of a razed city—the oldest and greatest the world has known. When Imrryr the Beautiful fell, there must have been many who wished great suffering upon you.' Elric emitted a short laugh. 'Possibly,' he agreed, 'but these are my people and I know them. We Melnibonéans are an old and sophisticated race—we rarely allow emotions to interfere with our general well-being.' (page 79)*

Yes, a people so sophisticated but which nevertheless have not mastered the idea of "burn me once, shame on you; burn me twice, shame on me." That's really hard to imagine. Can he actually close the deal? Maybe he has a combination of excessively high charisma, brilliant diplomacy, or even Jedi mind tricks? Let's see:

> *'There should be no contact between you and your people. We are wary for you, Elric, for even if we allowed you to lead us again—you would take your own doomed path and us with you. There is no future there for myself and my men.' 'Agreed. But I need your help for just one time—then our ways can part again.' 'We should kill you, Elric. But which would be the greater crime? Failure to do justice and slay our betrayer—or regicide? You have given me a problem at a time when there are too many problems already. Should I attempt to solve it?' 'I but played a part in history,' Elric said earnestly. 'Time would have done what I did, eventually. I but brought the day nearer—and brought it when you and our people were still resilient enough to combat it and turn to a new way of life.' (pages 84-85)*

That argument goes over about as well as you'd think. But his countryman ends up getting persuaded anyway. You see, the guy that Elric wants to take down had done something nasty to a Melnibonéan once, so he's owed payback. Why that would be enough to tip the balance is something that I couldn't tell you. But whether you find him to be a sympathetic character or not, he really appears to be the worst negotiator in the history of pulp adventure. Consider this exchange:

> *'Who sent you here?' 'Theleb K'aarna speaks falsely if he told you I was sent,' Elric lied. 'I was interested only in paying my debt.' 'It is not only the sorcerer who told me, I'm afraid,' Nikorn said. 'I have many spies in the city and two of them independently informed me of a plot by local merchants to employ you to kill me.' Elric smiled faintly. 'Very well,' he agreed. 'It was true, but I had no intention of doing what they asked.' Nikorn said: 'I might believe you, Elric of Melniboné. But now I do not know what to do with you. I would not turn anyone over to Theleb K'aarna's mercies. May I have your word that you will not make an attempt on my life again?' 'Are we bargaining, Master Nikorn?' Elric said faintly. 'We are.' 'Then what do I give my word for in return for, sir?' 'Your life and freedom, Lord Elric.'*
> *(page 93)*

Notice that he gets caught in a lie just moments before his life depends on whether or not this guy takes his word. And all he can do is smile. (Is this what sophisticated people are like?) I can't imagine why anyone would deal with him for anything. But nobody in these stories seems to care that he tells lies and breaks promises whenever it suits him. They keep on trying to deal with him in good faith.

I suppose that whether or not this destroys a reader's willing suspension of disbelief hinges on the world view of the beholder. I've seen plenty of people rave over these Elric stories, so it clearly doesn't bother *some* people. This is one of those things that people will just have to disagree on, I guess. A much easier question would be whether or not this kind of moral incoherence is representative of what goes on in fantasy role-playing games. Certainly the early computerized games do not reflect this. You can steal from store keeps in both *Ultima I* and *Nethack*, but if you're caught, the consequences are liable to be both swift and violent. To be sure, the city guards will not be brushed off with a condescending laugh.

The stereotype of the typical tabletop gamer runs towards the "Chaotic Neutral" murder hobo that adventures only so he can kill things and take their stuff. In reality, players are very much concerned with questions of morality even when their personal views on politics and religion would seem to run counter to that. It would be a rare group, for instance, that would fail to argue about the rightness of killing orc babies in "The Keep on the Borderlands." Exploring the consequences of whatever the players choose is the stuff of any long-running campaign that ventures beyond the routine of, as players put it, "cleaning out dungeons."

In games like the early versions of *D&D* which tend to have a high challenge level and high rates of player-character mortality, a new factor emerges to cause players to take a different view towards morality than Elric's. Success in the game depends entirely on the players' capacity to cooperate with one another. Nobody plays a superman. "Army of one" tactics ensure not just a greater chance of an individual fool to come to a bad end, but also increase by an order of magnitude the chances of a total party kill.

What this means in practice is that the players' party as a whole is a fairly rough crowd that, at best, become heroes only in scenarios such as *The Magnificent Seven*. If the players break trust with a king or a non-player-character ally, they *know* that they need to either move on to another domain or else find new friends. And if one of the players fails to behave like a real team player, then when he steps away from the table to get a snack, he's liable to come back to a group that has worked out a fail-safe way to frag him at the very next opportunity.

It is true that men cut from the same cloth as Tolkien's Riders of Rohan—men who "do not lie, and therefore they are not easily deceived" rarely show up as player-characters. And if there is a consensus among gamers, it would be that playing evil is more fun and that good is dumb. (I mean really. Just how often do you see people who are gung ho to play "Lawful" goody two-shoes types?) Nevertheless, there is a certain baseline of trustworthiness that is assumed when it comes to tabletop role-playing games. The party may be incredibly diverse and it may be hard to imagine anything that would give them a reason to work together like they do, but they always seem to set aside their differences enough that they can cooperate in whatever crazy scheme they get involved with. No, they are not idealists. Like Han Solo, they expect to be well paid.

Elric, though, is another case altogether. In a run of the mill game session, his contempt for loyalty and honesty would get him at best ignored and at worst murdered. Player-characters might be rowdy cutthroats, but there is a certain strand of honor among them. Elric's contempt for it simply would not fly. His short laughs and faint smiles would do little to protect him, either.

While it's not quite true that there is simply no place for a guy like him at the tabletop, a character like him would mostly just provide a nemesis that players wouldn't feel bad about killing. Players might actually spare the innocent orc babies, sure. But not Elric.

The Legion of Space
by Jack Williamson

Jack Williamson is another one of those names on the Appendix N list that, for too many people, simply doesn't register as being of any significance. The fact that his career spans nine decades means little now in terms of fame and recognition. That will seem outrageous to some, but I ask librarians and bookstore clerks about his work, and all I get for my efforts is blank stares from them. The same thing is true for most of the other Appendix N authors with the obvious exceptions of Burroughs, Lovecraft, Howard, and Tolkien, but it's tough seeing someone of Williamson's stature treated this way. That he published a novel as recently as 2005 and won a Hugo Award in 2001 doesn't seem to make the slightest difference.

In the early days, he had to get an attorney with the American Fiction Guild to wrangle payments out of Hugo Gernsback. From there, he went on to get writing tips from John Campbell. The really big moment for him was when he got a letter from A. Merritt asking to see the carbon copy of his second published story.[1] (The guy just couldn't wait for the next installment!) He would later become so prominent in the field that he could provide that same sort of kick to someone else: for instance, by sending a postcard to a young Isaac Asimov, who was just starting out as a science-fiction writer.[2] If that's not enough to make clear just how big a deal this guy was, Ray Bradbury declared him to be one of the greats, and Arthur C. Clarke put him on a plane with Asimov and Heinlein.[3]

I've spent a lot of time trying to understand how writers like Fritz Leiber and Fred Saberhagen could go from being nigh unto ubiquitous to being essentially unknown within a single generation, but I don't have any explanation for Jack Williamson's lapse into obscurity. It blows my mind. Outside of an increasingly white haired segment of fandom, there is sort of a received wisdom that implies that science fiction essentially got started with "the big three" of Heinlein, Clarke, and Asimov. Except for H. G. Wells and Jules Verne, just about everything from before those guys may as well be an undiscovered country. I think more people would want to know what's out there, but first they have to realize that there's something there to be rediscovered! Really, though, the writers that were just shy of these highest ranks are still quite good.

Cracking open the first novel in Jack Williamson's first series, we see a snapshot of a medium in transition. *Legion of Space* was hitting the pulps at about the same time as Stanley G. Weinbaum's stories, so the latter's influence is missing here. Both, however, have moved beyond the single planet focus of Edgar Rice Burroughs's John Carter stories in order to present a solar system with colonies at just about every conceivable location. While Williamson's aliens are mere boogeymen not unlike the monstrous invaders from *War of the Worlds*, he does accomplish one thing here that Weinbaum did not touch on: he presents a rather elaborate future history that is precisely in line with the sort of thinking that would serve as the backbone of Heinlein and Asimov's works.

And while Williamson does present an entirely conventional two-fisted hero that would have been anathema to Lovecraft, he also seems to anticipate another sea-change: an emphasis on a more cerebral scientist-type figure as a legitimate hero in his own right. Of course, even as he points to the future of the medium, he continues the Edgar Rice Burroughs practice of framing his tale in such a way that it could actually be a real account:

"Yes, Doctor, I've a son." His thin brown face showed a wistful pride. "I don't see much of him, because he's a very busy young man. I failed to make a soldier out of him, and I used to think he'd never amount to much. I tried to get him to join up, long before Pearl Harbor, but he wouldn't hear of it. No, Don never took to fighting. He's something you call a nuclear physicist, and he's got himself a nice, safe deferment. Now he's on a war job, somewhere out in New Mexico. I'm not even supposed to know where he is, and I can't tell you what he's doing—but the thesis he wrote, at Tech, was something about the metal uranium." Old John Delmar gave me a proud and wistful smile. "No, I used to think that Don would never accomplish much, but now I know that he designed the first atomic reaction motor. I used to think he had

no guts—but he was man enough to pilot the first manned atomic rocket ever launched." I must have goggled, for he explained: "That was 1956, Doctor—the past tense just seems more convenient. With this—capacity of mine, you see, I shared that flight with Don, until his rocket exploded, outside the stratosphere. He died, of course. But he left a son, to carry on the Delmar name." (pages 11-12)

(Of course, given the direct mention of Pearl Harbor, it's clear that this opening chapter could not have been written when the story was first serialized in the thirties. Just as with the opening story in the first Foundation novel, this was written specifically to flesh out the novelization of the old pulp material.)

The action presented here is exactly what George Lucas was going for with the first *Star Wars* movie: a group of adventurers going from one cliffhanging situation to another in order to rescue a space princess from an alien installation and who must then use her technological MacGuffin power to save the last holdouts of an otherwise doomed rebellion. It's the fact that the protagonists are all members of the legion that gives the work its dated feel though. The reading is almost ponderous at times; there are no scoundrel character to add spice, no goofy droids to add comic relief, no zen master to add gravitas, and no farm boy type for adolescent boys to invest in. Nevertheless, this book's proximity to earlier works of science fiction seems to lend it an energy which more than makes up for the characterizations.

Phobos is downright scenic, for instance:

John Star had heard of the Ulnar estate on Phobos, for the magnificent splendor of the Purple Hall was famous throughout the System. The tiny inner moon of Mars, a bit of rock not twenty miles in diameter, had always been held by the Ulnars, by right of reclamation. Equipping the barren, stony mass with an artificial gravity system, synthetic atmosphere, and "seas" of man-made water, planting forests and gardens in soil manufactured from chemicals and disintegrated stone, the planetary engineers had transformed it into a splendid private estate. For his residence, Adam Ulnar had obtained the architects' plans for the Green Hall, the System's colossal capital building, and had duplicated it room for room. But he had built on a scale an inch larger to the foot, using, not green glass, but purple, the color of the Empire. (page 45)

The final climatic moment conveys precisely the same feeling we all felt the first time we saw the Death Star blow up on a gigantic movie screen:

Her voice was perfectly calm, now without any trace of weakness or weariness. Like her face, it carried something strange to him. A new serenity. A disinterested, passionless authority. It was absolutely confident. Without fear, without hate, without elation. It was like—like the voice of a goddess! Involuntarily, he drew back a step, in awe. They waited, watching the little black flecks swarming and growing on the face of the sullen Moon. Five seconds, perhaps, they waited. And the black fleet vanished. There was no explosion, neither flame nor smoke, no visible wreckage. The fleet simply vanished. They all stirred a little, drew breaths of awed relief. Aldoree moved to touch the screws again, the key. "Wait," she said once more, her voice still terribly—divinely—serene. "In twenty seconds... the Moon..." They gazed on that red and baleful globe. Earth's attendant for eons, though young, perhaps in the long time-scale of the Medusae. Now the base of their occupation forces, waiting for the conquest of the planets. Half consciously, under his breath, John Star counted the seconds, watching the red face of doom—not man's now, but their own. "... eighteen... nineteen... twenty—" The Moon was gone. (page 186)

No, we don't get a look at what the consequences of the moon's disappearance would be on the earth. And this ancient alien menace could be right next door at Barnard's Star and could loot planet after planet for its own diabolical ends: we never find out why it was that they would have left Earth alone for all those millennia when humanity could do absolutely nothing to protect itself!

But no matter. The story ranges from Earth to Mars to Phobos to Pluto to beyond our solar system and back. There are all manner of daring raids and impossible escapes. There's space piracy, treks across alien wilderness, jury-rigged repairs, and A-team style inventiveness. *Traveller* adventures don't tend to play out like this, and that may be to their detriment. But the sequence of more or less stand-alone puzzle situations presented here *is* reminiscent of certain strains of text adventure design. There is a great deal of playable gaming material here.

Jack Williamson is not just the author who coined the terms terraforming and genetic engineering.[4] He played a significant role in helping to move science fiction away from the conventions of planetary romance and on toward a medium of interstellar polities and galactic empires. Looking back at *The Legion of Space*, it's hard not to see anticipations of everything from *Star Wars* to *Star Trek* to *Firefly*. But there's something exciting about going back and seeing what it was like when science-fiction writers were having their characters take their first flights outside the solar system. This is relevant not just to those that want to see how we got to where we are today but also for those that want to recapture the kind of wonder that we can no longer take for granted.

Notes

1. For more on Jack Williamson's contact with Hugo Gernsback, John Campbell, and A. Merritt, see Larry McCaffery's *excellent* interview.

2. According to Infogalactic, this is recounted in Jack Williamson's autobiography, *Wonder's Child: My Life in Science Fiction*.

3. According to Eastern New Mexico University's website, Ray Bradbury was quoted as saying this in the *Los Angeles Times*.

4. See the SF Site's "Conversation with Jack Williamson" for more on this.

Sign of the Labrys
by Margaret St. Clair

Margaret St. Clair's formula for an original novel is to start with a realistic dystopian near-future, then layer in a major fantasy element for counter-point, incorporate widespread drug use and hallucinations, and finally throw in at least two over-the-top science-fiction elements that (in comic book fashion) fail to disrupt either the setting or the plot overmuch. It's a potent combination that so dazzled her publishers that they could only explain her writing talent as being due to her feminine proximity to the primitive, her consciousness of the moon-pulls, and her Bene Gesserit-like awareness of "humankind's obscure and ancient past."

But it is more than just a great read. Within its pages is a contribution to tabletop gaming that is on par with Jack Vance's magic in *The Dying Earth*, Poul Anderson's law to chaos spectrum in *Three Hearts and Three Lions*, and the adventurer-conquer-king sequence that is at the heart of Edgar Rice Burrough's John Carter and Robert E. Howard's *Conan* stories. However, unlike those other inspirational works that played a significant role in the creation of the first fantasy role-playing game, Margaret St. Clair's influence is largely unrecognized.

Take, for example, this recent comment from game blogger DM David[1]:

In the fantasies that inspired the game, no character explores a dungeon. At best, you can find elements of the dungeon crawl, such as treasure in the mummy's tomb, orcs in Moria, traps in a Conan yarn, and so on.

This is just not the case. The archetypal Gygaxian dungeon really does have a literary antecedent, and it's here in this book.[2] Each level has a different theme, from living areas for survivors of the apocalypse to scientists and their unusual wandering monster creations, and on to the VIP level, where everyone is doped up on euph pills. Exploration is a key part of the plot as the lower levels are only connected by secret passages. At the same time—just like in the best dungeon designs—there is also more than one way to get from one level to the next and sometimes ways to bypass levels entirely. Finally, the action of the novel is focused on exactly the sort of thing that consumes the bulk of so many game sessions to this day: a battle within a dungeon by two rival factions.

Taken together, it's clear that some of the most offbeat aspects of what we take for granted in the standard gameplay of classic *D&D* and its descendants predate the game's publication by over ten years. It's uncanny, really. But there's more. The really weird puzzles of the classic Infocom text adventures are anticipated here as well. If you're wondering just how it is that the programmers at Infocom could come up with things like *Zork*'s Flood Control Dam #3 or *Enchanter*'s utterly devious Engine Room, Margaret St. Clair was coming up with puzzles like that almost two decades before 8-bit home computers became ubiquitous:

> *I had been absently watching the movements of the goldfish. There was something oddly regular in the paths their swimming took. One group seemed, as far as I could judge, to mark out a series of figure eights, and another moved around the pool in a large ellipse. I bent over and put one hand out directly in the path of an oncoming fish. It did not move aside or try to avoid my fingers. I closed my hand over it, brought my hand up through the water, and held my catch on my palm for the other two to look at. All this time there was not a wriggle or a twitch from the fish. We exchanged glances. "It's not alive," Despoina said. She poked it with one finger. "Metal, or plastic with a metallic coat. What makes it move, then, Sam?" I said slowly, "if something is tracing out lines of force on the underside of the pool..." Ross's eyes lit up. "I've seen something like that.... Wait—yes, I know now. There's a matter transmitter under the bottom of the pool." (page 98-99)*

Figuring out how to operate this machine requires not just using a screwdriver to drain the pool but also lying down in the correct position, arranging the fish just so, adjusting the dials, and then pushing the right buttons. If something like getting the rocket to fly in the game of *Myst* ever struck you as being contrived, realize that that sort of thing was perfectly normal to an author like Margaret St. Clair.

And while she's audacious enough to drop an uplifted dog and an anti-gravity pit into the middle of a fantasy story and then never revisit their implications again, her depiction of witches and witchcraft comprises a concentrated dose of the zeitgeist of the sixties. These are not cackling, broom riding hags. They are more like incredibly groovy people intent on sticking it to the man through some kind of quirky insurrection. Here's a sample of their shtick:

- *Wicca are people who know things without being told.* (page 92)

- *We Wicca know how to be happy even in a bad world. But we are not content with a bad world.* (page 94)

- *We Wicca do not consider "the seeing" extra-sensory.* (page 108)

No, these are not cultists intent on sacrificing children in order to summon some sort of horrific Elder God. At the same time, they are rather unconventional folk. Their concepts of good and evil, right and wrong are quite fluid, as this passage indicates:

"Despoina," I said, "what did you mean when you said, "I am not above the law?" "That there have been… witches who thought they were." "Who? You must have meant somebody." I could feel her considering whether to speak. "Kyra," she said at last. "Kyra? My half-sister? What did she do?" "We didn't know whether to admire her or to punish her. Kyra… loosed the yeasts." (page 116)

The witch Despoina goes on to explain here that before the big blow-up, Kyra was a lab assistant researching fungi for possible use in biological warfare. When she discovered a plague that was wiping out her guinea pigs, she chose on her own to unleash it on an unsuspecting humanity. The hero is, of course, shocked by this revelation.

"Consider the situation, Sam. Have you forgotten? Nuclear war seemed absolutely inevitable. Nobody knew from day to day—from hour to hour— when it would begin. We lived in terror, terror which was sure to accomplish itself. Nobody even dared to hope for a quick death. Kyra realized what had come into her hands. She acted. She took on her shoulders a terrible

responsibility; she assumed a dreadful guilt. She knew that plagues are never
universally fatal. She decided it was better that nine men out of ten should
die, than that all men should." (page 117)

The leaders of the Wicca folk did not necessarily disagree with the reasoning
of this rogue witch. They mainly took umbrage at the fact that the leaders of
the coven were not consulted before she killed countless numbers of innocent
people. It's only because this character *unilaterally* chose to bring about a
plague-fueled apocalypse that she must be punished with exile to the science
level of the dungeon more or less forever.

It's hard to fathom people blithely justifying this level of death and destruction in order to "save" the world. This is so rotten, in fact, that if there were
some sort of government agency or something that wanted to hunt them down
and remove their ability to pose a threat, that would strike me as a perfectly
rational response. And if I, like this protagonist, had grown up in the pre-
plague world and then seen practically everything I'd known destroyed by
horrible diseases, I'm not sure how charitable I could really be to the person
responsible for it. But the protagonist here doesn't really struggle all that much
with any of this.

This sort of thing really strains my capacity to suspend disbelief. Part of me
wants to go back in time and tell the author that she's writing this wrong. All
she had to do was change the big reveal to show that it was some paranoid
warmonger straight out of *Dr. Strangelove* that had inadvertently released the
plagues in an attempt to bring down the Soviet Union. The persecuted witches
of the world could then be united in a heroic attempt to keep totalitarian thugs
from wiping them out while they surreptitiously work out an antidote. Those
are the sort of changes that would have to be made if everything was going to
work out like it does in the movies.

But given that Margaret St. Clair was a devotee of Wicca, she really knew
precisely what she had to do to convey these sorts of people correctly.[3] And
witches should be attractive, seductive, and, above all, confusing; whether it's
in *Hansel and Gretel, Macbeth*, or *The Broken Sword*, they make the abandon-
ment of common sense seem like a good idea even as they blur the dividing
line between right and wrong. If they're going to play to type, they should
ultimately be able to make everything from the most cold-hearted revenge to
the most brutal mass killing seem good and right and smart and sexy all at

once—and the sultry, red-headed Desmoina really does manage to pull this off. Her blasé attitude toward the murder of ninety percent of mankind is actually right in line with the subject matter even if it goes against the grain of standard conventions of fantasy adventure.

No, after thinking this over, there is really not one thing I'd change about this book. From the publisher's bizarre back cover blurb to the original inspiration of the Gygaxian megadungeon, from the drug-infused apocalypse to the bizarre mixing and matching of science-fiction and fantasy elements, this book is a masterpiece. There's something intensely satisfying about the fact that conventions in tabletop games that we take for granted today sprang from something that was so fiercely original. This is a book that is so weird on so many levels that it really shouldn't even exist. That's why it's awesome.

Notes

1. See "4 popular beliefs Dungeons & Dragons defied in the 70s" for the complete post on this.

2. *Blog of Holding* has more on this point: "It is interesting to note that just going down a set of stairs doesn't guarantee that you're going into a deeper 'level': a complex that's 150 feet deep, and composed of several tiers, can be considered a single level if it's part of the same ecosystem. And that is, I think, how early dungeons were designed. Each level was its own conceptual unit: it might or might not be composed of several floors. The author goes on to explain something else puzzling about Gygaxian dungeon design: levels aren't always stacked one above another."

3. Andrew Liptak at Kirkus says, "She and her husband led a comfortable life in California, where they owned a house with an extensive library, gardened and became Wiccans shortly after its introduction in the 1950s."

The Best of Fredric Brown
edited by Robert Bloch

Fredric Brown's stories are impeccably well crafted. He really is a master of the short story form. From the opening hook, through the pulse of each development, and on down to the final kicker, there is not one extraneous word or sentence. His tales usually have twist endings in the same style as, say, the old *Twilight Zone* series. A few of them are little more than elaborate jokes. But more often than not, the total effect ranges from delightfully thought provoking to downright chilling. Fredric Brown stories make you think, and they stay with you long after you've closed the book.

Reading these stories is a transporting experience for a few incidental reasons as well. Coming out from the mid-forties to the early sixties, they really capture the gestalt of post-war American conventionality. In "The Geezenstacks," intact nuclear families are taken for granted as sort of a default baseline. In other stories, Jesus and Satan are as liable to put in cameo appearances as archetypal aliens that walk up to people saying, "Take me to your leader." Alcohol is ubiquitous and an essential part of practically every social interaction. And in the background of all of this hangs an omnipresent threat of nuclear war side by side with the conviction that man will conquer the stars in spite of it.

The most striking thing about the characters is that they are nearly all *adults*. And I mean adult in a way that you just don't see too much anymore. Reading about them, it's clear that they are the sort of people who wouldn't even have a clue as to what science fiction was for instance. ("Oh, you mean that Buck Rogers stuff?") If these sorts of people had known Robert E. Howard personally, they would have considered him a freak. They all are very careful with how they conduct themselves for fear that people might ever think *they're* crazy. I wonder how much of this conveys the times as they actually were and how much of it was due to a need to meet editorial expectations. The fact that Fredric Brown wrote for both *Playboy* and *Dude* in addition to the usual science-fiction and mystery magazines may well have had something to with it.

But if there is a question of what the author really thought in terms of mid-century American culture, it shows up when he attempts to project what life in America would be like in the eighties as he does in "Pi in the Sky" (1945). Not only is an astronomer character described as smoking cigarettes excessively, but a cab driver ends up drinking a fair amount Scotch *while behind the wheel.* Canada is depicted as experimenting with prohibition. The advanced technology featured in the tale incorporates vacuum tubes that are liable to blow out—just like the ones in people's radios. All of this pales, however, in comparison to his prediction of what eighties music would be like:

> *A radio was blaring out the latest composition in dissarythm, the new quarter-tone dance music in which chorded woodwinds provided background patterns for the mad melodies pounded on tuned tomtoms. Between each number and the next a frenetic announcer extolled the virtues of a product. (page 94)*

You know, I can't really fault the guy for failing to anticipate Devo or Milli Vanilli. I can even forgive him for failing to extrapolate from radio to television to music videos. And you have to give him credit for coming up with new ideas for musical instruments, even if he fails to present them as some kind of weird space-age gadget. And yes, he does in fact correctly guess that music will be important primarily for its utility in conveying a payload of advertising along with it. But his conviction that dance music and the couples-dancing of the Big Band era could still be a norm after all those decades is kind of sad. To Brown, the future was going to keep getting hipper over time, and it's not just that we'd have our own Charlie Parkers lighting things up, but we would have a culture that could dig that sort of thing as well!

At the other extreme, there's the eerily prescient "Etaoin Shrdlu" (1942). A Linotype machine becomes sentient after a mysterious foreigner uses it to print what can only be some sort of magic scroll. Not only does Fredric Brown anticipate modern word processing and print-on-demand technology, but he also manages a fairly convincing forerunner to *Tron*'s Master Control

Program. Needless to say, with action that amounts to a mashup of *The Sorcerer's Apprentice* and *Little Shop of Horrors*, this story puts all of the people who dutifully tend to their cell phones at all hours and circumstances in a fairly creepy light.

Meanwhile, the alien civilization featured in "Puppet Show" (1962) is right in line with several that were presented in the somewhat later *Star Trek* television series. They are privy to "fundamental social sciences" that can enable mankind to overcome his warlike nature. But in order to qualify for admission into the Galactic Union, mankind must first pass tests that measure how xenophobic he is. Right in line with Andre Norton's *Star Man's Son*, overcoming racism is presented as *the* primary task for humans to solve if they ever want to avoid Armageddon and create an interstellar civilization.

A counterpoint to this theme is one of the most mind-blowing stories in the collection. "Letter to a Phoenix" (1949) features a Lazarus Long-style character who has lived "four thousand lifetimes" and has seen just about everything. And unlike every other cautionary tale from the era that I've seen, in this one, it turns out that mankind's capacity to blow himself up periodically is precisely the key to his collective longevity:

> *Only a race that destroys itself and its progress periodically, that goes back to its beginning, can survive more than, say, sixty thousand years of intelligent life. In all the universe only the human race has ever reached a high level of intelligence without reaching a high level of sanity. We are unique. We are already at least five times as old as any other race has ever been and it is because we are not sane. And man has, at times, had glimmerings of the fact that insanity is divine. But only at high levels of culture does he realize that he is collectively insane, that fight against it as he will, he will always destroy himself—and rise anew out of the ashes. The phoenix, the bird that periodically immolates itself upon a flaming pyre to rise newborn and live again for another millennium, and again and forever, is only metaphorically a myth. It exists and there is only one of it. You are the phoenix. Nothing will ever destroy you, now that—during many high civilizations—your seed has been scattered on the planets of a thousand suns, in a hundred galaxies, there ever to repeat the pattern. (pages 170-171)*

For someone expecting the authors that inspired Gary Gygax to be primarily oriented toward high fantasy or swords and sorcery, having Fredric

Brown show up on the list is going to be a surprise. On the other hand, there are more than a couple of authors there that are known primarily for their science fiction, planetary romance authors like Edgar Rice Burroughs and Leigh Brackett are at least as influential on the original fantasy role-playing game as J. R. R. Tolkien, and entire swaths of Gygax's recommended books fall under the heading of science fantasy. But Gygax just wasn't one to think of science fiction and fantasy as being completely separate genres and consumed both with equal alacrity. When he described himself as being "an avid reader of all fantasy and science fiction literature since 1950", it's well to remember that it was actually humanly possible to do that in his day.[1]

A common topic of discussion whenever the Appendix N list comes up is who should be purged and who should be added to it. And I admit, it is a perfectly ordinary list that would not have been in any way unusual or offbeat when it was first published. For one thing, none of the works was at all obscure at the time like they are now. But like it or not, these are the works that Gary Gygax cites as having helped shape the form of his game. You can make your own game with its own list of carefully curated authors backing it up, but you don't really get a say in what it was that ultimately inspired this particular game designer back in the seventies.

Gygax said that dungeon masters would be able to "pluck kernels from which grow the fruits of exciting campaigns" from these old books, and that's certainly true of Fredric Brown. His mastery of the short-story lede is certainly worth careful study. Of course, at the tabletop players of role-playing games typically tune out whenever the DM describes the background at length or reads overly long box text sections out loud. To keep people engaged, it's crucial that they are given just enough of a hook to grab their attention so that they can drive play with their own questions, concerns, and interests.

Brown's mastery of the twist ending is going to be harder to apply consciously given the wide open nature of role-playing. But given the sheer number of variables, happenings, and interactions that go on in the typical game session, it's inevitable that something like this will happen from time to time. For instance, in one game I ran the player-character that was in the right place at the right time to hear a critical clue from a dying alien had a personality quirk that he was unable to remember names. And, of course, the clue that he had to tell the other players was the name of the person who they had to see for help! And while players are liable to blow past room after room with nothing particularly crazy happening, there are other times where they collectively decide to do the exact wrong thing for a given set of circumstances. The DM will be embarrassed to run the game and will want to show the players later sections from the module that prove he wasn't just arbitrarily messing with them!

But if you really want to have an experience that mirrors the satisfying nature of a brilliantly executed Fredric Brown story, my advice is this: let the players fail and (if need be) let them die. Consider the XP awards that were handed out over the course of thirteen sorties into my *Dwimmermount* campaign:

177, 43, 53, 175, 442, 403, 15, 192, 668, 874, 69, 27, 2240

This was a dungeon that was so large that the first several sorties were taken up largely with exploration. The fifth and sixth delves where they got over four hundred XP? That success was their downfall. They got lax and cocky and disorganized, and the very next run they got their noses bloodied big time. This more than anything got them to rethink what they were doing, actually formulate a plan, and then work together to pull it off. And even then, it took a couple tries before they achieved a significant success again. The fact that even at that point in the game not everyone in the party had leveled up—even after all that!—seemed to give the players a kind of determination that I've rarely seen in any kind of gaming.

The result of that kind of investment is that the reactions to both successes and failures get magnified well beyond what you'd think that they'd merit. *This* is the part of the game that ends up feeling reminiscent of a story. And it emerges in the most straightforward sessions involving randomly generated low-level characters that have barely even a twenty percent chance of surviving a half-dozen game sessions.

Classic *D&D* is a game that requires multiple decisive victories occurring over the course of multiple game sessions before the players can really see tangible benefits from their efforts. And the character that has spent six sorties working towards leveling up is often just as likely die as the freshly rolled-up henchman. People don't design games like that anymore—not if they're intending to make a top-tier game that will be carried by the big chain bookstores. Not everyone has moved on, but there nevertheless persists a widely held misconception that this is an overly simplistic hack-and-slash game that people will eventually grow out of before they will move on to the *serious* role-playing games like *GURPS* or some other flavor of "story game."

But the fact is that Gary Gygax *did* come up with a game that combines a surprising degree of investment with highly textured and nuanced narratives. If the players are winning, the game feels like a monster movie, with the players taking on the roles of monsters engaging in a triumphant rampage. If the players are doing so poorly that they face a significant chance of a "total party kill," then death for each player-character carries with it the same impact of the suspense you see in Ridley Scott's *Alien*. And either way, players know what they want. You can see it when, after losing a character, they immediately sit down to roll up a new one. When they come back to the table, they'll have a vision of what they want from the game. They will be spoiling for round two with *something*. They'll have a plan, even if they can't be entirely sure how it will go. But no matter what happens, *a story will emerge*. And if they are truly role-players at heart, they won't want it to ever stop!

Notes

1. *Black Gate* reports that Gygax canceled his subscription to *The Magazine of Science Fiction & Fantasy* in 1963.

Stormbringer
by Michael Moorcock

Fantasy role-playing games from their outset have included the possibility of epic-level play. And though players often passed over these possibilities in their campaigns, it was nevertheless integral to the zeitgeist of the medium. In first edition *Tunnels & Trolls*, player-characters could raise their attributes to godlike proportions as they leveled up. In *AD&D*, the spell slots of clerics and magic users kept increasing all the way up to level 29, and the default campaign world is littered with artifacts that could rival Tolkien's One Ring. *Deities & Demigods* includes rules for the ascension of player-characters so that they can join the pantheons of their game settings. And the classic Mentzer boxed set series of the eighties included two installments beyond domain-level play: *Master* and *Immortal* rules. Even when a campaign was destined to last only for a summer instead of the years of weekly sessions required for this sort of achievement, the potential for this sort of thing remained a core part of the game's appeal. For most characters, a pit trap in the next hallway could very well be the end of them, however, they still strode across the game world as if they were temporarily embarrassed demigods.

Looking over the literary inspirations for classic *D&D*, there's actually not a whole lot there that reflects this sort of thing. While Conan and John Carter follow the classic "adventurer, conqueror, king" sequence to a T, godhood is beyond the scope of their respective retirement plans. Roger Zelazny's *Chronicles of Amber* and Philip José Farmer's *World of Tiers* series present godlike protagonists, but neither is consistent with the end games presented in classic editions of *D&D*. There's pretty much just one author who is responsible for god-like achievements being the default destiny of those rare player-characters that can actually survive years of almost constant gaming: Michael Moorcock.

If you want to see the original template for this premise, then there's really only one book you need to read: *Stormbringer*.

The surprising thing about this is that, more than anything else in the Appendix N list, the plot of this book is a railroad after the fashion of the worst sort of role-playing adventure module. In retrospect, this is maybe to be expected; after all, by this installment of the Elric series, the hero not only has a sword that can instantly kill any mortal, but he also gets hold of a magic horse that eliminates terrain effects altogether and a shield that can protect him from the attacks of even godlike beings. When a character progresses to the point where neither the combat system nor the wilderness travel rules can provide any sort of challenge for him, how on earth do you craft a suitable scenario for him?[1]

Moorcock's solution to this problem will be immediately recognizable to anyone that's spent much time role-playing. This novel really is a great summary of what *not* to do as a game master:

- Have the forces of Chaos break into the player-character's castle to kidnap a loved one. Provide just enough clues as to what's going on that the player has no choice but to go on a wild goose chase. (Note: if your players' characters don't have any friends, love interests, or extended family, this is why!)

- Draw the player into a massive battle where he is preordained to lose. As the player flees the battlefield, leave only one avenue of escape. Have the enemy forces cover every other direction than the one where the next adventure situation lies.

- Introduce an epic-level NPC that can dole out missions on whatever basis fits the game master's preparations. With the nature of reality at stake, the player has no choice but to comply. (This sort of format pretty well steamrolls any influence the players might have had on the direction of the campaign. While it does simplify preparation requirements, it comes at the expense of player autonomy.)

- Only rarely give a choice to the players, but make it a very limited set of options that always leads to the next adventure situation regardless of the outcomes. (This is perhaps unavoidable in some strains of computerized adventuring, but with real-life role-playing this is generally considered to be a table flipping level of offense.)

If this is the inevitable outline of epic-level adventuring, it's no wonder that most people over the years have spent far more time attempting to figure out how to get the maximum utility from their ten-foot poles, iron spikes, and 50-foot lengths of rope instead. On the other hand, role-players that are reluctant to push their game systems to the limits really are missing out. It's really not hard to see why game designers in the seventies were so smitten with Moorcock's use of extra-planar entities and godlike beings:

Further and further into the ranks he sliced his way, until he saw Lord Xionbarg in his earthly guise of a slender dark-haired woman. Elric knew that the woman's shape was no indication of Xiombarg's mighty strength but, without fear, he leapt towards the Duke of Hell and stood before him, looking up at where he sat on his lion-headed, bull-bodied mount. Xiombarg's girl's voice came sweetly to Elric's ears. 'Mortal, you have defied many Dukes of Hell and banished others to the Higher Worlds. They call you god-slayer now, so I've heard. Can you slay me?' 'You know that no mortal can slay one of the Lords of the Higher Worlds whether they be of Law or Chaos, Xiombarg— but he can, if equipped with sufficient power, destroy their earthly semblance and send him back to their own plane, never to return!' 'Can you do this to me?' 'Let us see!' Elric flung himself towards the Dark Lord. Xiombarg was armed with a long-shafted battle-axe that gave off a night-blue radiance. As his steed reared, he swung the axe down at Elric's unprotected head. The albino flung up his shield and the axe struck it. A kind of metallic shout came from the weapons and huge sparks flew away. Elric moved in close and hacked at one of Xiombarg's feminine legs. A light moved down from his hips and protected the leg so that Stormbringer was brought to a stop, jarring Elric's arm. Again the axe struck the shield with the same effect as before. Again Elric tried to pierce Xiombarg's unholy defense. And all the while he heard the Dark Lord's laughter, sweetly modulated, yet as horrible as a hag's. 'Your mockery of human shape and human beauty begins to fail, my lord!' cried Elric, standing back for a moment to gather his strength. (page 236-237)

This is as thrilling a battle sequence as anything in the entirety of the Appendix N list and it's just getting started. We haven't even gotten to the part where this Duke of Hell's mount is dispatched or where his feminine leg is replaced by an insect-like mandible. If you've never run anything like this in a tabletop role-playing game, then what are you waiting for?[2] If your concept of fantasy hinges almost entirely on Frodo and Bilbo's "there and back again" journeys, then this sort of thing is liable to be inconceivable to you.[3] But reading this, it really makes it clear just why gamers back in the seventies took it for granted that game masters would want hard and fast stats for gods and godlike beings.

Ironically, the most epic aspects of classic *D&D* are in this instance tied directly to what is perceived as being one of the lamest aspects of the game: alignment. As it's presented in my battered *Basic* rulebook from 1981, Law is little more than a lifestyle choice for law-abiding, truth-telling team players. Chaos, in contrast, is "the belief that life is random, and that chance and luck rule the world." Its adherents will (just like Elric) keep promises and tell the truth only if it suits them. With chaotic player-characters, the needs of the one outweigh the needs to the many; and most importantly, they will (just like Elric) leave their friends high and dry at the drop of a hat.

Over the decades, alignment has often ended up being the source of arguments at the tabletop. Few people want any restrictions on their character's actions, but everyone seems to have a different opinion on how adherents of each perspective would actually behave. Play can grind to a halt as players heckle each other over whether or not their actions are in character or not. In practice, this really is the least "epic" aspect of tabletop role-playing. It's not heroic fantasy. It's armchair psychology. And not only does it not make sense, but it also has a tendency to lead to hard feelings. But even a brief look at Michael Moorcock's handling of the concept makes it obvious why it could have been taken for granted that something like that belonged in a fantasy game:

> As they approached, Elric was soon in no doubt that they were, indeed, those ships. The Sign of Chaos flashed on their sails, eight amber arrows radiating from a central hub—signifying the boast of Chaos, that it contained all possibilities whereas Law was supposed, in time, to destroy possibility and result in eternal stagnation. The sign of Law was a single arrow pointing

upwards, symbolizing direction and control. Elric knew that in reality, Chaos was the real harbinger of stagnation, for though it changed constantly, it never progressed. But, in his heart, he felt a yearning for this state, for he had many loyalties to the Lords of Chaos in the past and his own folk of Melniboné had worked, since inception, to further the aims of Chaos. But now Chaos must make war on Chaos; Elric must turn against those he had once been loyal to, using weapons forged by chaotic forces to defeat those self-same forces in this time of change. (pages 154-155)

The key to making alignment relevant then is to tie it to spiritual forces that are active on the prime material plane. Turn them loose to the extent that they end up having sweeping effects on the campaign map, and the players will start to care very quickly about this venerable aspect of the game. This can range from evil sorcerers with dreams of world domination to friendly godlings that have clues about where all the best magic items are. Upset the balance between these competing forces sufficiently, and player-characters will have to take a stand one way or the other. Faced with the prospects of mankind being twisted into monstrous beings while the earth itself buckles and heaves as the laws of nature lose their coherence, and even selfish anti-heroes like Elric can be inspired to do the right thing.

The problem for classic *D&D* is that Tolkien's approach to fantasy actually won out over Michael Moorcock's. In the minds of most gamers and fantasy fans, it seems perfectly natural to keep beings like Eru Ilúvatar and the Valar safely offstage. This trend didn't stop there either. Over the decades, "true faith" has ceased having to correspond to anything real; its main requirement is that it be some sort of sincere faith in about just about anything. In some urban fantasies, even a *pentagram* works as well as a cross against vampires so long as its wielder truly *believes*.

People take these sorts of assumptions for granted and then look back at the older games and jump to the conclusion that people must have been just plain weird back then. They say it is simply not how we do things anymore. But maybe the authors and game designers from back then weren't so weird after all. Maybe *we* are. And maybe our humdrum naturalistic approach to fantasy really isn't as *fantastic* as it could be.

Notes

1. Game blogger Goblin Punch has weighed in on this in "Keep Dungeon Threats Threatening."

2. Seriously, if you're consciously saving this sort of thing, you need to get with it because as the 1d30 blog can tell you, "You don't have time to build up to something great."

3. Nerd-O-Mancer of Dork phrases the conventional wisdom on this point like this: "I like that they do not include stats for their gods. Gods are omnipotent beings and shouldn't be degraded to yet another (if high leveled) monster for the characters to battle." On the other hand, as Blood of Prokopius points out, if your conception of the gods is derived from pagan sources, this actually is a theologically correct way to deal with them: "These gods are quantifiable because they are part of creation. Ancient creation stories repeat over and over again how all the various bits and pieces of the world are made from some part of the gods themselves. Creation always happens from some kind of pre-existant matter—everything is quantifiable."

Battle in the Dawn
by Manly Wade Wellman

Pulp fiction gets a really bad rap.

Whenever the media wants to invoke classic science fiction and fantasy from the thirties and forties, they go out of their way to dredge up a particularly lurid magazine cover from the period. Sure, even fans of the stuff get a chuckle out of the crazier ones. But the subtext is always the same: the pulps were all tacky, predictable, and full of not just stereotypes that have since become unfashionable but also loaded with mediocre writing and tiresome clichés.

Of course, every time this topic comes up, somebody will point out that 90% of everything is crap. Based on that, one might argue that the insinuations of the journalists are, therefore, pretty accurate. And it would certainly not be difficult to find examples of *bad* stories from the period. But the fact remains that people brought up under the steady pulse of this sort of negative advertising could never be prepared for the vividness of the writing of someone like Robert E. Howard. They would never conceive that scope and the depths of Lovecraft's stories are even possible. They would not anticipate just how striking Margaret Brundage's cover paintings could be. The reason is that they'd been led to believe that all of it was on the level of the worst sort of comic books.

This sort of thing doesn't damage the legacies of the greats all that much. And I know for myself that I used to worry about what I'd do when I'd finally gotten through all of Howard's and Lovecraft's material. But the fact is that those guys were far from being the only ones producing great stories during the pulp era.

Picking up a copy *Battle in the Dawn*, I was prepared for the worst. (That smear campaign in the media really does work!) Judging by the cover, I was in for another cheap Conan knock-off like the ones which crowded the book racks of the seventies. What I actually got was a backward extrapolation of a hero that could have been the inspiration for the mythical figure Hercules. And what's more is that everything is consistent with the science and archaeology of the author's day. The resulting stories combine elements of science fiction and fantasy in a striking manner that is unlike anything I'd expect to find on the shelves at the library or bookstore.

But this isn't some kind of academic exercise. And sure, the descriptions of hunting and javelin-throwing ring true. For instance, tricks like using a cord to put a spin on a javelin so that it flies farther and faster are something you don't see in a lot of fantasy literature. But the excitement that infuses the pulp stories of the thirties and forties is here as well. Mixed in with fictionalized versions of the first Homo Sapiens, monstrous Neanderthalers, and the diminutive Piltdown Men are depictions of lost worlds, elephant graveyards, and even Atlantis itself!

Yet Manly Wade Wellman's Atlantis is not some sort of crazy science fantasy metropolis either. No, he looks at the volcanic rock at present-day Gibraltar and concludes that an ancient volcano could have kept the ocean out of the basin in which the Mediterranean Sea currently resides. From there he imagines an advanced society developing in what would turn out to be the worst possible location. And had they, as some myths indicate, discovered the recipe for gunpowder, they would not only have had the means to rule the entire world as de facto gods, but opened the door to their own demise.

While the Hok stories are consistently this well thought out, that doesn't mean Wellman is opposed to epic-level action. In fact, he managed to write a literary antecedent for the climax to *Big Trouble in Little China*!

"This fellow flouts us, he is a madman," grumbled the deep voice, and its owner sidled his horse out to join the leader. This second speaker was squat and black-bearded, and even at the distance Hok saw that he was fierce of face and sharp eyed. "If I am mad," Hok threw at him, "I may come down and make you fear my bite." With an oath, the bearded one lifted himself in his seat, whirled a spear backward, and launched it at the defiant Hok, who stood still to watch the course of the weapon. It was a sure case, but not too strong, according to cave-man standards. As it came at Hok, he swayed his big, lithe body sidewise, shot his right hand like a snake, and seized the

flying shaft by the middle. Whirling it end for end, he sped it back the way it had come, with all the strength and skill of his mighty muscles behind it. Forty throats whooped, in startled anger as the black-beard spun off his beast, transfixed by his own weapon. Hok's answering shout of laughter defied them. It had all happened in two breaths of time. (page 52-53)

Granted, the way that Hok just so happens to both be the guy that invented the bow and the sort of guy that could "accidentally" create a sword from a molten meteor similarly strains belief. But it's how he combines his strength, cunning, and technological advantages that make the story. Because he comes back against all odds against not just Neanderthals but also a Loki-like figure and even an octopus "god," his daring raids deep into territory controlled by hostile factions never fail to entertain.

But if I'm going to read stories about cavemen having epic adventures, I'm not going to be satisfied unless I get a veritable menagerie of prehistoric beasties. And yes, Wellman's Imperial Mammoth is positively majestic:

Gragru the mammoth, tremendous beyond imagination, marched with heavy dignity to the enticing breakfast Hok had set him. A hillock of red-black hair, more than twice Hok's height at the shoulder, he sprouted great spiral tusks of creamy ivory, each a weight for several men. His head, a hairy boulder, had a high cranium and small, wise eyes. His long, clever trunk sniffed at one snack of juniper, and began to convey it to his mouth. (page 150)

Hok's battle with an entire flock of pterodactyls is fantastic:

Hok had notched another arrow, and sped it into the chest of one. Before he could seize a third shaft, the other Stymph was upon him. Its talons made a clutch, scraping long furrows in his shoulder. He cursed it, and struck a mighty whipping blow with his bow-stave that staggered it in mid-flight. Clutching the supporting branch with his legs, he tore his axe from its lashing at his girdle, and got it up just in time to meet the recovering drive of the brute. Badly gashed across the narrow, evil face, the Stymph reeled downward, trying in vain to get control of its wings and rise again. More Stymphs circled this third victim of Hok, and tore several bloody mouthfuls from it. A loud clamor rose over Hok's head—the smell of gore was maddening the flock.

Slipping his right hand through the thong on his axe handle, he looked up. The sky was filling with Stymphs. Though never a man to recognize danger with much respect, Hok was forced to recognize it now. (pages 172-173)

And if I had any doubt that Hok was a convincing interpolation of a possible real-life inspiration of Hercules, I was completely won over with Wellman's take on the classic battle between the Greek hero and the wild boar of Eurymanthis. The boar, in this case, turns out to be one of the last surviving *Dinocerus ingens*:

Its monstrous bulk, clad in scant-bristled hide of slate gray, stooped above the carcass. Its shallow, broad-snouted skull bent down, and powerful fangs tore the hairy hide from Gragu's flesh, exposing the tender meat. That head lifted as Hok came into view, a head larger than that of a hippopotamus. Two small hooded eyes, cold and pale as a lizard's, stared. The mouth sucked and chewed bloody shreds, and Hok saw down-protruding tusks, sharp as daggers. Upon the undeveloped brow, the swell of the muzzle, and the tip of the snout were hornlike knobs—three pairs of them. (page 158)

This is exactly the sort of stuff I wish I could have read before running the classic "expert" *D&D* module "The Isle of Dread." The combination of pulp adventure with a synthesis of science and myth is eminently gameable. One reason it's so good is that Manly Wade Wellman had first-hand life experience with de facto Stone Age people. Even though the science is out of date in places, I really can't think of a better resource for a DM who is going to run a lost-world-themed role-playing campaign.

While today we tend to look back on the pulp era with more than a little condescension, the fact is that it wasn't during the forties that Poul Anderson felt compelled to write an essay pointing out how excessively derivative and unrealistic fantasy was liable to be the end of an otherwise popular subgenre.[1] It was the *seventies* when the mediocrities began to overwhelm the good stuff— all culminating into a multi-genre extinction event. The fact that publishers and fans could accord Wellman with the degree of honor and recognition that they did really says a lot about them. They had far better taste than they are typically given credit for.

Notes

1. This is a modest example of what John C. Wright refers to as "The Parochialism of Anachronism". This subject is difficult to discuss with people because the fact of just how good the pulps were goes against the narrative of social evolution.

The Complete Compleat Enchanter
by L. Sprague de Camp and Fletcher Pratt

There is an odd passage in the book of Hebrews where the author rattles off a list of all the things he's *not* going to talk about.[1] The subjects he takes for granted as being too straightforward and elementary to spend much time on happen to include things that have been hotly debated for centuries. (It's funny, really.) There's a similar passage in the first edition of the *Tunnels & Trolls* game that strikes almost exactly the same cadence:

> *There are recognized laws of magic that we have mostly ignored in dreaming up these spells—the Law of Contagion, the Law of Similarity, the principles of necromancy and control of spirits, preferring instead to base most of these spells on inherent abilities of the magic-user a la Andre Norton.*

Notice that this is basically an apology. The designer is convinced that his magic system will not function the way people expect. There are laws of magic that he presumes everyone is familiar with and that are foundational to the topic. And while he can't take the time to spell all of this out in such a small booklet, he feels compelled to acknowledge this before moving on to the nuts and bolts of his game's spell system.

Unlike in the case of the epistle to the Hebrews, we *do* have enough documentary evidence that we can easily unpack every turn of the phrase here. Most people reading fantasy or playing fantasy games today are just not going to be that concerned about the Laws of Contagion and Similarity, but the fact is that it was perfectly reasonable to assume that people in the mid-seventies would. The guys that had defined magic for that generation as much or more than J. K. Rowling has for us today were of course de Camp and Pratt. And they did it with their Harold Shea stories, a mainstay of *UNKNOWN* magazine.

It's hard to underestimate just how influential this series of books was in gaming. Do you ever wonder why it could make sense for a Green Dragon to breath chlorine gas instead of fire? Or why giants would necessarily come in three main varieties: hill giants, frost giants, and fire giants? Those mainstay *D&D* tropes go back to *The Roaring Trumpet*. Do you ever think about why Gygax used the ponderous term "somatic" to denote the hand motions a magic-user needed to use in order to cast a spell? Again, it's due to de Camp and Pratt:

> *Half an hour later: "… the elementary principles of similarity and contagion," he was saying, "we shall proceed to the more practical applications of magic. First, the composition of spells. The normal spell consists of two components, which may be termed the verbal and the somatic. In the verbal section the consideration is whether the spell is to be based upon the command of the materials at hand, or upon the invocation of a higher authority." (page 271)*

Some might argue that this is merely a coincidence. It is possible that there was some other inspiration which was shared by both de Camp, Pratt, Gygax, and St. Andre. On the other hand, de Camp and Pratt are not only mentioned in the "Forward" (sic) to the original *Dungeons & Dragons*, but they are also singled out by Gygax as being among "the most immediate influences" of *AD&D*. If that isn't convincing, then note as well that there are very few fans of classic *D&D* that will not immediately recognize this place:

> *The door banged shut behind them. They were in a dark vestibule, like that in Sverre's house but larger and foul with the odor of unwashed giant. A huge arm pushed the leather curtain aside, revealing through the triangular opening a view of roaring yellow flame and thronging, shouting giants…. Within, the place was a disorderly parody of Sverre's. Of the same general form, with the same benches, its tables were all uneven, filthy, and littered with fragments of food. The fire in the center hung a pall of smoke under the rafters. The dirty straw on the floor was thick about the ankles. The benches and the passageway behind them were filled with giants, drinking, eating, shouting at the tops of their voices. Before him a group of six, with iron-gray topknots and patchy beards like Skrymir's, were wrangling. One drew back*

his arm in anger. His elbow struck a mug of mead borne by a harassed-looking man who was evidently a thrall. The mead splashed onto another giant, who instantly snatched up a bowl of stew from the table and slammed it on the man's head. Down went the man with a squeal. Skrymir calmly kicked him from the path of his guests. The six giants burst into bubbling laughter, rolling in their seats and clapping each other on the back, their argument forgotten. (pages 62-63)

This is, of course, the Great Hall from Gygax's "Steading of the Hill Giant," which tends to end up being the site of an utterly titanic battle for players undertaking the most iconic module series of the *AD&D* game. And while it may be a coincidence that one of the giants in that game supplement is indeed pictured as having a topknot, there is another homage in "Hall of the Fire Giant King" here. Both de Camp and Pratt's story and the adventure module place trolls as guards in the fire giants' dungeon. I think it's safe to say that Gary Gygax really, *really* loved these stories.

How far was Gygax willing to take this sort of thing? Further than a lot of people would think. Most people, for instance, tend to think that the guy was simply being eccentric when they discover that the original name for the "fighter" class was "fighting-men." The reality is that it's easier to list the Appendix N books that *don't* use that term than it is to pick out the ones that do. And that's far from the only example of particular turns of phrases being lifted from the designer's favorite books. As I've pointed out previously, the thief in *AD&D* has a "hide in **shadows**" skill and an uncannily good ability to climb walls because of the way the thief character is depicted in Roger Zelazny's *Jack of Shadows*. By the time I'm flipping through my well-worn Moldvay *Basic D&D* booklet and note that White Apes from Edgar Rice Burroughs' *A Princess of Mars* are shortly followed up with the green slime monster from Sterling Lanier's *Hiero's Journey*, I begin to assume that anything in the Appendix N books that wasn't nailed down by aggressive legal protections was more than likely bolted onto the game at some point.

And that's why it gives me pause when I come across passages like this:

"Very fine girl, provided she doesn't put an arrow through you and cut your ears off for trophies. I confess my taste runs to a somewhat more sedentary type of female. I doubt whether I can stand much more excitement of this sort." Shea said: "I know how you feel. Traveling through Faerie is just one

damned encounter after another." His two narrow escapes in one day had left Shea feeling like a damp washcloth. Chalmers mused: "It is logical that it should be so. The Faerie Queen *indicates that this is a world wherein an endless and largely planless concatenation of encounters are a part of the normal pattern of events.... (page 173)*

I'm not the only game master who has run entire game sessions using little more than a few wilderness encounter charts. Is it possible that such a significant chunk of the original fantasy role-playing game could have been directly inspired by a passage like this? Well, given that the nuances of a Gygaxian style megadungeon level are plainly laid out on in Margaret St. Clair's *Sign of the Labrys*, why not? But it is worth noting that there are wilderness encounters in Avalon Hill's *Outdoor Survival* game, so de Camp and Pratt are not the only potential source for this particular element.

The point here is that literature was a primary inspiration to tabletop game designers in the seventies in a way that's very difficult for a lot of people to comprehend these days. When Marc Miller sat down to adapt the original three *D&D* booklets into a similarly organized science-fiction game, he didn't think to channel the old *Star Trek* television series or the *Planet of the Apes* movie franchise. No, his inspiration came from books by H. Beam Piper and E. C. Tubb. When Steve Jackson sat down to design Metagaming Concepts' flagship MicroGame *Ogre*, he had Keith Laumer's "Bolo" stories and Colin Kapp's "Gottlos" at the forefront of his mind.

It isn't like this anymore. And no, it's not that you can't find old-school games that have healthy reading lists attached to them. There are a pair by Alexander Macris and Ron Edwards that I can recommend, for example. And *GURPS Time Travel* is loaded with recommendations of iconic works from Appendix N authors as well. But for the most part, it's not short stories and novellas and 180-page throwaway paperbacks that dominate the collective consciousness of today's gamerdom. Most people get their notions of science fiction and fantasy from a handful of top-tier properties. When you game master a role-playing game at a convention for a group of strangers, your common frame of reference is not the written word, but a collection of blockbuster movies. And when game designers begin a new project, it's natural for them to think in terms of pre-existing games rather than synthesize something from the work of an incredibly diverse set of authors.

The seventies were not like that. When you look at the most enduring game design work of the period, you're looking at the product of a culture that has ceased to exist. And the generation gap that has emerged since then is exacerbated by the fact that so many of the authors have become unaccountably obscure in a surprisingly short period of time since then. This makes it doubly hard to comprehend some of the old games, as not only is their cultural context now largely unimaginable, but in some cases, the designs assumed that game masters would have a wealth of diverse literature to support their own creativity.

Some people try to dismiss this as being a topic that's worth looking into. "Eh," they say, "times change; this sort of thing is inevitable, really." Other people diminish the study of the Appendix N by claiming that the books that inspired the Appendix N authors would be far more edifying. But here's the thing that these sorts of people don't understand: *the "Appendix N" of Appendix N is embedded in Appendix N!*

If you want to reach back into the truly foundational stories of Western fantasy, look no further than de Camp and Pratt's Harold Shea series, which takes a psychologist from the twentieth century and thrusts him into adventures in fantasy worlds ranging from Scandinavian mythology to Spencer's *Fairie Queen* to *Orlando Furioso* and on to *The Kalevala* and Irish mythology. And these guys were far from the only Appendix N authors to do something along these lines; even Michael Moorcock invokes Roland in his Elric stories.

But more than betraying a fluency in "real" literature, the Appendix N authors were themselves highly influential to each other. The now virtually unknown A. Merritt occupied the same spinner racks as seventies icon Roger Zelazny. He was a primary inspiration that led Jack Williamson to launch a nine-decade long career writing science fiction. When H. P. Lovecraft wrote his signature story "Call of Cthulhu," he was pretty well writing A. Merritt fan fiction. And on the weird fiction side of things, Lord Dunsany was a major influence on Lovecraft, though we might not even know Lovecraft's name were it not for the efforts of August Derleth. Indeed, much of what we call Lovecraftian today is, in fact, Derlethian. Finally, Edgar Rice Burroughs inspired not just other authors on the Appendix N list, but countless numbers of scientists and technologists as well.[2]

These authors' books really were present in the seventies in a way that's hard to imagine anymore. When John Eric Holmes, the editor of the first iteration of *Basic D&D*, wrote a series of novels, he didn't think anything of using Burroughs' *Pellucidar* books as the starting point. That cost him in the end, as he never received permission to publish his third novel in that series. The *Pellucidar* books debuted in 1914 and were dated in every way imaginable—to the point of positing a sun inside of a hollow Earth—but were still effectively current, as were the numerous derivative works inspired by Robert E. Howard's stories from the 1930s.

Taken all together, it's clear that there was a wide-ranging canon of science-fiction and fantasy authors that spanned the better part of a century. The Appendix N list was a quirky subset of these that (by definition) focused on the books that inspired Gary Gygax's famous fantasy game. But even if he wasn't representative of fandom in general, his voracious reading habits were certainly held in common with other role-playing game designers of the time, Ken St. Andre and Marc Miller not being the least of these. Their games were in some sense a culmination of a conversation that had been going on not just for decades, but centuries.

But between the success of these designers, impending changes in publishing, and the dawn of home computers, that was a conversation that was on the verge of coming to an end. Whether the changes were for the better is largely a matter of taste. But in my opinion, something uniquely compelling was lost.

Notes

1. Hebrews 6: 1-2: "Therefore leaving the principles of the doctrine of Christ, let us go on unto perfection; not laying again the foundation of repentance from dead works, and of faith toward God, of the doctrine of baptisms, and of laying on of hands, and of resurrection of the dead, and of eternal judgment."

2. In an interview at *The Paris Review*, Ray Bradbury said the following:

   Burroughs is probably the most influential writer in the entire history of the world.... I've talked to more biochemists and more astronomers and technologists in various fields, who, when they were ten years old, fell in love with John Carter and Tarzan and decided to become something romantic. Burroughs put us on the moon. All the technologists read

Burroughs. I was once at Caltech with a whole bunch of scientists and they all admitted it. Two leading astronomers—one from Cornell, the other from Caltech—came out and said, Yeah, that's why we became astronomers. We wanted to see Mars more closely. I find this in most fields. The need for romance is constant, and again, it's pooh-poohed by intellectuals. As a result they're going to stunt their kids. You can't kill a dream. Social obligation has to come from living with some sense of style, high adventure, and romance.

The Hobbit and *The Lord of the Rings*
by J. R. R. Tolkien

The extent of Tolkien's influence on the formation of the *Dungeons & Dragons* game is the subject of countless arguments. Most of what Gary Gygax has said on this topic is generally dismissed out of hand as being a transparent effort to avoid legal hassles from the Tolkien estate.

Of course, the co-designer of the original fantasy role-playing game wasn't always under such pressure. Writing in 1972, well before any lawsuits could be a factor, Gary Gygax had this to say about his fantasy gaming supplement for the *Chainmail* miniatures rules:[1]

> Tolkien purists will not find these rules entirely satisfactory, I believe, for many of the fantastic creatures do not follow his "specifications," mainly because I believe that other writers were as "authoritative" as he.

The creatures he refers to are (in this order) halflings, sprites (and pixies), dwarves (and gnomes), goblins (and kobolds), elves (and fairies), orcs, heroes (and anti-heroes), wizards (including sorcerers, warlocks, magicians, and seers), wraiths, lycanthropes, trolls (and ogres), treants, dragons, rocs (including wyverns and griffons), elementals (including djinns and efreets), basilisks (and cockatrices), giant spiders and insects, giant wolves, and wights (and ghouls).

This list has been held up as conclusive evidence of Tolkien's influence on the formation of original *D&D*.[2] When taking all of the game's influences into account, it's just not that convincing though. Certainly, players of this rule set would have been able to recreate the Battle of Five Armies and the Battle of the Morannon. And unlike anything you'd see in the coming *D&D* rule sets, Bard the Hunter's ability to take out a flying dragon with a single shot is accounted for. But while wraiths here are clearly inspired by the Nazgûl, raising the morale of their allies, causing their foes to make morale checks, and paralyzing men with fear, these special abilities also failed to survive the transition from the miniatures supplement to the role-playing game.

Other staples of the *D&D* zeitgeist are in evidence even at this early juncture: the chromatic dragons are out in force, along with the chlorine gas-breathing variety from de Camp and Pratt's *The Roaring Trumpet.* The clearest example of Tolkien's diluted authority in Gygax's views would be in the matter of trolls. "What are generally referred to as Trolls are more properly Ogres," he explains. To Gygax, "true Trolls" are more in line with the one in Poul Anderson's *Three Hearts and Three Lions.*

Similarly, the wizards of the *Chainmail Fantasy Supplement* are unlike anything from Tolkien's corpus; they unleash "Cloudkill" on enemy armies, create hallucinatory terrain, "haste" friendly units while "slowing" enemies, and disrupt the opposing force's command and control with "confuse." Tolkien's stark contrasts between good and evil are replaced with Poul Anderson's and Michael Moorcock's Law to Chaos alignment spectrum, with the most surprising implication of this system being that the question of whether elves will come in on the side of halflings or wraiths is determined entirely by the roll of the dice!

The inclusion of sprites and pixies takes things in a direction that would not at all have been to Tolkien's liking.[3] Even with no significant mechanical differences, the addition of gnomes, kobolds, and fairies into the lineup begins to nudge things more toward a fantasy equivalent of the cantina in Mos Eisley. The inclusion of the djinn, the efreet, and the roc accords first-class status to *One Hundred and One Nights* and presages Gygax's later tendency to incorporate creatures and beings from almost any tradition or mythology.

Gary Gygax really was more of a syncretist than a purist, and it shows even at this early stage. And as much as he distanced himself from Tolkien later on, there *are* examples of Tolkien's work slipping into the earliest edition of *Dungeons & Dragons.* A goblin's lair will have a goblin king, and his guard is just like what is seen in *The Hobbit.* Orc villages are liable to have high-level humans present who are serving as leaders in a manner reminiscent of Saruman or the Mouth of Sauron. But alongside these few examples are Lord Dunsany's gnolls, Sterling Lanier's green slime, de Camp and Pratt's hill giants, frost giants, and fire giants. Gargoyles are drawn straight from medieval architecture. Angry villagers are pulled directly from classic horror movies to provide a means for the referee to police the players during urban sequences. And on the same wandering monster charts that contain traditional mythological creatures such as minotaurs, unicorns, dryads, and pegasi, there are apts, banths, thoats, calots, white apes, orluks, sith, tharks, and darseen that come right out of Edgar Rice Burroughs's stories of Barsoom.

But the lists of monsters here are merely intended to be an aid in helping the referee get a game off the ground. They are a set of examples, they are not intended to be a restricted or canonical bestiary. Gygax insists that "there is no practical limitation to the variety of monsters possible" and rattles off examples from his own games: titans, cyclopses, juggernauts, living statues, salamanders, gelatinous cubes, robots, golems, and androids. Not even science-fiction elements are off limits here. Elsewhere, he writes that "some areas of land could be gates into other worlds, dimensions, times, or whatever. Mars is given in these rules, but some other fantastic world or setting could be equally possible." And as for the player-characters, there is no limit on them under original *D&D* either. Gygax states that "there is no reason that players cannot be allowed to play as virtually anything, provided they begin relatively weak and work up to the top."

Original *D&D* is explicitly wide open for adaption to almost any conceivable setting. There is nothing remotely like the Middle Earth style world that's assumed to be the default background of the game. The Tolkienesque style certainly overwhelmed the line during the eighties, but the game's original purchasers were simply not expected to sit down and work out a *Forgotten Realms* campaign map loaded with various kingdoms and adventure hooks and demi-human strongholds carefully demarcated more or less in imitation of the maps of Middle Earth. They weren't going to necessarily create their own fantasy languages as Tolkien did or work out elaborate campaign plots after the fashion of the *Dragonlance* novels either.

But they were going to have to be creative right from the start, and Gygax helpfully provided direction to those early Dungeon Masters concerning how they were to prepare for their campaigns:

> *The referee bears the entire burden here, but if care and thought are used, the reward will more than repay him. First, the referee must draw out a minimum of half a dozen maps of the levels of his 'underworld', people them with monsters of various horrid aspect, distribute treasures accordingly,*

*and note the location of the latter two on **keys**, each corresponding to the appropriate level.… When this task is completed the participants can then be allowed to make their first descent into the dungeons beneath the 'huge ruined pile, a vast castle built by generations of mad wizards and insane geniuses.'*

This is altogether unlike anything in fantasy literature.[4] If it *was* set in the world of an existing fantasy novel, it would be far more at home in Jack Vance's *Dying Earth* or Lin Carter's *The Warrior of World's End* than in Tolkien's Middle Earth. And while Gygax drew from all manner of stories, myths, and legends to populate his imaginary worlds, the heart of the thing he constructed was unprecedented. Consider just how off the wall his "mythical underworld"[5] really was:

- *"It is generally true that any monster or man can see in total darkness as far as the dungeons are concerned except player-characters."*

- *"Doors will automatically open for monsters, unless they are held shut by the characters. Doors can be wedged open by means of spikes, but there is a one-third chance (die 5-6) that the spike will slip and the door will shut."*

- *"Monsters are assumed to have permanent infravision as long as they are not serving some character."*

It's very difficult to imagine how some of this could even make sense. But original *D&D* is first and foremost a *game*—not a toy for frustrated fantasy novelists. If someone were to insist on finding literary inspirations that could justify these sorts of design choices, then the drug-infused strangeness of Margaret St. Clair's novels would necessarily be a much closer fit than anything of Tolkien's.

The central role of halflings, elves, and dwarves in the lineup of player-character options looks at first blush to be a prime repository for Tolkien's influence on the game. The dwarves in *The Hobbit* were certainly as greedy and shortsighted as the typical player-character party. And even if most games begin with chance meetings in a tavern rather than something more akin to the Council of Elrond, the diversity of race and class among party members certainly seems to have caught on as an enduring trope of the medium. Murder hobos they may be, but whatever else their faults, the adventuring party is most assuredly a fellowship.

But it may also be the case that the halfling was imported to the game from *Chainmail* not so much to ratify it as a central premise of the game, but to illustrate how a player's wish to play something offbeat could still be accommodated even with so minimal a rule set. The level limits on demi-humans are certainly harsh enough that Gygax seems to be discouraging them as much as he can. Meanwhile, the elf depicted in the original *D&D* rules must choose to perform as either a fighter or a magic-user at the start of each session—something quite unlike anything in the literary antecedents. And the elf's ability to spot secret doors and the dwarf's ability to detect sloping passages likewise make little sense outside the context of the bizarre funhouse dungeon environments that are so integral to the game.

The addition of the cleric class stands in stark contrast to this. This player archetype is much more of a first-class entity, with numerous original game mechanics developed for it. In contrast, the elf, dwarf, and halfling are presented as restricted variants of the fighting-man and magic-user classes with a game-oriented perk or two to compensate for the level restrictions. If this is indicative of Tolkien's influence on the game due to the *Chainmail Fantasy Supplement* being the original basis of the game, then the cleric illustrates how medieval history was considerably more of an influence.

The inspiration for the cleric's prohibition on the use of edged weapons originates in medieval tapestries depicting Bishop Odo fighting with a club.[6] The cleric's spell list is largely modeled after biblical accounts of miracles. But rather than being part of an organized effort to, say, take back the Holy Land from Saracens, the character class seems to take more inspiration from figures from horror literature such as Van Helsing. Indeed, a whole raft of undead creatures was added to original *D&D* in order to provide a more fantastic nemesis for clerics to contend with than what would have been available in the *Chainmail Fantasy Supplement* by itself. Compared to this lavish detail, the Tolkien-derived demi-humans amount to little more than an afterthought.

Needless to say, this sort of explicit religious element was something that Tolkien was at pains to avoid in his fantasy novels. And if the addition of the paladin from *Three Hearts and Three Lions* as a core class in *AD&D* was balanced by the inclusion of the Tolkien's rangers, it must also be noted that the incorporation of half-elves and the Dunedain is significantly watered down in comparison to their antecedents in Tolkien's stories. Indeed, the addition in *AD&D* of the monk class, which is largely drawn from seventies martial arts movies, seems to be a reiteration of the "play as virtually anything" principle from the original rule set.

Of course, you can list all of the literary influences on the game, and people will still see Tolkien as being a primary force in the formation of the game regardless of the actual proportion of his contributions. For a lot of people, he is such an overpowering figure in terms of his position as an author who effectively *defines* fantasy that it's difficult for them to grasp that other writers took a substantially different approach to the genre. Just like when game masters ignore rules that they don't understand or that are too cumbersome in actual play, so too will they gloss over anything that strikes them as being too far out of bounds of what seems them to be "reasonable" for fantasy.

The fact is that Tolkien was just *one* perspective on fantasy in the early seventies; he was just one voice among many and was far from being dominant. The fantasy world of the second role-playing game to be created, Ken St. Andre's *Tunnels & Trolls*, "was based on *The Lord of The Rings* as it would have been done by Marvel Comics in 1974 with Conan, Elric, the Gray Mouser and a host of bad guys thrown in."[7] The literary antecedents for the three character types of that game were Howard's Conan, Vance's Cugel, and Tolkien's Gandalf. As far as tabletop games were concerned, Tolkien was certainly a major influence. But he was far from the only one, and Gary Gygax himself acknowledged equal, or even more significant, contributions from other fantasy writers.

Add to this the fact that not even Tolkien was Tolkienesque in the seventies; the norm for fantasy was so different then, and Tolkien's ascendance was still sufficiently incomplete that his worlds and characters were sometimes portrayed in surprisingly incongruous ways. While it may not be all that surprising that Eowyn would get the Deja Thoris treatment at the hands of Frank Frazetta, it's striking to see how the book covers of Tolkien's works in the seventies were such a far cry from the Larry Elmore paintings that would come to dominate the eighties. In the Rankin/Bass adaption of *The Hobbit* to television, the elves look downright *weird*. From their alien appearances to their odd, long-legged proportions, they are nothing like the fair-haired, well-spoken sophisticates from Peter Jackson's more recent blockbusters.

People were different then. They thought differently. They took different things for granted. What we tend to think of as even being normal or inevitable for fantasy didn't even exist when original *D&D* was being published. And the fact remains that the best way to get inside of the heads of both the game designers and their intended audience is to read the books that they cited as their inspirations. We *do* have later works where *D&D* was adapted to fit the expectations of people who were bred on watered-down mass-market epic fantasy trilogies. But the earliest efforts in tabletop role-playing bore the marks of the older, wilder pulp fantasies that lapsed into obscurity in the mid-eighties.[8]

Dungeons & Dragons was a product of its times. And while Tolkien made his mark on the game at the earliest stages, there were a great many authors who did the same. As Peter Bebergal put it, "*D&D* is a living expression of pulp, science fiction, and fantasy literature, not merely an overly-complicated board game."[9] When Gygax asserted that "de Camp & Pratt, Robert E, Howard, Fritz Leiber, Jack Vance, H. P. Lovecraft, and A. Merritt" were "the most immediate influences upon AD&D", there's really no reason not to take him at his word.

Notes

1. See "1972 Gygax Article" at *Grognardia* for the full article.

2. See "The Primacy of Tolkien" at *Delta's D&D Hotspot* for more.

3. In Tolkien's essay "On Fairy Stories," he explains that the Oxford English Dictionary's association of diminutive size with fairies is a relatively recent development. He quite disliked the stories he read in that vein while growing up.

4. That paragraph has more in common with Infocom's *Hollywood Hijinx* (1986) and id Software's *Doom* (1993) than anything in science fiction and fantasy literature from before 1974.

5. See Jason Cone aka Philotomy's "The Dungeon as a Mythic Underworld" for more on this.

6. Rick Stump's "Misunderstood and Improperly Played - the Cleric" is a great post on this topic.

7. This is from the "Demon Issue Interview with Ken St. Andre" from 1986.

8. James Maliszewski has been asserting this for a long time; see "Some Words about Pulp Fantasy" for details.

9. "Dungeons & Dragons 5th Edition gets it mostly right" is over at BoingBoing.

Afterword: Appendix N Matters

It's difficult to find a stopping place with something like Appendix N. The forty-three installments in this series delve only into the books that Gary Gygax singled out in particular, and for the authors whose body of works he recommended, I only covered a single novel. Then there are the series that he highlighted. I stopped with those after the first volume when I sometimes wanted to put the entire project on hold to read them to the end. Finally, there are all the fantasy authors that wrote since the seventies that people think deserve a place on a list like this. People want to know if more recent authors measure up to these old classics. But even more, people really want to know which contemporaries of the Appendix N authors were snubbed by being excluded when they really deserved to be there.

By far the most often suggested names that come up when people discuss the Appendix N list are C. L. Moore and Ursula K. Le Guin. And while I can see how Moore at least belongs on just about any list which includes both H. P. Lovecraft and Robert E. Howard, I actually rather doubt that her omission is accidental. She wrote some of the greatest fantasy and science-fiction stories ever written, but her heroes lack the sort of "stamp"[1] that would have most appealed to the co-designer of *Dungeons & Dragons*. Northwest Smith is at times a little too passive, a mere foil for some other overwhelmingly feminine character. Indeed, Moore could even write disembodied brains that positively exude femininity. While it's positively astounding, it just isn't consistent with the spirit of early *D&D* in the same way that Leiber, Vance, and Moorcock are.

That so many people insist on Le Guin's *Earthsea Trilogy* perplexes me though. It's rather dull in comparison to the other Appendix N books. The opening scene of the first novel where a novice spell-caster saves his village with the equivalent of a cantrip or two is pretty good. And the part where he defeats several dragons might be useful for anyone looking for inspiration for running games. But the lack of connection to the real world that is so fundamental to the Appendix N books is missing, giving her work more in common with the derivative works of the eighties than anything in Appendix N. The way that the wizardly protagonist teams up with rather ordinary children in the second and third books is not just different from typical *D&D* stuff; it's a little weird. And defeating Lovecraftian terrors with the power of friendship *really* isn't how any *D&D* player adventures in a mythical underworld.

I really don't think that many of us on the wrong side of the canon gap even know what we're looking at when we see the list of Gygax's inspirations. I think the fact that people are so quick to suggest that significant authors like Lord Dunsany be removed so writers like Le Guin can replace them shows how they have missed the point of the appendix. They are simply not in tune with the times that produced the original book list. This preservation of a historical perspective is a small thing, perhaps, but it may be the most important thing that Appendix N preserves.

I say this because when I went and spoke to Ken St. Andre, who helped pioneer one of the earliest efforts in role-playing game design in response to and in competition with Gygax, his reactions were very different than what I see in most discussions of Appendix N. It almost sounded as if, to him, L. Sprague de Camp and Lin Carter were figures to be held in reverence. Books like Roger Zelazny's *Jack of Shadows* and Andre Norton's *Witchworld* novels were spoken of in much the same tone as *The Fellowship of the Ring*. And there, towering over all the other authors in both stature and influence, was the man that dominated both Gygax's and St. Andre's concepts of fantasy and world building. No, it wasn't J. R. R. Tolkien. It was Edgar Rice Burroughs. And the book series I needed to drop everything to go take a look at based on his advice? It was *Tarzan of the Apes*, a hero that dates all the way back in 1912!

The important thing to notice here is the undiluted zeal of St. Andre's for classic science fiction and fantasy. And yet, as the guy was confirming many of my suspicions and explaining things that I'd been trying to articulate for a long time, even I had trouble believing the full extent of it, even though I know that Tolkienesque fantasy isn't very much like Tolkien's actual work, even though I know that Lovecraftian horror has very little to do with what Lovecraft actually wrote and the swords and sorcery genre that we *think* we know is a far cry from what Robert E. Howard actually wrote. You'd think that by now that I'd be able to take a guy at his word that a classic pulp fantasy novel really is as undeniably awesome as he says it is, but somehow, it's not like that. Like everyone else, I remain a product of my own times.

But when I went and read the books he recommended, nearly every chapter had something in it that could surprise me. The savagery! The action! The oft-omitted details that actually make *sense* of a character's actions that are absent from so many derivative works. The nuance that the many smear campaigns against the pulps had convinced me would not be there. I was blown away. Repeatedly!

I'm not alone in this. I am far from the only one. I know, because people like Stewart Gee write in to explain how it is for them:

> *My father, long ago, made mention in passing of his enjoyment in the original Tarzan and some of the stories that followed. I never fully understood the sentiment, or would have equated such appreciation with a potential kinship of spirit in other characters like Conan... until now. He was from an older generation that saw two wars during its lifetime, and he harbored a deep love of both hunting and boxing. I find myself re-evaluating his tastes now, many years after his passing, and that is unsettling... but perhaps in this, he and I were more alike than I was willing to admit.*

This literary estrangement between the generations isn't normal. And it's not just that people in the seventies would have read many of the same science-fiction and fantasy authors that their parents and even grandparents did. The scope of things that fall within the black hole of the generation gap seems to be expanding almost exponentially now. Even things like *Bugs Bunny* and *Tom & Jerry*—I would have watched the same stuff that my big brother watched when I was a kid—and we were familiar with the same classic cartoons that our parents and grandparents would have watched. But that's changed now. And it goes well beyond older television shows quietly dropping off the radar and being forgotten. Millennials who will admit to never have seen them still somehow "know" that those old books and shows and films and authors were racist or something and deserve to be erased.[3]

When it was announced that the World Fantasy Award was replacing its iconic Lovecraft bust, Joyce Carol Oates declared that the literary canon is "saturated with racism, sexism, anti-semitism, anti-democracy... and lunacy." Oates graciously allows that "tossing it all out is no solution." But why wouldn't you toss it all out? If it really was as bad as people claim, you probably *would* do just that. Why would people read the works of such terrible authors? As it happens, they mostly don't. And if by some chance they do, their revulsion can be almost physical, as this woman describes it:[2]

> *I read a lot of Bradbury as a teen and thought his stories were wonderful. Rereading his stories now is actively painful to me. I'm a lot more able to pick up on those subtle cues, and less able to make excuses for them, that the author doesn't really see his female characters as important, or real, or three dimensional, or people.*

Are we really so advanced a civilization now that reading *The Martian Chronicles* should make us ill?

Older readers steeped in the classics will be tempted to dismiss her reaction as an outlier, but it really is a sign of the times. This attitude certainly shows up in a great many of the reviews of old works of fantasy and science fiction that pepper the Internet. It's almost as if there is a barrier in these peoples' minds. As soon as they get to something they have been trained to think of as being "problematic," they shut down. Very little in the way of any kind of analysis of the material can even be done because calling out and reviling everything from madonna/whore complexes to "black and white morality" is the sort of thing that passes for deep or sophisticated thinking.

The retiring of Lovecraft's bust from the World Fantasy Awards is therefore not so much reminiscent of statues of Stalin being pulled down in post-Soviet Russia. It's more a reflection of the Berlin wall *going up*. It used to be that reading centuries-old books was almost universally considered to be a very good thing, to the point of being the very definition of an education. Now, looking into works that are merely decades old is increasingly beyond the pale. People with this attitude will even go so far as to object to having to read Ovid at university, and college administrators—far from standing up to this—seem instead to be on the lookout to *accommodate* this sort of literary thought-policing.

In the not-too-distant past, the "dangerous visions" of the day could be enjoyed side by side with classic fiction by Lord Dunsany and A. Merritt. Professionals with highly divergent views on politics and religion could coexist within the pages of the same magazines. And people who were keen on challenging every imaginable taboo could get on within the same market where more traditional approaches to science fiction and fantasy were still given space on the spinner racks. People were free then in a way that's hard to even imagine now. Political correctness and its legions of freelance thought police were only beginning to gain a foothold in the arts, and at least some knowledge of the old ways and attitudes could still be taken for granted. That is clearly not the case any longer.

The Appendix N list therefore preserves more than a list of books that are of special interest to fans of classic *Dungeons & Dragons*. It is also a snapshot of what fantasy fandom was in the seventies. Don't let anyone tell you otherwise. While the list is not without its idiosyncrasies, it is nevertheless a representative sample of the authors who were popular at the time, and who would have been translated into foreign languages when other countries began importing the literary phenomena of science fiction and fantasy.[4]

For readers looking to go beyond the three biggest names in fantasy fiction of the 20th century, Appendix N is a great start. Our science fiction and fantasy heritage is greater than we know and far better than many would suspect. But this survey of works spanning the better part of six decades also reveals the surprising scope and rapidity of the changes within our culture. Even a brief survey such as this uncovers much that is barely conceivable to the current generation. And although these works were primarily intended to entertain, they nevertheless preserve a vision of courage, determination, and undiluted heroism we sorely need today.

Appendix N contains more than the story behind how familiar genres and games came to be. It also preserves a sense of who we were, and what we may yet become again, if we so choose.

Notes

1. See "Gygax on Tolkien (Again)" at *Grognardia* for more on Gygax's views on heroic figures of the Conan "stamp."

2. This is from a comment on Michael R. Underwood's "Science Fiction and Fantasy 101: Thinking Academically About Genre."

3. This observation is from Alex Kimball.

4. See my own "Fantacollana: Italy's Take on the Swords & Sorcery Canon of the Seventies" for more on this.

Appendix A:
Adventurer Conqueror King System
by Alexander Macris

The funny thing about this game is that, in many ways, it's one that I've already been playing for years. It takes the *Basic* and *Expert D&D* sets of my youth as a starting point and then develops from there. I've said before, those sets are the purest, most refined, best-designed iteration of the original fantasy role-playing game.[1] They look simplistic maybe and a bit clunky, but I get a surprising amount of mileage out of them. Under those rules, I've seen players completely fall apart facing "cream puff" monsters in "The Keep on the Borderlands" that characters from more recent systems would roll right over. I've seen "The Isle of Dread"[2] eat a large party of adventurers one by one as they made their way to its central plateau. I've seen high-level characters pull out every trick they could muster in order to survive a session-spanning combat in "Steading of the Giant Chief."[3] Even if I was otherwise indifferent, it's hard to argue with the fact that people will just flat out play this game.

So yeah, I'm glad to see that Alexander Macris and company had the savvy to use *my* version of *D&D* as the basis for their take on their iteration. Still, picking this up, I initially had to wonder how they could possibly improve on such a quintessential work. Can they entice me away from my beloved red book with the Erol Otus cover artwork? Or will I see things that I intend to steal for my own game and then somehow never get around to it? There's nothing for it but to check out what's inside and see how it stacks up....

Characters

The surprising thing here is that the most obvious changes were not made. Thieves still have only d4 hit dice. Clerics still don't get a spell at first level. Attributes are still rolled 3d6 in order without any monkeying around besides maybe dropping a stat by two points in order to raise a prime requisite by one. Most people can't leave this stuff alone. Heck, not even Gygax could leave this stuff alone. This is a very good start in my opinion because these choices mean that this is a *proper* version of *D&D* where the players don't get a lot of handouts and they're forced to learn how to work together. That's just how things should be in my book.

One subtle change is that the option to reroll pitifully low hit points or to possibly even throw out "hopeless" characters is eliminated. You know, maybe it is kind of tacky to set the character generation process up in such a way that the Dungeon Master has to start making judgment calls almost immediately. The solution presented here is that, if you want to be *sure* to get something you'll actually want to play—because you're a sissy and all, *obviously*—then you have to roll up **five** characters. You get to run with the best one, but you have to take the next best two as backups to use next when your favorite dies. *Then* you have to give the remaining two to the Dungeon Master so that he doesn't have to spend so much time creating non-player-characters like henchmen and hirelings himself. That's pretty harsh for some sort of mercy rule. If you want favors from the DM in this game, you have to be willing to lighten his workload! Heh.

The classes are going to be fairly familiar except that the halfling has been replaced with two new variations of the other demi-human classes: a dwarven cleric and a fancy elven thief/magic-user. (Note: there are halflings in the monster section, so you can still kill them for fun if you are of a chaotic bent.) These new demi-human options have fully developed class descriptions, and they are given first-class treatment throughout the rule book. These are not at all some kind of "multi-classing" type hack, though it's obvious they were put together from some sort of balanced and generic class toolkit. (I couldn't tell you if the loss in charm is made up for in flexibility or playability though. That's your call.) The other classes are adaptions of the assassin, bard, and ranger from *AD&D*. The one surprise here is the sword dancer, a female-only cleric variant.

Proficiencies

There are so many ways to mess this sort of thing up. It seems like every new version of just about every role-playing game has added more and more skills, feats, options, chrome, and cruft, often to the point where they become unplayable monstrosities. When I was a kid, I was a sucker for anything with "Advanced" slapped on the cover like anyone else. But as I grew older, I seemed to have less and less of a desire to turn this aspect of the game into a chore. I am quite happy to tell people that whatever it is they wanted to do *just worked*™. If they're asking for something that sounds iffy, I might ask them to roll a relevant attribute or less on a d20. That's the *Basic D&D* way, after all, and it works just fine. So I don't *need* this stuff.

But I will say this section accomplishes a great deal for the system in a mere ten pages. Firstly, a great many of the class abilities show up on these lists, including almost all of the thief skills. That means there is a very simple way to capture the gist of multi-classed characters without having to bolt on kludgey rules or gradually adding in an interminable series of custom character classes. Secondly, several things that often become the subject of house rulings are codified here. For example, people who want a way to give non-clerics a chance to patch people up after a fight have to give up some other perk in order to do that. Those who want a little something extra for combat-related advantages have to do without things that might make them more flexible or otherwise better fulfill their class role. Finally, many of the NPC specialists-for-hire from early editions of *D&D* have their skills broken down and explained here. This means you can not only work out how the players might take on various do-it-yourself type projects at less than expert-level proficiency, but you can also see how all of the specialist characters can be generated from "classless" normal human characters.

I have to say, there is some pretty deft design work here. The proficiency system captures a lot of the flexibility of point-build systems like *GURPS* but *without* sacrificing the overall accessibility of old-school gaming. At the same time, a lot of the undeveloped aspects of the old games are addressed with concise rules, saving the Dungeon Master from having to make ad hoc rulings in order to bring them into play. And we've already seen that proficiencies end up having a great impact on the mass combats of *Domains At War*.[4] And there are a few other nice touches such as how the fighters pick up new proficiencies at a much faster rate than mages, further differentiating the classes in a believable way. These rules add a lot to the game; they solve a problem I don't really have, sure, but you wouldn't have to twist my arm too hard to get me to use them.

Magic

The big change here is that magic-users can cast from any of their known spells. This is an incredibly common modification in rule sets that came after classic *D&D*, so it's not really a surprise to see it crop up here. But it *is* a surprise that a rule set that keeps such venerable traditions as the d4 thief and the spell-less first-level cleric would go down this decidedly "new school" path. This just isn't how *real* Vancian magic works, after all.

In this variant, the concept of repertoire is introduced, and what is actually kept in spell books is more carefully delineated. The idea is that each mage will have a small set of spells in active rotation. Your spellbook might be full of all kinds of esoteric formulas, but you cannot just cast them willy-nilly until you've done the work to get them into your routine. It's like a musician who could conceivably play just almost any piece of music that's at his skill level, but to actually *perform* them, he has to do a significant amount of work first. If you want to change your magical repertoire, though, you're looking at spending one week and 1,000 gp per spell level. This is yet another example of the designer giving players what looks like a "free" perk when he's simultaneously taking something significant away that they would otherwise take for granted.

But by setting things up this way, the designer also has an opportunity to address a longstanding problem. Everyone seems to think that a mage with high intelligence should be able to do a much better job than his not-so-bright competitors. In the *Greyhawk* supplement and again in *AD&D*, Gygax took a stab at incorporating this idea by having the players roll a chance to know each spell based on their intelligence score. It's cumbersome and wonky and rarely used in actual play. In *these* rules, though, the mage gets a number of randomly chosen first-level spells in his repertoire equal to his intelligence bonus. I have to say, I really like this rule because it preserves the simplicity of the old *Basic* rules, it allows players to start the game with their beloved "Sleep" spell, it gives a significant but not overpowering edge to high-intelligence mages, and it also gives an avenue by which some of the less commonly used first-level spells might come into play. Not bad!

But even that's not the most significant rules change here. If you'll recall, the classic *Basic D&D* rules forbid magic-users from both moving *and* casting spells within a single combat round. If you play out your combats in the old "theater of the mind" style, this may not be that big of a deal. But as soon as you switch to using miniatures, it has the profound effect of turning the magic-users into artillery units. You practically have to limber and unlimber them in order to get them into position to cast a combat spell! Another lesser-known aspect of the game is that there is no explicit way to spoil a spell caster's casting within the Basic D&D rules. This is pretty much a staple of fantasy gaming, and finding a way to work that in requires some creative interpretation.

Adventurer Conqueror King preserves the old rule of forbidding a mage from moving on the combat round that he casts a spell, but if he decides to cast a spell, he must declare his intention to do so before initiative is rolled. If anything happens to him that causes him damage or to forces him to make a saving throw, his spell is not only spoiled, but *also counts against the number of spells he can cast each day!* Come to think of it, I'm just not entirely sure how I would have adjudicated a duel between rival mages under my well-worn *D&D* booklets. Even better, just as in Steve Jackson's classic microgame *Wizard*, a mage with a high dexterity is a force to be reckoned with!

I admit, I'm as much of a purist as anyone. The past several years, I've been more interested in seeing what happens when you assume that classic *D&D* is not broken than in fixing any of the perceived problems with it. I'm just not that big on house ruling my games. And when I play "new school" games, I really chafe at how clerics, for instance, don't have to pick out specific spells when they do their morning prayer thing. But the restrictions on mages' repertoires and the explicit rules for spoiling spells are so devious that I think I can be convinced to set aside my normal preferences for this rule set. These design changes are not changing things in the manner of the typical house ruler. Several related things are being fine tuned at once here in order to produce a very specific result. I would never have been inclined to make any one of these rules changes. (I would *never* think to embrace individual initiative on my own, for instance.) But I have to say, I quite like the way they all work together. It's like "real" old-school gaming is suddenly snapping into focus into something tighter and cleaner.

One more thing: from the standpoint of a student of the Appendix N reading list, one rule here particularly stands out. In *AD&D*, magic-users can only gain new spells for their spell books by copying them from scrolls and so forth, but here—starting at the fifth level—mages can research spells that they don't have formulas for without having to luck into them in a treasure horde or purchase them from some sort of guild. If a mage has amassed a sufficiently large library of magical tomes, he can work it out for himself if he dedicates time, money, and makes a Magical Engineering proficiency check. Those wonderful "shelves stacked with volumes, folios and librams" that you read about in Jack Vance's *The Eyes of the Overworld* now have an explicit application in these rules. That's really cool.

Conclusion

Okay, I haven't even gone into how the domain game is addressed in this system. Yeah, there's a lot here for that, but you probably won't want to touch it if you can't abide the relatively radical changes I've covered here with regard to character generation, proficiencies, and spellcasting.

I admit, though, what's particularly nice about this game is how you can instantly determine how many mercenaries, specialists, and henchmen are available at a given Market Class. Similarly, you get a breakdown of how many spellcasters are available for hire, what their rates are, and the rate at which they can cast spells of a given level. Both of those things are something I've had to pull out of thin air for nearly every adventure I've ever run, *and I finally have playable rules that do that which actually make sense!* Basic campaign demographics are also covered in detail, and you can tell at a glance the number of NPC's of a given level that will be in a particular realm. Whether you want to start fighting battles at the domain level or whether you want to set up a thieves or assassins guild at a major metropolis, there are concise rules here to help get you started. And there is comprehensible advice for converting real-world kingdoms and existing campaign settings into the *Adventurer Conqueror King* system.

On the whole, it looks like the things that are added to the game solve far more problems than they create. Even if you don't leave classic *D&D* altogether, there are plenty of things in this volume that can help you run your game. It is clearly written for modern gamers, and many common things that players today would ask for are incorporated into the rules, but this is nevertheless done in such a way as to preserve the elusive old-school flavor of the earliest editions of the game. Even though a great many aspects of the old games are nailed down in a systematic way, these new systems seem to be able to account for the *feel* of a great many fragments and oddities from the old editions in a coherent manner. This is not the result of some sort of grail quest to find the authentic, "totally for real" ur-*D&D* that was **actually played** in the seventies. But it *is* a game that will let you tackle the themes those old grognards seemed to take for granted even though they never really explained **how** to do it.

In short, this is a very fine product that deserves every ounce of praise and buzz that it has generated in the gaming blogs and on social media. It may sound like an oxymoron, but the state of the art in old-school gaming really is moving forward. *This* is the sort of thing that helps make this the best time ever to be a tabletop gamer.

Notes

1. See my post "Snappy Answers to Trollish Questions" for more on this.

2. See "Exploring the Isle of Dread, session three" for details.

3. My post "G1 with B/X: Slumber Party in the Hill Giant's Throne Room" has the complete story.

4. My review of *Domains at War: Battles* is over on the *Castalia House* blog.

Appendix B: *Dwimmermount*

by James Maliszewski, Alexander Macris, and Tavis Allison

This book is a monster. Clocking in at over four hundred pages, it has everything you'd need for a long-running campaign: background, history, game-mastering advice, a stocked wilderness area, a fully described "Keep on the Borderlands" type of base for the players to use, new spells, new monsters, new magic items, and one of the biggest and most elaborate dungeons ever published. It's positively brimming with references, developments, and applications of material drawn from Gary Gygax's Appendix N reading list from *Advanced Dungeons & Dragons*. If you've wondered what fantasy role-playing adventure would look like if someone revisited its foundations and took sort of a neoclassical approach to it, this is it!

The overall tone is much closer to the science fantasy[1] of Jack Vance than the glam/goth/punk mashup in evidence in recent incarnations of the *D&D* franchise. The exact same willingness to mix in science-fiction elements that are in evidence in classic game products *Greyhawk*, *Blackmoor*, and "Expedition to Barrier Peaks" is here in spades. It is perhaps an homage to Edgar Rice Burroughs that the underworld sprawls to the extent that it does. Much more explicit are Robert E. Howard's Hyperborean barbarians exploding out of the north to smite a sorcerous and decadent empire. It's A. Merritt that provides the most impact on the material, however: not only is there an actual moon pool in the dungeon, but there are also frogmen about as well. (To be fair, the latter do seem to be more out of Lovecraft than anything else, but given that Lovecraft also claims a spot in the Appendix N list, this is still a win for fans of weird fiction.) Finally, the old three-point alignment system from Poul Anderson's *Three Hearts and Three Lions* is adapted here to this world with neither faerie nor Christendom; it is thoroughly integrated into both the general world history and the specifics of the adventure. Its ramifications are thought through and consistently applied in everything from the most obscure lore and setting history to traps, encounters, and magic items.

The real payoff for going back to the pulp roots of the game for inspiration is that it no longer feels like something that's derivative of watered-down Tolkien ripoffs. Everything feels much more alien and mysterious. All the classic adventure gaming tropes are here, but you really can't take anything for granted in this new context. Old standbys like dwarves and elves are here more or less as you'd expect; a set of variant cleric classes have been detailed here that are more or less along the same lines as the ones introduced way back in the second edition *Advanced Dungeons & Dragons Player Handbook*. But both the demi-human races and the cleric classes are wedded directly to the campaign setting and the dungeon's backstory. Figuring out the history, origin, and nature of these things is a big part of the game. At the same time, they're not loaded with the gratuitous detail that failed novelists gravitate toward when they take solace in adventure design. Everything here on the races and classes is different enough to be intriguing while still being easy to pick up and run with.

Traveller has long been praised for creating a style of play where the players are primarily motivated by a desire to learn more about the nature of the game universe.[2] *Dwimmermount* manages to integrate that sort of premise into the context of classic *D&D* adventuring in a really significant way. Sure, if the players don't have any real leads to follow up on, they can always go back to the default m.o. of killing monsters and taking their stuff. But gold isn't the only thing that will motivate the players to keep rappelling down this particular rabbit hole. Indeed, there is an experience point value on information that is equal to that which can be gotten from retrieving treasure! That's the sort of incentive that even the most hardened dungeon delver can grasp immediately.

But this is by no means an ordinary dungeon crawl. You cannot clear this thing. Coming back alive from the place with a bunch of loot is liable to be a very big deal; it can inspire non-player-character parties to try to get in on the act. The players can make a lot of money (and thus experience) just selling maps that they make of the place. Doing so will help them level up a lot faster, but it will also generate additional attention and activity on those levels by rival adventuring groups. It's possible for rooms to get restocked between sessions, and it's possible for rooms to get looted before the players even find them!

Not that it has to get that wild and woolly. Sure, there are tools and advice on how to make the dungeon a living, breathing world. But you don't have to over-complicate things. By default, each room is set up to provide a solid and interesting situation. You can assume most of the time that the players happened to get there just as those things are playing out. This creates a bit of a quantum effect[3] to some extent, but it's a lot easier than trying to extrapolate out the action on eight or nine dungeon levels as the players gradually make their way down.

There are multiple factions on each level. And a lot of these don't just stay on the level that they're "supposed" to be on but are active on several of them simultaneously. Figuring out what these groups are up to, which ones to cooperate with, and which ones to wipe out is not an easy question. If you wish you could have done something a little more creative with the various factions of the iconic Caves of Chaos, you'll have plenty of chances to rectify that with this module. In any case, a lot of these monster groups are willing to talk and deal, and you get plenty of details to help you run them intelligently.

Another thing you can expect is a whole lot of *weird* stuff. If you've ever rolled up a dungeon randomly with your trusty *Basic Set* booklet, you not only got a surprising amount of empty rooms but a whole lot of "specials" as well. I was never that creative, so I ran out of ideas for those things rather quickly back in the day. After reading a few hundred pages of room descriptions from this dungeon, that is not a problem anymore! Without giving anything away, you can expect all kinds of contraptions, idols, and statues… most with some sort of puzzle associated with them. Most of the puzzles are optional, so they're not necessarily going to bring play to a halt when the players don't understand how they're supposed to work. I can easily see the players pass some of this stuff by, figure something out at a lower level, and then rush back to previous locations to try again to solve what stumped them before.

If you liked old text adventure games like the *Zork* series, *Planetfall*, and *Suspended*, then you'll get a lot of enjoyment out of this stuff. (I know I felt like a genius when I first figured out Flood Control Dam #5.) Best of all, you don't have to wade through several tedious levels with the standard goblin, kobold, and skeleton-type encounters. Every level has a blend of politics, danger, and strangeness. And all of it ties into the overarching mystery. There's a lot here, and it just goes on and on and on and *on*…. Well, that is kind of the point of a gigantic, sprawling monster dungeon like this. But going through each of these levels, at some point, my mind just couldn't be blown anymore. There's just so much awesomeness that I began to worry that the last few levels might not be able to provide anything like a real payoff. Fortunately, I was wrong.

Again, not to give too much away, but there *is* something down there that is on par with the audaciousness of the "domed city" on the final level of the old sample dungeon from the Holmes Basic Set rulebook. We now know that the drawing was by Tom Wham.[4] We also have the sample dungeon cross-section that J. Eric Holmes himself had intended to be used in the book.[5] A lot of design principles that can be garnered from these iconic maps are in evidence in *Dwimmermount*, sure. But I have to say, seeing something like this completely thought through, worked out, tested and developed... finally having it in my hands and ready for play... having all of those preceding levels and the background information and the history... it's just positively breathtaking. It's equally astonishing to see the things I speculated on in my retrospectives on *At the Earth's Core* and *The Moon Pool* pretty much all here and in an even more immediately playable format than I had imagined could be done.

But that doesn't mean that there's nothing left to create for a campaign that features this material. For starters, there are plenty of treasure maps within *Dwimmermount* that will give the players an excuse to go tromping about the wider world. There are portals and pointers to what are essentially entire new worlds, just like what I observed in *Changeling Earth*. And there are notes on how to continue the adventure into new dungeon levels beyond what are covered here. This is a framework that could easily support an entire line of supplements and modules.

One thing missing from all of this is an epic battle—something like the Battle of Five Armies on the slopes of the titular mountain or something like the climatic battles from the end of *A Princess of Mars* or the epic wars from Middle Earth's First Age, with legions of monstrous and demonic entities from all over the multiverse clashing as "Carmina Burana" blares in the background. Still, individual referees shouldn't have too much trouble whipping something up along those lines if that's their bag.

The *ACKS* edition of *Dwimmermount* is fully fleshed out with complete stats for each of the domains, including market class and the exact compo-sition of their military forces. And even though I am a staunch advocate of minimalist old-school gaming, I have to say that I quite like the way that the

ACKS proficiency system is used to flesh out the non-player-characters. It isn't just gratuitous chrome either but is fully integrated into the room descriptions and puzzles. And though I tend to lean toward doing initiative by side, I admit I am keen on running some of the combats from the lower levels with the *ACKS* individual initiative system, where there are explicit means of spoiling mages' spell-casting attempt.[6]

It's hard not to wonder though... is this thing so big, so richly detailed, and so complex that it is impossible for a mere mortal to run it? I don't think so. The leveling system—both in terms of the character development and in how the dungeon is organized—means that the complexity and detail are doled out steadily from session to session. The nuances of the competing factions are something that becomes clear just by playing; you don't have to figure it all out beforehand. Still, this is not Michael Curtis's *Stonehell*. You're not going to be running this like it's a one-page dungeon. You're not going to be taking levels from *Dwimmermount* and then dropping them into totally different campaign settings either, at least, not without a lot of retrofitting.

If you do want a little extra help keeping up with the campaign and running sessions, the "*Dwimmermount* Dungeon Tracker" PDF presents the dungeon maps with the room names marked directly on them opposite space to mark when random monsters turn up. It also has a brief summary of the level's background, factions, and oddities. Note that while the level maps from the "*Dwimmermount* Map Book" have neither the annotations nor the tracking aids, the companion booklet does contain a four-page extra large wilderness map and set of illustrations that break down the order in which the various levels were constructed.

Altogether, this is a pretty amazing set of products. The scope is so large that it's hard to believe that this ever got completed. And while the old grognards might have taken it for granted that tabletop adventure gaming should be something like what is presented here, the old guard never actually published anything of this scale. All those little kids looking at that "Skull Mountain" megadungeon map in their brand new Holmes *Basic Sets*... only a fraction of them had the skills to create something like that, and *none* of them had the option to just up and buy one. Now we not only have something like that available, but we also have one that incorporates decades of gaming experience. That's awesome. This is just one more reason why there's never been a better time to be playing tabletop games.

Notes

1. For more on science fantasy in the "Appendix N list, see D&D's Appendix N Roots Are Science Fantasy" over at *Roles, Rules, and Rolls*.

2. For more on this point, see the sidebar on page 81 in *GURPS Traveller* by Loren Wiseman.

3. See the *Quantum Ogre* series at *Hack & Slash* for more information on this well-known design issue in role-playing games.

4. Check out "Skull Mountain by Tom Wham" at *Zenopus Archives* to get the full story.

5. See "A Missing Link: A Miniature Megadungeon" over at *Semper Initiativus Unam* for details.

6. I know now that those rules were right there in the Cook/Marsh *Expert* book all along, but because they were never explicitly laid out in the sequence of play, I never got the chance to experience them. In any case, they were not in the Moldvay *Basic* rules at all, so it's really no wonder that I ended up playing it "wrong" for so many sessions. Doh!

Appendix C: *The Annotated Sorcerer*
by Ron Edwards

Before I review this work, I have to be upfront about the fact that I am not the target audience for this sort of product. I am perfectly happy playing vintage role-playing games like *Classic Traveller*, Moldvay *Basic D&D*, and *Car Wars*. I am simply not looking for a replacement for those games, and I feel like the RPG industry (such as it is) left me at some point rather than the reverse. Furthermore, when I run games with my kids at home and at conventions, I end up game mastering for all stripes of people. Because of that, incorporating the explicit adult and occult-type themes of *Sorcerer* just isn't in the cards for me. In spite of this, I have to say that Ron Edwards is far more interesting than the self-styled pundits of gaming make him out to be. While he is more often associated with the experimental new wave of role-playing that emerged at the tail end of the twentieth century, he nevertheless came up on classic games like *The Fantasy Trip* and *Champions* and played the heck out of them. He not only knows his Robert E. Howard and H. P. Lovecraft better than the run-of-the-mill *D&D* fan, but he has also crafted game mechanics that bring their respective takes on the mystic arts to the tabletop in ways that few games have even come close to attempting. And given the horrors that develop whenever game masters attempt to **impose** story on the medium of role-playing games, it actually is pretty interesting to see what exactly he's done in order to encourage story to **emerge** naturally in the course of gameplay.

While I now readily admit that Ron Edwards is a far more significant game designer than I imagined before reading through this groundbreaking game, I also have to say that I am really irritated with the whole premise of these annotations. I mean, I have an annotated edition of Robert Louis Stevenson's *Treasure Island*; it's incredibly handy to have some of the language and cultural differences spelled out there. But this game's not even two decades old; it's just a bit much to see it get the "study bible" treatment. Sure, that's basically a gazillion years ago in Internet time; I just don't see why a revision, a designer's notes article, a retrospective, or even the addition of *GURPS* style sidebars wouldn't have been good enough to handle the problems created by the text's relative antiquity.

Yet even though the format bugs me, I have to admit that the information contained in the annotations really is essential to understanding the implications of the system. This game really is different from just about every other role-playing game I've seen. The rules are not tied to a specific setting. In fact, they could just as easily be adapted to playing swords and sorcery, a gritty blend of *Twin Peaks*, *Highlander*, and *Miami Vice*, or even science fiction and cyberpunk. At the same time, this is not a generic game. It is completely focused on themes of forbidden knowledge, demon summoning, relationships with those beings over time, and the balance between risk and corruption in a dangerous world. While the game leaves nailing down the exact nature of magic and the supernatural as an exercise for the referee, it nevertheless requires a world where sorcery is both rare and secret. So while there is no "official" *Sorcerer* setting, the rules nevertheless imply a great deal about *your Sorcerer* setting. You do not turn dials to adapt the system to your tastes as in *GURPS*. It's yours to change and modify as you please, of course, but the primary avenue through which a referee adapts the rules to his campaign is via defining the game's terms. This gives the game an almost Euclidean level of applicability, and it's really instructive to see how the designer pulled that off.

The Heart of the Game

The core mechanic of *Sorcerer* is interesting in that it only comes into play for the sort of thing *GURPS* players would call "a contest of skill." The vast majority of skill checks and so forth that other games would make you do are simply declared to *just work*. They're literally hand-waved in the players' favor. The basic throw of the game is each character's player rolling a certain number of dice based on the relevant stat. (The actual type of dice used doesn't matter as long as everyone is using the same thing; now's your chance to break out a big mess of d12s!) Success goes to the person with the highest showing value. (Yes, there are allowances for tie-breakers.) That person's degree of success is "the number of dice that show higher values than the highest of the loser's dice." (Don't get crazy and try to line the dice up in order like in *Risk*; just read them exactly like I just said there.) The degree of success is folded into the subsequent rolls as bonus dice, encouraging players to try to set up difficult tasks by playing to their strengths with one action before following through with another.

The number of dice a player throws in these opposed roll situations is also modified based on how dramatic the player is being, whether or not the action is specific and well described, how smart the move is, and whether or not the action moves the plot along. (But *not* the plot the game master has envisioned in advance for the session, mind you.) It reminds me somewhat of how character point awards are handed out in *GURPS* at the end of each session: there are a couple of points the game master is supposed to award based on how well he thought the players role-played. I for one am loath to make a completely arbitrary judgment call like that, yet *Sorcerer* seems to be making me do it on *every stinking roll.* What's worse, the game is supposed to be set up in such a way that the players really have to be getting these bonuses in order to have any chance of succeeding or even just living. There's no way around it! Ron Edwards himself even criticizes his own system as falling into the "whoring for dice" trap, but he takes pains in the annotations to spell out that the bonus dice *are not incentives.* They are supposed to be handed out based on an objective assessment of how much fun has increased and whether or not a player-driven story is actually emerging.

Can this core mechanic actually deliver on what it promises to do? Does this work with regular, non-beret wearing types? I don't know! But I really want to emphasize that this system takes something I tend to avoid at all costs when I referee my more traditional role-playing games… and then goes and makes it central and fundamental to gameplay. I'll say it again: *I really do not like having to make assessments or judgments on how people actually role-play or imagine or engage.* That's a really personal thing. I mean, I'll kill your characters with cycle gangs, spiked pit traps, and aliens exploding from their chests and then laugh at you while you work up a new one. In a heartbeat even. But I would never single out Bob's funny voices as being inferior to the way Sally's hi-jinks end up creating this insanely funny scene that somehow gets everyone engaged in the action and hanging on every die roll even though they have disastrous tactical consequences in terms of what the game is "supposed" to be about. Sally rocks my table, no doubt. At least, *I* enjoy the zany action that ensues when she sits down to game with me. But who am I to decide that this is best for everybody when everyone else might be too nice to point out the complete lunacy of her actions directly? And how can I tell that any given action of hers is the thing that's going to make the entire adventure *a thing*? Can I openly make calls on that sort without making people feel bad or jealous or unappreciated or snubbed or left out?

You know, honestly… I tend to play to an emerging group dynamic, not to individual players. I love it when someone goes all "army of one" and then dies a completely ignoble, undramatic death. I love it when someone is not being a team player and then when the other players have had it, they collectively decide to frag that guy as soon as they get out of the dungeon. And I absolutely despise this notion of "spotlight time" that everyone seems to think they're entitled to now. (Since when?) On the other hand, the biggest thing I see the players of role-playing games mess up on is that they play the rules as they think them to be rather than the game as the referee runs it. Time and again, I see players start to do something awesome, then remember some odd nuance of the rules, then think out loud about it for a moment while bringing play to a halt, and then finally retract their action without once asking the referee what *he* thinks about all of it. Why can't they just describe their actions or explain what they want to do and let the game master tell them how it is in *his* game? It's like these people don't know what role-playing games are or how they actually work! They are certainly cutting themselves off from the sort of exciting things that set the medium apart from every other type of game in existence.

So what then is the fundamental thing that these rules *do* to get the emergent story going without having the game master baby it along all the time with railroads and sleight-of-story tricks? First, everything that isn't essential to developing conflict and action is hand-waved. ("It just worked!" and "Okay, you're there.") Second, the players are immediately rewarded for **describing their actions** and playing in terms of imagination rather than a byzantine mastery of some kind of gaming codex. Finally, the game master is pushed outside of his role as a neutral judge and encouraged to actively pour fuel on the fire whenever things are clicking and players are doing things that increase the engagement and immersion levels of everyone at the table.

After numerous false starts and countless play-test sessions… *this* is the basic outline of what Ron Edwards discovered could solve the problem of creating story in the context of a role-playing game session. Whether his answer is your thing or not, there is no doubt about the fact that his innovations are born out of actual play and refined through an iterative design approach. And even if you don't adopt his methods wholesale, there are insights that can be garnered here that can be just as easily applied to more traditional games. However, I would argue that a lot of good game masters are already running their games along these lines even if their rules don't explicitly back them up in this or encourage it.

Character Creation

Perhaps the most pleasant surprise in store for people unfamiliar with this game is that Steve Jackson's 1978 MicroGame *Wizard* provides the basic overall foundation for it. If you aren't familiar with that classic piece of Metagaming history, it was an inexpensive tactical combat game that orig-inally came in a small plastic baggie. Instead of rolling up characters, you designed them with a simple point-build system. Instead a lot of strange ratings and odd-sounding "saving throw" scores, just about everything in the game derived from three core character attributes. Instead of combat being played out loosely in the "theater of the mind" style with rules geared toward miniatures wargames that would have been nearly incomprehensible to the average role-player, everything in *Wizard* was played out on a hex map with concise rules and comprehensible range and movement specifications. Instead of being a game that you had to be initiated into by people who already knew how it was supposed to work, *Wizard* could be learned by kids straight from the rule book and played at the lunch table at school.

The game was a masterpiece, but it is not well known outside of a few ded-icated fans of vintage games. Some will argue that it wasn't really a true role-playing game, but in practice, anything that isn't directly related to characters and combat can be made up on the spot. A great many game-mastering tomes boil down to little more than props. Its release was a landmark event in game design history, but it just is *not* the sort of game that I would associate with the sort of people who are usually into indie role-playing games today. It is almost dumbfounding to consider it, but all of the wild theory and experimentation that came out of the indie-RPG community at the Forge over the last decade can be traced back to one guy who was eaten up with how awesome this game was, and was using it as a vehicle for addressing one of the biggest open problems in role-playing game design.

Players in *Sorcerer* have ten points to divide between three attributes: Stamina, Will, and Lore. Each score is also given a **descriptor** which explains why the score is what it is. I don't see any direct application for them per se, but somehow they turn what would otherwise be a meaningless list of numbers into a real character that is very easy to imagine. (It's subtle but similar to how you end up imagining a real person when you roll up a character in classic *Traveller*'s "life path" style-generation system.) Instead of a detailed list of mundane skills and social advantages, the character gets a catch-all **cover** score with its own descriptor. (That's another place where the game's implied setting shows up again: sorcery is necessarily both secret and uncommon in this game.) Instead of hit points, there is a **humanity** score which can be lowered due to the practice of dark magic-related acts and raised when a player-character banishes a demon that isn't bound to him. What it actually means is something that the game master has to nail down at the start of the game, and even the meaning of what "dropping to zero humanity" entails will be different from campaign to campaign. Instead of choosing from a menu of diverse disadvantages that are difficult to keep up with in the heat of a session, a sorcerer character chooses a single **price** that levies a stiff one-die penalty in a fairly large range of situations. Finally, a **telltale** is also chosen that gives away the fact that the player-character is a sorcerer to acquaintances who notice it.

The most challenging part of character design in *Sorcerer* lies in the choice of a **kicker**. One thing you see in a lot of role-playing groups is that everyone comes up with exactly the character they want to play... and then when they get together, the group has this problem of figuring out why the player-characters are together and why they would bother with whatever the game master has in mind. This is exactly what the concept of a kicker is supposed to help address. It might be a shocking discovery that launched the player-character on an adventure where he is in need of an unlikely set of allies. It might be a crazy opportunity that has turned up that makes the player-character get involved in something wild. It might be a bizarre mystery that scares the pants of anyone that knows about it: *the player-character has to do something, or who knows what will happen!* The idea behind this aspect of the game is to set things up in such a way that stories and action and mayhem can emerge from the course of play right from the get-go without it having to be imposed unilaterally by the game master via some sort of stock scenario structure. It's also one of the key features of the game that makes it better suited to just three or four players; juggling five or more might not be workable.

The typical *Sorcerer* game just won't begin with each character meeting at a tavern to hear from the little old man what the adventure is about. Each character is liable to end up beginning play getting into trouble individually, with the players ultimately joining forces later on as the situation develops and their stories get entangled. If a character resolves his Kicker, he is out of the game unless he can work with the game master to come up with a new one. Instead of potentially endless grinding resulting in a default story of "zero to hero," *Sorcerer* is designed to focus on the same kind of story arcs that characters in movies and novels traditionally follow.

Demons and Magic

The character-creation rules are thus little more than a few stats, some color, a bit of background, a disadvantage, and a sort of "story" instigator. That is only half of the process, however, as your character is not complete until you've also designed his associated demon and played through the binding process.

Now, before we get into this I have to point out that this stuff is actually unnerving if not actually scary. Seeing as it's just a game, I'm trying to think why that's the case, and I can only explain it by way of analogy. *Car Wars* is something I've played countless times and in spite of its relatively brutal theme—televised vehicular death matches—its gameplay is still relatively tame. I would have thought that Peter Dell-Orto's *Deathball* would have been right up my alley as well, but I just... couldn't... play it. There's something about having more fully realized characters with more or less realistic damage effects and hit locations that make the game far more gruesome and graphic than what I'd normally be up for. For some reason, *Car Wars* just doesn't seem like real violence when the focus is squarely on little cars swerving, skidding, shooting, rolling, and catching on fire. You can enjoy the intensity of the contest without getting hung up on the poor penniless autoduelists that get rushed to the local Gold Cross facility to have their brains scanned for imprinting on a new clone.

Really, it's more distressing that these guys don't have enough petrol around to keep their 1973 Ford Falcon XB GT Coupes running. Almost as bad is the fact that they have to eat algae instead of hamburger. Those poor saps!

Likewise, it's obvious that the people responsible for the *D&D* hysteria of the early eighties had no direct experience of the world's most popular fantasy role-playing game. I mean, there is not the slightest hint of real occult or witchcraft elements involved in the casting of the game's "Sleep" or "Magic Missile" spells. Vancian magic is, of course, an artifact of science fantasy, it is not even remotely similar to genuine magical traditions or myths. *Sorcerer*, in contrast, has all of the game's powers, advantages, and special abilities locked away in these demonic entities that are controlled by the game master. That right there is evil in and of itself just from a game design standpoint, but it gets worse. These creatures are each assigned a **desire**, which amounts to a vice for which they pressure their associated player-character. Further, they also have a **need**, which is often gross if not outright wicked. If these *things* are not getting what they want, they become gradually more unreliable, if not actively dangerous, to the character they ostensibly serve.

I have to say that these demonic creatures are nuanced enough that I don't know right off how to whip one up under *GURPS*. Are they an ally or an enemy? *Yes!* And every interaction with these things is through ritual magic which actually has to be described and played out. This is not a system where magery comes off as a stand-in for technology. It's time consuming, difficult, unreliable, and costly, and it takes its toll. I could see a Van Helsing-type character retaining some semblance of humanity while **banishing** demons, **containing** them, and **punishing** them. But executing the **contact**, **binding**, and **summoning** rituals sound utterly horrific—not just because of what these creatures represent but also because of how many ways these things can go awry. It's bad enough that a player-character might sacrifice an animal in order to improve his chances of summoning a demon. But a character that does so will likely accrue greater and greater penalties to his ability to banish demons. The possibility that a demon will end up poorly bound is similarly frightening: the number of victories it obtains on the roll become a penalty for every subsequent interaction with it!

Of course, as far as what this game is attempting to achieve, this is all gasoline on the fire. You've already got three or four player-characters, each with their own kicker driving the play toward "the bangs" (that's Ron Edward's term for engaging scenes) right from the start. You also have these creatures tied to each of the players pushing them toward mayhem and various sketchy activities. The players are describing their actions and attempting to increase the level of group interaction on every single roll. And to top it off, the players are going to be in grave danger due to whatever BAD STUFF the game master has turned loose. The players will end up in situations where they *have* to use sorcery in order to have a chance to deal with their problems, which in itself is not entirely predictable and is even liable to go terribly wrong. When a group sits down to *that*, there is just no way that they could have even a remote idea of how it will all play out in advance.

Combat: Initiative and Sequencing

Every role-playing game does this a little bit differently. Some games do initiative by side; others do individual initiative. Some games reroll initiative every single round; other games keep whatever sequence is established in the first round until the end of the combat. *GURPS* did away with initiative entirely and just had everyone go in order of their Basic Speed attribute. (The fact that everyone gets a "free" defensive action by default is what allows for the elimination of something that would otherwise appear to be integral to the tabletop role-playing idiom.) Combat games like *Car Wars* and *Star Fleet Battles* worked up elaborate phased movement systems, often with numerous points where secret and simultaneous declarations had to be managed by the referee. In contrast, *BattleTech* produced an almost chess-like feel with each side alternating the execution of a unit's full movement and then again taking turns to execute torso-twists and then attacks. Other games with a similar degree of granularity worked out elaborate systems for interrupts in order to allow players to cover certain regions with their rifles and so forth.

Sorcerer, though, opens each round with everyone declaring their actions at once. If people hear something they don't like or get a better idea based on what everyone else is choosing, they can alter their choices as much as they want. This goes on until everyone is satisfied with how things stand. A similar method was recently used to simplify *Federation Commander* and make it more playable than its progenitor *Star Fleet Battles*. From there, the game master determines how many dice each character gets to roll based on the relevant scores and modifiers. Actions are then resolved in order from best to worst rolls, as determined by the core mechanic. The highest number wins, using other dice as tiebreakers if necessary. If a player ends up being attacked before he can execute his declared action, he has the option to change it to a defensive move. If he doesn't, he's liable to be taken out before he can act.

The "free and clear" stage where everyone is declaring their actions at once combined with the many bonuses for role-playing even in combat can do a lot to create more cinematic action than what tends to happen in "I go, you go" systems. As it's described in the annotations, it's possible to perfectly capture scenes like you see in Quentin Tarantino movies where everyone is pointing a gun at someone else and everyone is threatening to shoot at once. It's even possible for the initiative rolls to come up and then everyone opts to defend instead of shooting one after another. This drama comes at a price because working out what happens, and when, is a bit fiddly, because the game master will have to make flowchart diagrams in order to keep up with it every round. Other than that, this is an extremely lean system that accomplishes a great deal with very few rules. Also note that this system can be applied to non-combat situations.

Now what's so interesting about this is that it is terribly old school. It may even be that the original fantasy role-playing game was meant to be played somewhat like this. I'm not sure; the rules for the sequence of play were always a bit of a hash and I don't think I've ever quite played them exactly as intended. Just going by what Matt Finch says in his "Quick Primer for Old School Gaming," a lot of people had a problem with combat in early editions of *D&D* just dissolving into "I roll to hit. They roll to hit. I roll to hit." His advice for how to avoid that is quite clearly in the same spirit as the combat rules in this section, but the difference is that Ron Edwards has completely nailed down understandable rules that can be implemented in order to consistently produce the kind of freewheeling action that Matt Finch upholds as the *sine qua non* of old school gaming. I know I've enjoyed it when combats happen to play out in ways that no rules system could ever completely account for. It appears that Ron Edwards is cognizant of exactly what that *je ne sais quoi* is; even better, he can explain how to harness it without going all zen on us. That's significant.

Conclusion

I am actually afraid to play this game—and not just because its rules are engineered from the ground up to push game masters like me out of our comfort zone *and then keep us there.* The convention where I'd be best be able to try this out is frequented by nice, geeky teenage girls, many of whom would be liable to be on the lookout for their chance to try out role-playing games for the first time. Being of sort of a conservative purist bent, it's more my style to bring someone into the hobby the same way I was: by being asked to roll 3d6 in order six times and then facing down a fairly strong chance of a total party kill. That's not just because there would be an off-chance that one of the players' dads would be eavesdropping from the next table, either.

I am not entirely comfortable with getting inside of the mind of a demon-like character, even one in a setting that has been stripped of the standard Christian connotations that people in the West typically bring to the subject matter. It's one thing to read *The Screwtape Letters.* But playing all this out? I'm leery... and I still come across people who hold all role-playing games in the same degree of disdain they view ouija boards and people playing Led Zeppelin records backward. Of course, that stuff is not half as scary as the fact that this game directly undermines almost every tool and technique that I lean on in order to keep control of a role-playing game session. I mean... I *thought* I ran a wide-open game where the players could do whatever they wanted. Now I have to wonder just how much of that is an illusion!

Still, I have to say that this game was almost the perfect vehicle for kicking off a new scene of independent role-playing game designs. I can see now why the *Forge* could take off the way it did, and why it became the center of discussion about role-playing theory. Reading this book makes *me* want to design a role-playing game myself, very much like the many people who heard the Soft Boys' album *Underwater Moonlight,* then went off and started a band. This game challenges assumptions about the medium that I didn't know I held. It provides a vocabulary for talking about what actually goes on in sessions that I've never seen before. Finally, it takes some of the core elements of iconic games like *The Fantasy Trip* and *Champions* and then goes off in a direction with them that I could never have anticipated. But the roots of this game go even further back than that. Ron Edwards says in his list of inspirational reading section, "If you haven't read the original, 1930s

Conan fiction before, try it; it's never been imitated successfully." *Sorcery and Sword*, a follow-up supplement for this game "is based almost entirely on the conventions established by pulp fantasy fiction in the 1930s and 1940s by authors such as Robert E. Howard and Fritz Leiber." If you're keen on really bringing the staples of the Appendix N literature into your tabletop adventures, then this is something you'll want to seriously take a look at.

The real value in this game is not just in how well it captures the horrific nature of "real" sorcery. Yes, even if you stick with your preferred game system, just reading through this can really flesh out and juice up the bad guys your group's player-characters are out to beat up on. But beyond that, this short book is packed with wisdom that applies to most any role-playing system. This passage, for instance, completely captures how I run everything from *Basic D&D* to *Traveller* and *GURPS*:

> *The game works wonderfully when you use what's there, and it will make you suffer horribly if you try to beat it. In fact, I urge you to accept damage, including defeat, to interpret it merely as changing the arena of conflict. Remember how often the characters in the source material fail and suffer. When that happens to your character, let go of how you planned to win, because now, your story is about the guy who won anyway, or went down in glorious flames in trying. This is quite a subversive concept in role-playing, both to let go of the present and how you want or expect your character to look at the moment, and to let go of the future and of your dreams for what the character might become. (page 112)*

That is some of the best advice that a novice game master is liable to ever be given. I wasn't too clear on what all Ron Edwards had really accomplished before I sat down to review this game, but just based on that one paragraph alone, it's clear that he is an asset to the role-playing hobby. If you are a connoisseur of role-playing excellence, you really owe it to yourself to see what he's accomplished.

Appendix D:
A Conversation with Ken St. Andre

I recently contacted Ken St. Andre in order to confirm some of the claims I had made regarding the literary antecedents of his *Tunnels & Trolls* role-playing game, the *second* role-playing game ever created. Before he'd talk to me, he wanted to know why I was so interested in this, so I mentioned that I was working on a book about the stories that inspired the earliest RPGs. In the course of our email exchange, he not only answered all of my questions, but he also graciously agreed to allow me to publish it all as an interview.

Jeffro: My first question has to do with your reference to the Law of Contagion and the Law of Similarity on page 21 of first edition *Tunnels & Trolls*. Now... I realize this is written a long time ago. Those laws aren't something people tend to think of nowadays in regard to magic, but I'm pretty sure I know which stories you were referring to there. If you happen to recall what you were thinking of forty years ago with that... please fill me in and either confirm of disprove my suspicion!

Ken St. Andre: You should understand that when I created the first edition of T&T, I was already 28 years old with a master's degree in library science, not some teenager just getting into fantasy. I had been reading and collecting all the fantasy I could get since I was 12. I'd also been studying real world Magic (not stage magic) for over a decade. I knew about the Laws of Contagion and Similarity. If there was a source for mentioning them, it was probably *The Dark Arts* by Richard Cavendish, although I may also have been thinking of *The Incomplete Enchanter* by L. Sprague de Camp, or *Three Hearts And Three Lions* by Poul Anderson.

Jeffro: Well, my guess was *The Incomplete Enchanter* as the source, but I see that it's not quite as clear cut as I would have liked.

You don't mention a specific author or resource when you mention "the principles of necromancy and the control of spirits," but you do mention

Andre Norton as being the model for how spells in *Tunnels & Trolls* are based "on inherent abilities of the magic-user." Now... I just got an omnibus of what I think you were referring to there in the mail. Can you confirm which Andre Norton books you had in mind there so that I can be sure I have the right books?

Ken St. Andre: References to Norton would go back to the *Witch World* series. That was her best fantasy available in the 70s. *Star Man's Son* also had a psychic powers system indistinguishable from magic. Necromancy would have been Clark Ashton Smith most likely. However, it would be hard to overstate the influence of both de Camp and Carter back in the mid-seventies.

Jeffro: I try to explain how big a deal de Camp was back then... but it's really difficult to get it across. His stuff is just so different from how people think of fantasy now. He has all these stories where a really smart archaeologist or psychologist travels to ancient Rome or the world of Orlando Furioso or an alternate earth where scientists study history by staging incredibly huge reenactments with brainwashed citizens.... It's just crazy.

I mean, this is fantasy and all... or maybe science fantasy in some cases. But there's no dark lord, no odd bunch of demi-humans trotting off for an epic quest to find or get rid of an ancient artifact just in time. There's not even an Arnold Schwarzenegger-looking guy running around in a loin cloth. It's all so different and varied. Were you conscious of how wild some of this stuff was at the time? Because looking back, it's really hard to get into a frame of mind where L. Sprague de Camp and Fletcher Pratt could be major players in fantasy.

Ken St. Andre: You are talking about some of de Camp's best and most original work, but there was so much more. He and Carter teamed up to finish unfinished Howard stories about Conan. There was also *The Tritonian Ring* (1953), *The Goblin Tower* (1968) and *The Fallible Fiend* (1973). Plus, he was instrumental in finishing and publishing *Tales of Conan* (1955) and *Conan the Adventurer* (1966). That's not even mentioning his work with Fletcher Pratt or his historicals that were almost fantasy. De Camp was a very big deal in fantasy back in the 60s and 70s.

Jeffro: And yet these guys aren't mentioned too much these days... except to point out how awful their Conan stories were in comparison to Robert E. Howard's. Lovecraft fans are upset about de Camp's biography of their favorite author. Lin Carter's writing is routinely savaged. And many of the more recent reviews of what you call de Camp's best and most original work can be summed up as someone simply saying, "ewwwwwww."

Now… I'm less interested in some of the scholarly nit-picking than I am the large and relatively rapid shift in the culture. When you talk about these authors, your enthusiasm is infectious. These guys really defined fantasy for an entire generation. How do you think they could lapse into obscurity as quickly as they did?

Ken St. Andre: How did they get obscure?

1. They died.

2. Wave after wave of new writers redefined fantasy in their own image.

The greats of yesteryear—forget them! Most of it comes down to TOO MUCH GOOD STUFF. There is really only room for a couple of old legends to exist, so Howard, Lovecraft, Tolkien. That's 3 biggies from the ancient first half of the 20th century. Forget, gloss over people like Carter, de Camp, Leiber, Anderson, Norton, Jakes, and dozens of others. That's just the way it is. You think anyone will remember me or *Tunnels & Trolls* in 50 years? Nope, it will be all Gygax with the purists remembering Arneson as well. I, Stafford, Miller, Peterson (both of them), Henderson, and dozens of others will all be written off or ignored as imitators.

Jeffro: I think you sell yourself short. Even fifty years from now, I fully expect people to still praise *Tunnels & Trolls*'s flexibility and the singular way it frees the game master from the need for endless rules books. And what about your work on *Stormbringer*?!

I love playing the classic RPGs myself. The way that they encapsulate the older, wilder sort of fantasy is just really compelling to me. For instance, your idea of the rogue character type is very different from the way most people would do that sort of thing today. But a guy that has access to spell abilities without the benefit of formal training? That's just fun. And it's not just Jack Vance's Cugel spilling over into the game there, but Fritz Leiber's Grey Mouser as well. I'd go so far as to say that those old characters are right in line with *Tunnels & Trolls*'s freewheeling and irreverent attitude. Certainly, a guy that was bred on only Tolkien and his imitators would have a harder time grasping where your game was coming from there.…

Ken St. Andre: You seem to be well-grounded in fantasy yourself. Mentioning Cugel and the Mouser gets you points with me. You might also consider Zelazny's *Jack of Shadows*. Go ahead and ask anything you want. I'm not a mind reader, and I have no particular horse to ride, especially since I have no idea what the scope or theme of your book will be.

Jeffro: Well… here's one of the more controversial points that I've stumbled into in the process of looking into this topic. From what you've said here, it's clear that you read pretty well the same science fiction and fantasy books that Gary Gygax did. The thing that's striking is that while Tolkien is in the mix of what you guys were kicking around, he was far from being the prime determinant of your assumptions about how fantasy ought to work. In fact, guys like Roger Zelazny and Michael Moorcock and a half dozen other authors that are now relatively obscure would have been on par with Tolkien in your minds.

Now… saying that around some fantasy fans… it really makes their heads explode. They almost can't imagine it. And the thing is, it's very easy to talk about Tolkien's influence on the RPGs of the seventies and how it was relatively limited in comparison to what came later. It's harder to talk about fantasy fans in the seventies in general. So people will dismiss you guys as being representative only of gamers or else somehow being out of step with your own times.

So I guess what I want to know is… what do *you* think? Were RPG designers like you back the seventies typical fantasy fans of your time? Or was there something different about you guys? Or did the requirements of RPG design influence who showed up and filter out only a particular sort of fantasy author that would have been different from what "normal" people were reading?

Ken St. Andre: I suppose you could consider people like Gary and me to be super fantasy fans of the time. But we weren't all that unusual. There was a fantasy boom going on in SF publishing. Publishers like Ace and Ballantine were doing all they could to bring anything fantastic back into print. And I don't think there were any requirements of design.

Fandom was a much smaller subset of society than it is now. Those of us who were in fandom thought we were pretty special. A lot of us were also gamers, although gaming fandom didn't really exist yet. However, it was taking off at the same time. It was all part of the fantasy explosion.

Gary and I were in the mainstream. People like M.A.R. Barker and Greg Stafford were more original and more creative, but even they shared in the fantasy explosion of the time.

Jeffro: How would you have known you were a part of fandom? Was there an initiation rite? Did a parent give you a set of Narnia books? Or did a hippy loan you a copy of *The Lord of the Rings*? Or did you just know you were "in" if you subscribed to a couple of short fiction magazines and maybe bought a two-hundred-page novel every week or so?

Ken St. Andre: I was brought into fandom by a friend who was already in it. He showed me some fanzines, explained the concept. Fandom wasn't hard to join—you just had to be willing to write a letter now and then. As I got more involved, I started writing and printing fannish things that further expanded my circles. No, no initiation rites per se. Maybe you could say that attending my first science-fiction convention counted an initiation rite, but actually, my first one was LerpreCon I here in Phoenix, and I was one of the people who made that happen.

Jeffro: Can you describe what participating in the fanzines was like? (My impression is that it was akin to many of the discussion fora on the internet today. You'd have the same sort of flame wars that we are familiar with today, but they'd be stretched out over the course of months or years.)

Ken St. Andre: Participating in fanzines is just like subscribing to *Wired*. Except more participation was expected. If you had any talent, writing or artistic, you were expected to contribute. Yes, it was very much like participating the fora, only at the speed of the U.S. mail instead of electrons and computer code. You level up when you join an APA. I've been a member of three APAs. The Wild Hunt, Rehupa, and some Tarot APA I've forgotten the name of. I was also a member of the Burroughs Bibliophiles during the 70s.

Jeffro: One of the things that strikes me about the early RPG designers was just how eclectic their tastes were. For instance, you were a member of the Burroughs Bibliophiles over twenty years after ERB's death. The thing that explains the obscurity of all these authors now—i.e., death and time and replacement—didn't really happen in your day. You guys read New Wave stuff like Moorcock and Zelazny just as much as you did old school planetary romance.

And your games… they pulled all kinds of stuff into them. I mean… when I try to describe Trollworld to people, I say it's "the Mos Eisley cantina of fantasy." It's loaded. Jam-packed. Wide open. Full-throttle. This is something that's completely alien to a lot of people who are under forty or so. Can you speak to this aspect of the times somehow? Did it just seem like a good idea at the time... or is there something objectively awesome about it even though that style rapidly fell out of fashion with the rise of the Tolkien pastiche as the dominant form of fantasy?

Ken St. Andre: Eclecticism? I don't know what I, or anyone, could say about that. That's just the way it was back then. We were all young, and the world was full of wonders—and it still is—and we just took everything and did stuff with it.

I think you're maybe trying to over analyze things when getting into the topic. We weren't analyzing anything back then. We were just looking for fun, and creating it in a thousand different ways. Young people are still doing the same thing today as far as I can tell, though I'm no longer part of those groups.

Jeffro: Well, I've taken up quite a bit of your time here. I'm grateful for everything that you've managed to clear up for me. This has truly been a blast.

For my final question, are there any other books in particular that you'd like to call out or fantasy authors that you'd recommend for someone who is looking to get into the mindset of those times when role-playing games were a brand new thing and you were right in the middle of it all? Anything that I might have overlooked or that I should be sure not to miss—anything else that you think might have particularly gotten your creative juices flowing?

Ken St. Andre: In my opinion, a lot of the background and tone in role-playing games comes from non-fantasy sources—or at least a different sort of fantasy. The influence of Edgar Rice Burroughs really can't be overestimated on my work. And also the romances of the Middle Ages. The legends of Arthur and Charlemagne are really important. You want book titles? *Tarzan of the Apes*, *A Princess of Mars*, *Le Morte d'Arthur*, *The Volsunga Saga*, *King Solomon's Mines*, and Foster's *Prince Valiant* comics to name just a few. You already know about Tolkien, and Howard, and Leiber, and Moorcock, but for both Gary and me there were 100 other sources equally important: Vance and de Camp and Carter and Malory and Homer and *Beowulf* and the *Arabian Nights* and on and on.

Jeffro: I know I said that was the last question, but if you can explain how Edgar Rice Burroughs influenced you, that would be a huge help. People, in general, can maybe wrap their heads around his mass popularity enduring well into the seventies… but again, the claim that he was a primary influence on early fantasy RPGs to a greater extent than perhaps even Tolkien is not something that many people can readily accept.

Ken St. Andre: I first discovered "escape/adventure" fiction through the book *Tarzan And The Ant Men* when I was bicycling through Sunnyslope, Arizona (now a part of north Phoenix) and found their public library. I was in the summer between 6th and 7th grades, so that would have made me about 12 and the year 1959 or 60. I loved *Tarzan And The Ant Men*. Edgar Rice Burroughs immediately became my favorite author. His books were hard to find in the 50s and early 60s.

Many people don't realize that *Tarzan* is fantasy. Raised by apes but grows up to be superhuman—yeah, like that's ever gonna happen. Discovers prehistoric worlds, becomes immortal, finds lost civilizations including Opar, an outpost of Atlantis, talks to and understands animals, gets shrunk down to 6 inches in size. Fantasy, pure fantasy. The settings from Edgar Rice Burroughs helped create the settings of Trollworld—jungles, deserts, caverns, prehistoric cities. The fauna from Edgar Rice Burroughs made up a large part of the Trollworld fauna—lions, crocodiles, apes—all part of my original list of monsters. The idea that technological anachronisms could be part of the world comes directly from Edgar Rice Burroughs. He takes rifles and airplanes to Pal-Ul-Don. He has super scientists doing genetic manipulation on gorillas in the African jungle. All sorts of strange things happen in his books.

Jeffro: Thanks so much for taking the time out to talk to me like this. This has been really, *really* awesome.

Ken St. Andre: Thanks for talking to me, Jeffro, and for giving me an opportunity to talk about my influences in creating *Tunnels & Trolls*. I'm always happy to set the record straight, and turn people on to the great fantasy fiction of the world.

———

Ken St. Andre was born April 28, 1947, spent most of his life goofing off, and is planning to never die. So far, so good! You can find out more about him on his Infogalactic page. A range of his game design work is available through RpgNow, including the deluxe edition of *Tunnels & Trolls*. He is rather proud of *Deep Delving, Dwarf World, Dewdrop Inn,* and the spell books that he did this year: *Rock and Rule, The Spellbook of Shancinar,* and *The Spell Book of the Uruks.* You can find a wealth of information about his work at the *Tunnels & Trolls* website and at Trollhalla.

About the Author

Jeffro Johnson is a lifelong fan of science fiction, fantasy, and tabletop games. His researches into the origins of role-playing games lead him to rediscover the forgotten pulp fantasy canon. At the conclusion of his survey, he inadvertently set off a literary movement. He has blogged for over a decade at Jeffro's Space Gaming Blog and is editor of the Castalia House blog, for which he has received Hugo Nominations for Best Related Work and Best Fanzine.

CPSIA information can be obtained
at www.ICGtesting.com
Printed in the USA
BVHW041242190523
664481BV00002B/36